Lougheed Library
125 Route 340 Sparkill, NY 10976

# The St. Thomas Aquinas College National Center For Ethics and Social Responsibility

## DATE DUE

# THRESHOLDS
## OF
# MOTIVATION

*The Corporation as a
Nursery for Human Growth*

# Copyright Permissions

# THRESHOLDS
## OF
# MOTIVATION

*The Corporation as a
Nursery for Human Growth*

**V S MAHESH**

*With a Foreword by*
**WILLIS HARMAN**

**Tata McGraw-Hill Publishing Company Limited**
NEW DELHI

*McGraw-Hill Offices*

**New Delhi** New York St Louis San Francisco Auckland Bogotá Guatemala
Hamburg Lisbon London Madrid Mexico Milan Montreal Panama
Paris San Juan São Paulo Singapore Sydney Tokyo Toronto

Third Reprint 1994

RCDACRBJRXLRR

**ISBN   0-07-462232-3**

Published by Tata McGraw-Hill Publishing Company Limited,
4/12 Asaf Ali Road, New Delhi 110 002, typeset at
Interpress Magazines Pvt. Ltd., and printed at
Rajkamal Electric Press, B 35/9 G T Karnal Road, Delhi 110 033

*This book is dedicated with love and gratitude*
*to*
*my parents*
*Viakalathur Sundaresa Shankar*
*and*
*Vidya Shankar*

# Foreword

Few doubt that the corporation is being thoroughly redefined, in some way influenced by the changing marketplace, the rising aspirations of workers, and the looming challenge of global environmental and other dilemmas. Many attempt to respond to these influences and even to anticipate what they mean in terms of the future. Only a very few—V. S. Mahesh being one—have had the insight to identify as the keystone in this redefinition a shift in the prevailing view of the essential nature of human beings.

The modern Western paradigm underlies the institutions of business and industry wherever they may be in the world. With its materialistic story of evolution through natural selection of the most competitive organism, and its conviction that the loftiest thoughts and feelings are nothing but the functioning of a physical brain, it has tended to support an ignoble concept of human motivation. However, that is now changing. There is ample reason to believe that the prevailing view of human nature is shifting rapidly, for an assortment of reasons, to one that is far more extravagant in terms of the ultimate potentiality of human beings, and far more noble in its concept of what people ultimately desire in terms of the meaning of their lives.

It is somewhat ironic that at the same time India has experienced a strong tendency to "modernize" and allow the Western materialistic emphasis to impinge on its value system, the West has seen its materialism challenged by an infusion of a new transcendentalism, coming partly from the East. This "new paradigm" emphasizes a purposive, conscious universe unity of the intercommunicating parts of the perceived reality; a balance between outer and inner, intuitive and rational, masculine and feminine.

It may well be that the picture that ultimately emerges, at a global level, will be based on three legs and—like a three-legged stool—will have a stability not found with only one or two legs fully developed. The three "legs" to which I refer are the emphasis on individuation and self-determination of the West; the inward-looking emphasis of the East; and the oneness with Nature so strongly emphasized in the traditions of the indigenous peoples of the world—and now so badly needed to counter our newly recognized proclivity for destroying the very ecological systems we depend upon for life support.

This challenge to the modern worldview is far more profound than is generally appreciated. Modern culture has for a long time been trying to manage a society based on two incompatible pictures of reality—one scientific-economic, and the other humanistic-spiritual. The former tends to deny the spiritual, and the latter finds science irrelevant to the important questions of life. The British author C.P. Snow wrote of the phenomenon in a much-discussed book, first published in 1959, entitled *Two Cultures*. The scientific worldview was, and is, powerfully influential in the political, economic, and industrial institutions of modern society. People tend to live their lives, however, by the other, competing worldview. Since the two worldviews are completely incompatible, it should not have come as a surprise that modern society presently finds itself in serious trouble.

There now appears to be a profound change of mind taking place in the modern world. It is reflected in survey data and book sales; in the new emphasis on values in the women's movement; in the ecological, peace, and alternative lifestyles movements; in the Green political movements in various countries; in new approaches to spirituality, including the suddenly fashionable "12-step" programs for dealing with addictions and "co-dependency". A new attitude toward spirituality is manifested both in the broader society (in involvements in various meditative disciplines and religious philosophies; and in the nature of some of the newer forms of executive development seminars) and in the scientific community (somewhat surreptitiously, in the form of research on consciousness and related topics).

The cultural shift is characterized by a repudiation of the competition, exploitation, materialism and consumerism of modern society, and an increased emphasis on alternative values—on quality of relationships; humane, ecological and spiritual values; cooperation, caring, and nurturing; oneness of humanity; social justice; respect and caring for the other creatures on the planet. It includes an assertion of the importance of the feminine—not only of women, and a feminine point of view, but of the feminine side of all humans. It involves a weighting of relationships over things, of wholeness over parts; it recognizes the authenticity of inner knowing. It implies a new, non-exploitative relationship to nature and a return to the spiritual centre.

This "global mind change" is bound to have a profound effect on the business corporation, in whatever country. In the oneness perception though we may compete, we are nonetheless each part of a unity, so that no one of us "wins" unless we all do. The affirmation of inner wisdom, authority, and resources challenges the predominant scientific materialism of the earlier part of the century. The rising appreciation of the feminine implies a total change of corporate culture. The value emphases in the new picture of reality are at total variance with the economic rationality which dominated the old. The *meaning* of work assumes far greater importance compared to financial reward, employee benefits, and even the quality of the work environment.

The practical importance of this shift in basic premises does not dawn on one immediately. Modern industrial society, like every other in history, rests on a set of largely tacit, *basic assumptions about who we are, what kind of a universe we are in, and what is ultimately important to us.* The scientific materialism which so confidently held forth its answers to these questions a couple of generations ago is now a dying orthodoxy. Its basic positivistic and reductionistic premises are being replaced by some sort of transcendentalist beliefs that include increased faith in reason guided by deep intuition. In other words, a respiritualization of society is taking place, but one more experiential and non-institutionalized, less fundamentalist and sacerdotal, than most of the historically familiar forms of religion. Such a change in basic assumptions must inevitably be accompanied by a long-term shift in value emphases and priorities. *All institutions can be expected to go through major changes, including particularly industrial, economic and financial institutions.* These changes will challenge assumptions we have held to be true throughout our lives. The coming decades will be exciting, if not totally comfortable, ones.

Mr Mahesh's book addressed this challenge. It is unique in that it first defines the emerging picture of essential human nature, and then applies that to the task of managing the corporation—concluding that the successful corporation of the future will be "a nursery for human growth". This conclusion emerges, not as a result of personal bias or caprice, but because it follows by inescapable logic from the new view of human motivation and the new appreciation of the need for the corporation to be viewed as, not an entity competing in a hostile marketplace, but part of a global ecological system.

WILLIS HARMAN
Institute of Noetic Sciences
Sausalito, California, USA

# Acknowledgement

There are thousands of people to whom I owe debts of gratitude. This book would never have seen the light of day were it not for the conscious and unconscious help of all of them. In choosing but a few of them here, I know I have to commit gross errors of omission. I pray that I am forgiven on the count that limitations of space have imposed too severe a restriction upon my urge to express my gratitude. I wish to express my thankfulness to:

* The large, extended families of my grandfathers, Sundaresa Iyer and C. Subramanya Ayyar, who have been a source of great strength and support. A consistent family vision of what constitutes a good life—a combination of low *threshold limits* and a joyful pursuit of one's vocation—has taught me more about psychology and philosophy than all the books and teachers could;

* "Master" C.P. Seshadri, Sharad Jakatdar and Arun Maira, by trusting and investing in me, enabled me to learn about human motivation in the raw—in the editorial room of a Daily, on the shop floor of a no-nonsense automobile company and in the rarefied atmosphere of HRD respectively;

* My former colleagues in the House of Tatas, in whose development and growth I was concerned with. They taught me, with great conviction, that far from there being anything wrong with it, human potential is the personification of Perfection itself: From fellow officers of the Tata Administrative Service to Laxman, the driver, Nannai Maharaj, the union leader, and Ajit Kerkar, the unquestioned numero uno of the Taj Group of Hotels, I learnt how life and its foibles can shape human potential to take different forms—from that of a saint to a criminal;

* The management of Indian Hotels Company, who so gladly granted me a sabbatical to pursue my research and writing in England;

* The University of Buckingham, in beautiful, quiet Buckinghamshire, England who received me as a Visiting Fellow in their School of Accounting, Business Studies and Economics during my sabbatical. In particular, I thank the then Acting Vice-Chancellor, Peter Watson and the Business Studies faculty, Tom Baum, John Bicheno and Douglas Stoddart, all of whom read and commented on the manuscript. Their encouragement and feedback were invaluable;

* Ronnie Lessem of the City University, London, and Sylvia Balmer, then with the Highbury College, Portsmouth, who invited me to present my "East-West Model of Motivation" to their business management students and benefit from the latter's response and feedback. Ronnie is due another special "thank-you" for his advice on the conceptual framework of the book, for his critical editing of the early chapters and for suggesting the title of the book;

* Dorine Munn in Buckingham and Eugenea Menezes in Bombay were an ideal pair of secretaries to provide the support I needed. Their patience and meticulousness have been of immense value in the preparation of the manuscript;

* My new colleagues in WIPRO Corporation, whose buoyancy and an avant garde high-tech–high-touch approach to business helped provide the icing on the cake as it were for the book;

* Jack Gilles, of the Institute of Cultural Affairs, with whom I have had several discussions stretching over the years on the subject matter of the book. His comments, insights, and feedback on the manuscript have added great value to the book;

* Ranjan Kaul, Tata McGraw-Hill's former indefatigable Manager for Business and Professional Books whose persuasive skills and patience were primarily responsible for my taking time off from an executive career to write the book;

* Poonam Kasturi, who quietly took charge of the design and art work for the book and set her own high standards. I am grateful that she chose my book as the canvas for her talents to find true expression on;

* Willis Harman, for having so readily agreed to my request to write the Foreword for the book: I could not have hoped for a more appropriate person to do it; and

* My old friend, philosopher, guide and inexorable critic, Hem, but for whose never-failing support, affection and unsolicited counsel, I would not have written even a page of this book.

V S MAHESH

# Introduction

CORPORATE EXCELLENCE THROUGH HUMAN
SELF-ACTUALIZATION

This is a book on the intrinsic nature of human beings, and how internal and external forces affect the unfolding of this nature. It is also about the demonstrated fact that business corporations, in fact all organizations of men and women, can achieve sustained excellence in performance only by enabling the organizational members to find the means to actualize their full potential through the quality of their endeavour and life.

This book is not, however, a Pollyanna book that calls for an abiding, blind faith in the goodness of all human beings at all times. In the last decade of a century that has witnessed two world wars, suffered at the hands of men like Hitler and Stalin, and which could end with a major ecological disaster brought about by the infantile, short-sighted behaviour of millions of people around the globe, such calls are unlikely to get any meaningful response.

Within the corporate world, there are almost identical examples of human behaviour too: internecine quarrels and organizational warfare that threaten to, and sometimes actually do, tear up organizations; autocratic managers who attempt to perpetuate their individual glory by obliterating all who dare to oppose or compete with them; and grossly negligent attitudes that ignore the effects of one's actions on the physical and social environment. Such micro images of the larger reality of the world outside constantly reconfirm to us that there is an apparent consistency in human behaviour. That people within organizations have caused less damage than their political counterparts could be ascribed to the simple fact that they were by and large occupying smaller stages, and had less destructive weapons at their disposal. Even that comfort is gradually being eroded, as multinational corporations become larger and nation states begin to splinter, bringing the size of their stages, and their potential for destruction, within comparable limits.

## THE PERENNIAL DEBATE OVER HUMAN NATURE

Therefore, when we are told that it is in the nature of human beings to be cruel, petty, selfish, or destructive, and that the few who do not appear to be so are masking their true nature, some of us do find it difficult to refute the statement.

Many of us, however, silently and deep within ourselves, reject the explanation as being incorrect. For, we remember that there have been many occasions in our lives when we have ourselves felt an inner thrust towards achieving perfection in our endeavour, merely for the joy of doing it; we also remember having witnessed altruistic, noble behaviour among colleagues, friends and relatives in shared experiences. We have also read, heard or observed that the Japanese attribute their success in the corporate world to the manner in which people in their organizations are given freedom to participate in all aspects that concern them.

In India, as early as in 1943, while initiating the creation of a Personnel Department in the Tata Iron and Steel Company in Jamshedpur, India, Mr JRD Tata wrote to his fellow directors on the Board of the company,

> I firmly believe that greater efficiency and co-operation can be got from men who are allowed to use their intelligence and initiative and who are made to feel that the company appreciates the value of their brain as well as of their brawn, than from men whose sole motive is fear of punishment . . . Individual employees would thus be encouraged to take an intelligent interest in their department as a whole, and to develop a sense of personal responsibility for the success of its operations.

Half a century later, TISCO was still the largest and among the most respected corporations in India, having established an impeccable record of sustained excellence. Their humanistic approach to management had become a byword in Corporate India.

On the evidence of this alternative set of observations and facts, we are tempted to believe that intrinsically human nature is capable of achieving perfection; it is the circumstances and events of life that lead to negative behaviour. This debate about human nature has existed for several millennia, since the time when the Vedic seers in India propounded their philosophy that Man's instinctive urge towards perfection is merely a symptom of his true, godly nature. Over the centuries, almost every generation has debated the same question: *Is nobility and perfection a natural quality in man, and cruelty and pettiness an aberration, or vice versa?*

Over the past twenty years, by working at different levels in corporations, from that of an apprentice to a senior executive's, I have had the opportunity to learn first-hand that nobility and perfection are intrinsic to human nature. Nine of these years were spent in the Tata Engineering & Locomotive Company's green field plant at Poona, where the corporation was engaged in research and development in automobiles, design, manufacture and assembly of special-purpose machine tools, transfer lines, press tools, material handling equipment, and a range of automobiles. The last decade was spent in the Indian Hotels Company, who manage the successful Taj Group of Hotels, a chain of five-star deluxe hotels spread over four continents and 12 countries.

Since October 1991, I have been the Corporate Vice President (Human Resources) of WIPRO Corporation, a conglomerate with diverse interests covering consumer products, engineering, information technology, lighting, financial services and medical instrumentation and systems (which includes a 50 : 50 joint venture with GE).

As a practising executive in such diverse businesses, I have been able to make *a priori* assumptions on the subject of human nature and motivation, put it to effect and satisfy myself that given the right conditions, human beings can be helped to find their true nature of perfection. That efforts to enable the unfolding of human potential are consistent with, and are a prerequisite for, achievement of corporate excellence is a fact that I have learnt from experience.

With active industrial undertakings as a testing ground for my assumptions and understanding of human nature, it was possible to test out the theoretical models available, and selectively accept or reject them. Unlike many behavioural scientists, who have had to rely on simulated conditions for observation of rats and pigeons, for subsequent theoretical extrapolation to human behaviour, or psychiatrists who have had to rely on observation of behaviour exhibited by their patients, I have had bright, young, ambitious people to interact with. I have also had my share of interacting with entrenched trade union leaders, power hungry executives, insecure adults who could see their limitations standing in the way of winning through healthy competition, and leaders whose existence appeared to depend upon fomenting inter-group rivalries. But, with the reality of corporate performance and free market competition outweighing individual pettiness, there was always a thrust for achievement of quality results. It became increasingly clear to me that there was an obvious correlation between the unfolding of human potential and quality of performance. Once I managed to pin this correlation down, it was possible for me to evolve a model that enables individual and corporate development in a mutually supportive manner. This is the model that I wish to present through this book, a model that seeks to

- Explain the process by which human nature unfolds itself to its full potential;
- Indicate the respective roles of both an individual and his corporation in facilitating this process;
- Identify and explain the crucial link between the quality of endeavour and the stage of development of a human being;
- Explain why so many people do not reach their full potential, and suggest remedial measures;
- Integrate some of the major schools of thought in psychology, and explain how such a holistic understanding could be used towards facilitating individual and corporate growth;
- Provide corporations with a framework for human resources management as well as empowering leadership that will enable human self-actualization within the context, and in support, of corporate success; and
- Integrate, at a higher level, with what Willis Harman terms "the second Copernican revolution", or the paradigm shift taking place in the very belief structure of the industrialized world.

## VALIDATION OF THE UNIVERSALITY OF THE MODEL

That this model is perfectly workable in India, I knew from personal experience. When I presented this model to an international audience in Mexico in 1988, the overwhelmingly positive response tempted me to validate its universal applicability: the audience there had consisted of Americans, Latin Americans, Europeans, Africans, Australians and Asians, of different ages and backgrounds, and there were about as many men as women.

To further develop it and test it adequately, I went on a sabbatical during the autumn and winter of 1990/91. For the duration of my sabbatical, the University of Buckingham in England accepted me as a visiting fellow in their School of Accounting, Business Studies and Economics.

## AN EAST-WEST MODEL OF MOTIVATION

A few months of theoretical research, spread between the Franciscan library in Buckingham and the Bodleian in Oxford, helped me correlate my model with the works of many others, and develop it further into its current form, the *East-West model of motivation*. I was most happy to find that the model could integrate the main features of three of the major schools of psychology—the Freudians, the behavioural scientists and the humanists—as also those of the classical, Eriksonian model of child psychology. At the same time, the original features of its practical roots, and integration of Western Thought with Eastern models of creative aspirations in Man, remained well intact.

Simultaneously, I was also involved in designing and teaching a course on service industry management at the University of Buckingham. I integrated some essential features of my model in the course, and was struck by the ease with which the young business studies students accepted the relevance of the model within the context of service industry management.

To further test the validity and acceptance of the model, I first presented it at a seminar in the University of Buckingham, and later, at the City University, London, the Highbury College of Technology, Portsmouth, and at an organizational development program for working executives held in Sussex. Irrespective of the nature of the audience, which ranged from higher national diploma, graduate and MBA students to practising managers and faculty members, the response was overwhelmingly and uniformly good. In particular, the international mix of audience in Buckingham, London, and Portsmouth—with over thirty nationalities represented—added further strength to my conviction that the model was indeed universally valid.

Capping the entire process of correction and validation was a fortunate and timely session I had with Professor S. Chandrasekhar of the University of Chicago who happened to be giving a series of lectures in Oxford when I was in Buckingham. Himself an erudite scholar, thinker and writer on the subject of motivation, albeit in the pursuit of science, his candid response and critique of my model was of great value.

## TARGET AUDIENCE FOR THE BOOK

In putting my thoughts down on human nature, and describing the East-West model of motivation, I decided to write it in a manner that any uninitiated student of management, or practising executive could read and understand. In fact, even a lay person who has never worked in a corporation should be able to read the book and put it to use, either to understand himself better, or to help others better understand themselves.

I have attempted to give brief sketches of some relevant historical developments, so that what is sought to be presented in this book is understood in its right context. Even advanced students and practitioners of management may find the perusal of the background sketches useful, particularly since I have endeavoured to use original sources for all references, including the fascinating, *Kavyamimamsa*, the 10th century work of Rajasekhara's.

I have derived immense satisfaction in writing this book. Its subject matter has been so close to me for over a decade now that I have a feeling that I am bidding farewell to an old friend as I complete writing the book.

V S MAHESH

# Contents

## Conclusion

## Bibliographical Notes

## Index

# THE VICTORY OF HUMAN NATURE

The question, " Is nobility and perfection a natural quality in Man, and cruelty and pettiness an aberration, or vice versa?" is likely to be answered very soon in favour of human nature being intrinsically capable of unfolding its potential for perfection. The reasons for such optimism lie in some significant changes that have taken place globally, which have collectively led to the phenomenon that Alvin Toffler calls the Third Wave.

Several millennia ago, Man was a hunter, and lived by that skill. The discoveries and events that led to his changing his mode of living to being a settled farmer constituted the First Wave. In the seventeenth and eighteenth centuries, when Man the farmer was transformed into an industrial worker, his mode of living changed completely. The mega changes that occurred then were termed the Second Wave. A similar change, of a gigantic and fundamental nature, has begun and is likely to engulf Man in the form of a Third Wave before the century is over.

We will consider some of the critical aspects of the Third Wave, focussing specifically on a set of interconnected problems that, I believe, has been forced on the management of Third-Wave corporations. In seeking solutions to these problems, industrial organizations will find that they have no option open to them other than to *believe* in, and *facilitate* the unfolding of human nature to its full potential for perfection.

## ALTERNATIVE SOURCES OF ENERGY AND DECENTRALIZATION

The most significant change is in the exploration for alternative sources of energy required to drive industry. The days of mindless exploitation of non-renewable sources of energy— oil, coal and other fossil fuels—are fast coming to an end. The last few decades have seen massive efforts being mounted to tap energy from renewable sources such as sun rays, tides, winds, ocean currents and biological compounds. This change in the source of energy utilized for industrial activity will reduce the need to have dense concentrations of men labouring in traditional factory settings, and increase the thrust towards *decentralized production, service and information centres* that can exist on such renewable energy sources. The resultant effect on decentralization of managerial authority and control is too obvious for any further comment.

## NATURE AND FOCUS OF INDUSTRIAL ACTIVITY

It is more than evident that there is a major shift from industries such as steel, automobiles, textiles and chemicals to Third-Wave industries such as electronics and computers, information and services, biological compounds, ocean sciences, space exploration and genetic engineering—a vast majority of which are low-energy-consuming—and *dispersed businesses*.

As we will see later, all these industries have either or both of two features:

- Provision of increasingly customer-centred services, calling for sensitive front-line staff who have the knowledge, skills and authority to instantaneously respond to customer demands; and

- Rapid generation, collation, analysis and dissemination of increasingly complex arrays of information, calling for high skilled, knowledgeable employees who have the freedom and authority for independent and instantaneous decision making.

Simultaneously, the nature of activity in the traditional industries is also changing rapidly, with service and information being bundled with traditional manufactured products, thus blurring the differences between traditional and modern industries. The discussions that follow will elaborate how this is taking place.

## The growth of the service industry

In most countries, corporations that offer services as their products have far outstripped those who offer traditional, manufactured goods as products, in terms of growth rate, employment and share in GNP. In India, during the 1980s, while total employment in the manufacturing sector accounted for just 7% of the additional employment generated, service industries accounted for over 70%. Since 1985, the total employment in manufacturing industry actually reported a marginal negative growth. In the USA, the total aggregate employment in the manufacturing industry in 1988 was the same as in 1968. That this has been a world-wide trend is not open to argument any more.

The nature of services offered has also changed considerably. While traditional services, such as those provided in hotels, transportation and banking continue to account for a high proportion of employment generated, it is knowledge-based services, such as financial services, management consultancy, research & development and training, that are rapidly increasing their share of additional employment generated. That the shift to such knowledge service industries has been profitable is also clear from facts. In 1990, *Forbes* magazine reported that seven of the ten richest American billionaires were those whose fortunes had been made in providing computer and information services.

## The bundling of manufactured products with information and service

Traditional manufacturing corporations have begun to bundle their products with high-tech information and customer-sensitive services, as a means towards beating competition: customers are

3

insisting on their individual preferences being catered to, and these corporations have had to respond faster, with smaller batch sizes of production, greater variety and the requisite service back-up. In Motorola, a customer needing a paging device can today specify his requirements to a front-line staff member, who will directly feed in the information through a hand-held computer device. The production will be immediately started and finished in 17 minutes, shipped within one hour thereafter, and delivered to the customer's place in a day. The front-line staff member is empowered to take decisions on the spot and commit to the customer that his product will be delivered within two days.

On the one hand, advances in robotics and automation have been reducing the need to employ people for repetitive, simple tasks; on the other, customers are increasingly insisting on dealing only with those who have the knowledge and authority to respond to their changing needs. As a result, the nature of employment is shifting from jobs that are done with hands to those done with the head. Barring a minimal number of unskilled jobs, the lowest echelon in manufacturing organizations is being filled with knowledge workers. They create, analyze and generate—as well as respond to—information and knowledge, or provide service, or do some of both.

Production, according to Bateson, is being replaced by what he terms "servuction", where the customer is an intrinsic part of the production and service system. The gaps and edges between design, manufacturing, assembly, delivery and consumption are blurring and disappearing rapidly, with most of these functions being done real-time, in the presence of, and in sensitive response to, the customer.

## The information revolution

The growth and advancement of the computer industry, major changes in telecommunication and a revolution in printing technology and the audio-visual medium of communication have significantly changed the volume, quality, variety and rate of flow of information from and to individuals. "Information" as a product is fast increasing its share in total trade. A series of interconnected events arising out of the information revolution is going to substantially change the quality of life and expectations of both customers and employees. Let me highlight some of them.

As the cost of petroleum and other transportation costs spiral up everywhere, the price of telecommunication is shrinking spectacularly. Satellites have slashed the cost of long distance transmission, bringing it so near the zero mark per signal that there is already talk of "distance-independent" telecommunication costs. With computer power multiplying exponentially and the cost of electronic parts dropping substantially, backed by breakthroughs in fibre optics and allied technologies, it is clear that costs are going to dip further—per unit of memory, per processing step and per signal transmitted.

## Telecommuting v. commuting

Corporate executives already know that, on many occasions, it is far more cost-effective to telecommute than physically commute. When we can have conference calls connecting executives in Bombay, Paris and New York, and in the near future, audio-visually projected too, one can finish a conference in under an hour while sitting in one's office in South Bombay, in less time than it would take to reach the airport. Besides, one would have avoided the cost, effort, fatigue and jet lag that would have otherwise resulted from having that conference.

## Electronic cottages as workplace

It has been predicted by Toffler that this will also lead to many jobs being done by employees from out of their homes, making the 'electronic cottage' as much a part of the Third Wave corporation as the smoking chimneys were of the Industrial Revolution. Research workers, designers, computer programmers, sales executives and many others might end up working three to four days a week in their electronic cottages, and meeting with colleagues in a central, office location just once or twice a week.

In different parts of the globe, from Bangalore to Washington, DC, this is fast becoming a reality. A leading management consultant in Washington, DC realized that his down-town office was an unnecessary expenditure, for he was using it only for occasional meetings with clients, and for receiving telephone calls. By doing the former more effectively in the client's office, or in a restaurant, and the latter at his home, he began working out of his home. His business prospered, he had more time with his family, and the nightmare of daily traffic-jams was overcome. A modem, electronic mail system, a fax machine, and proper linking with customers ensured his availability for much longer durations of time, and instantaneously.

## High-tech–high-touch

The impact of such high technology, and the resultant distancing among people has given rise to a curious human reaction. People by and large are unhappy with too much of high-tech if it means too little human interaction. In fact, they wish to have the reduced amount of human interaction compensated for by much better quality of human interaction whenever it does occur. In predicting this, John Naisbitt called it the " high-tech – high-touch " phenomenon.

Naisbitt's predictions have come out to be correct. Banks that have introduced automatic vending machines, hotels that have introduced self-service, and departmental stores that have tried to eliminate human contact altogether, have all experienced this phenomenon.

Feargal Quinn, the pioneering Irishman who controls the Superquinn chain of stores, spends an hour every week, assisting his customers pack their purchased goods in bags along with his staff. He says that he learns as much about the customers and their concerns while doing so, as through poring over computer reports. A bank that pressurized their front-line to ensure that no customer spent more than five minutes while transacting his or her business, received complaints from customers that they felt that they were being rushed unnecessarily. The *personal touch* continues to be the cutting edge for competitive thrusts.

## Bundling "information" with service

As customers and employees become more knowledgeable in buying and using "information", and change their life style, corporations that offer "information" as a product must seek new and attractive ways to bundle information with *customer-and employee friendly service*. An outstanding example of this is the manner in which the Marriott corporation organized the concierge services in the 1800-room Marriott Marquis hotel in New York:

A few months before the hotel was to open, the corporation appointed eight local recruits, each from a different part of New York.

They were given information about New York that the guests might ask questions about, and the new recruits familiarized themselves with it. But Marriott did not stop there. They provided a simple system by which the eight new recruits could keep adding to and updating the information bank based on their interactions with guests. Within six months, there was eight times as much information available as had been originally provided. Besides, the new recruits rightly felt the pride of "ownership" of the information bank, as their knowledge, skills and commitment had created it.

While the Marriott concierges do have the information in plenty, it is their courtesy, efficiency and sensitivity that makes the guest wish to return.

It is a characteristic of the information industry that most of the employment generated in it is in the transmission of knowledge and information and in providing customer-sensitive service. In IBM, for instance, a mere 6% of employees are engaged in what would be traditionally described as manufacturing functions. The rest are providing service, either to an internal or an external customer. This is true of the information industry in India too. In WIPRO Infotech, the second largest information technology company in India, less than 10% are engaged in traditional manufacturing activities.

## A THREAT AND AN OPPORTUNITY FOR LESS DEVELOPED COUNTRIES

The manner in which traditional manufacturing industries are being converted into a Third Wave phenomenon, with information and service as its added value and competitive edge, will provide the Less Developed Countries (LDCs) with both a threat and an opportunity. What is increasingly becoming critical in this context is the vital question as to how rapidly, effectively and readily a corporation reacts to the information a customer provides with respect to his unique preferences. Let me illustrate with an example.

For the past few decades, corporations in the garment industry have found it profitable to locate their manufacturing units in countries that have had relatively low labour costs. Designs, made in anticipation of market preferences and needs, were typically sent with sufficient lead time for the manufacturing units to buy the appropriate cloth, make samples for approval, thereafter make the huge batch sizes, and ship them in time for the seasonal demand. In most cases, the cycle time for conversion of information on customer needs into a finished product in the customer's possession ranged from four months to a year.

In some countries now, the customers' preferences are changing so fast that many in the garment trade have decided that they can no longer afford the time taken for the earlier cycle of activity.

The Arrow Company, a US shirt maker, has recently transferred 20% of its dress production back to the US after 15 years of offshore sourcing, while Frederick Atkins, Inc., a buyer for US department stores, has increased domestic purchases from 5% in 1987 to 40% in 1990.

Levi Strauss, which required a lead time of nine weeks for making an average batch size of 1000 pairs of jeans, is now offering designer jeans that are made within a lead time of four days with an average batch size of six pairs.

Stalk and Hout have dealt with this phenomenon in their *Competing against Time*. Their analysis is worth dwelling upon. Let me highlight one of the examples they have given: Wal-Mart, whose stores move nearly $20 billion worth of merchandise every year, manage to replenish their stock about twice a week. Their main competitors average once in two weeks. Thus Wal-Mart is able to

- maintain the same service levels with one-fourth the investment in inventory;
- offer its customers four times the choice of stock for the same investment in inventory; and
- do some of both.

The authors have identified a clear, inverse relationship linking *suppliers' potential profit* and the *elapsed time between customers' decision to buy and product delivery,* . There is more of the former, i.e. profit, for those who manage with less of the latter, i.e. time taken to respond to customer need.

## TELECOMMUNICATION MODES ARE AFFECTING PHYSICAL RESPONSE TIME

Physical communication of people and goods has become too slow, cumbersome and costly, when compared to the speed, ease and low cost of telecommunication. Having got accustomed to the latter, the global customer has begun to demand that physical response should also become faster, easier and cheaper.

If the LDCs do not wish to lose out on this business, they should emulate "Italy Numero Tre" by organizing for themselves rapid transportation of goods, minimum administrative and bureaucratic delays and world standard telecommunication systems. What is happening in "Italy Numero Tre", or the Third Italy is this:

Using high-tech production methods, and hooked through sophisticated telecommunication to market demands and trends in far places, small establishments situated in rural areas are turning out custom-designed clothing, leatherware and furniture for overseas markets. In the Val Vibrata valley alone, over $1 billion a year is produced by such establishments, and that is only a small part of Italy Numero Tre.

Such establishments are normally family-run enterprises, fitting culturally and otherwise as perfectly in the larger context of their life and environment as was the farming activity of joint families in the First-Wave setting. Adaptation of such modes could lead, in India, to a Third-Wave solution along the lines of Mahatma Gandhi's insistence on a rural-centred life. This could be a way for LDCs to leapfrog directly from First-Wave settings to the Third-Wave, without going through the privations of an urban-centred Second-Wave society.

## THE NATURE OF THIRD-WAVE PRODUCTS

From the earlier discussions, it should be obvious that Third-Wave products fall in four broad categories:

- A bundle of manufactured product and customized service, with the built-in proviso of the "high-tech–high-touch" phenomenon;
- A bundle of updated, live information and rapidly responsive service;
- A pure customer-sensitive service, either traditional or knowledge-based; or
- Pure knowledge products, created by "knowledge workers".

Any corporation engaged in business today must realize that irrespective of its traditional concerns and foci, it is going to be irresistibly drawn into the vortex of the third-wave. Sooner or later, it is going to be competing for a position in the market place with a product or products that fall under one or more of these four categories.

## THE SEVEN ELEMENTS OF A NEW MANAGERIAL PROBLEM

As three of the categories contain elements of service in them, and the fourth is dependent on providing freedom and space for a knowledge worker to perform effectively, it follows that any corporation that wishes to survive, let alone excel, in the market place, must understand the peculiarities and difficulties that go with both service quality assurance and management of knowledge workers. I believe there are seven important elements that are fundamental to this extremely difficult managerial problem. Let us consider each of these elements:

### 1. Change in the role of the front-line employee

The most important element in the provision of service quality is the changed role of the employee who is in direct touch with a customer; the erstwhile, bottom rung employee who was supervised and controlled throughout his working time has now become the front-line employee interacting with the customer. What is more, research has conclusively proved that the customers' assessment of the quality of service he receives is critically linked to how well a corporation has empowered front-line employees. Every time a front-line employee says he has to check with his or her boss before responding to a customer, the corporation scores a negative point. Kenneth Blanchard suggests that service organizations should philosophically invert the organizational pyramid, with the responsibility vested with front-line staff, and the management looking at its role as being responsive to the needs of the front-line staff.

Whether a front-line employee is delivering pure service, or a bundle of "manufactured product with service", or a bundle of "information with service", he or she has to be more than merely a "submissive rule-observer". Teruya Nagao, professor of information and decision sciences at the University of Tsukuba, opines rightly that such rule-observers are actually "not good workers" in the current context. In today's fast-change environment, he points out, rules too, need to be changed more frequently than in the past, and the workers need to be encouraged to propose such changes. Asking questions, and challenging assumptions based on yesterday's reality, are crucial for both survival and success. And that has to be done where a customer meets an organization's representative with his needs.

## 2. The elusive nature of the *"Moments of Truth"*

Research has shown that over 90 % of such front-line – customer contacts take place beyond the eyes and ears of the management. For instance, airline ticketing and cabin crew staff, hotel reception-ists, waiters, bell boys, telephone operators, bank tellers, service mechanics, courier service staff, TV and radio interviewers and live reporters . . . all of them are directly interacting with customers, thinking on their feet, responding to unique customer needs and delivering service. It should be obvious to anyone at all that over 90% of such customer–front-line contacts take place in a manner and at a time when it is impossible, and undesirable, for a member of the management to be personally present. Jan Carlzon, the CEO of Scandinavian Airlines Systems, who pioneered many of the concepts now accepted as central to service industry management, refers to these contacts between front-line employees and customers as " moments of truth " for the service organization.

## 3. The silent customer

Research in traditional service industries like hotels, airlines and banking show that less than 5% of the unhappy customers bother to lodge a complaint about poor quality service received. Most hotels and airlines will consider themselves lucky if even 3% of their customers bother to fill out a suggestion folder, including com-plaints of poor service received. In knowledge services, such as financial services, dentistry and education, while major complaints are lodged through the courts of law, the majority of other complaints are silently and mentally recorded and acted upon in a manner that must chill the very blood of any entrepreneur entering the service industry. That is the next element in my list.

## 4. Word-of-mouth negative publicity

If there are a hundred unhappy customers of services provided by a corporation, as we have seen in (3) above, a maximum of five will give a feedback to the corporation. Research has established that out of the remaining 95, about 25 are likely to shift their clientele without giving any notice of it. All 95 are also likely to talk to an average of 10 people each about their unhappiness with the service received. Such word-of-mouth negative publicity is likely to be given with little malice by most people, for it is done as part of everyday conversation. To get back to our calculation, we see that for every five complaints that the management of a corporation learns of, about 950 strangers will have heard of the corporation's reputation as a provider of poor quality service, 250 of them hearing it from customers who have decided to shift their clientele as well.

Traditional methods of advertising are powerless against such an amplification of negative service received. In provision of service, the golden rule is, "Get it right the first time". And, as we now know, that has to be ensured by the front-line employee.

## 5. The indispensable employee

In the Second-Wave industry, an employee was dispensable. In fact, that was an essential part of Taylorian scientific management. In the Third-Wave setting, the rapidity of change can be coped with only by the initiated. The employees' skills in innovation, knowledge of the field and/or customer preferences, and mastery over the collation and dissemination of information unique to their organization, make them truly indispensable. If not indispensable, at least extremely costly to replace. In Fig. 1.1, I have suggested, based on the Replacement Cost Model of Eric Framholtz, a method of computing how much it costs to replace a knowledge worker.

Let me explain the model.

First, I have assumed that a knowledge worker ought to contribute at least twice his wage cost, after accounting for the expenditure on his existence. This appears to be a reasonable assumption to make, for most consultancy organizations use this as a minimum norm when charging their clients. Their billing is normally thrice the wage costs of consultants engaged in any activity.

On the x-axis, I have plotted time in months, and in the y-axis, money in rupees.

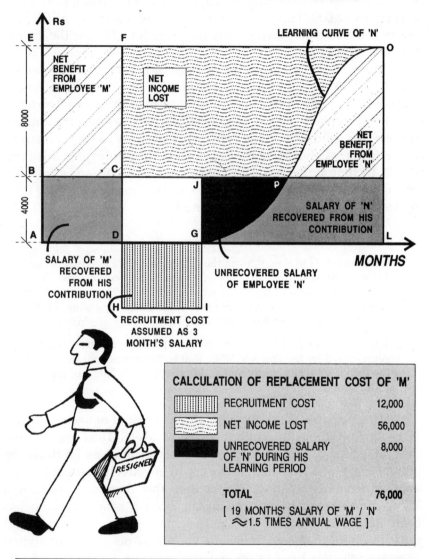

REPLACEMENT COST OF KNOWLEDGE WORKER

CALCULATION OF REPLACEMENT COST OF 'M'

| | | |
|---|---|---|
| ▦ | RECRUITMENT COST | 12,000 |
| ░ | NET INCOME LOST | 56,000 |
| ■ | UNRECOVERED SALARY OF 'N' DURING HIS LEARNING PERIOD | 8,000 |
| | **TOTAL** | **76,000** |

[ 19 MONTHS' SALARY OF 'M' / 'N'
≈ 1.5 TIMES ANNUAL WAGE ]

*Figure 1.1*

Let us first take the case of employee M. From time A to time D, when he is employed by a company, he is costing Rs 4000 by way of salary. This is represented by the rectangle, ABCD. During this time, the sales he generates is, according to the assumption stated earlier, Rs 12,000. This is represented by the rectangle, AEFD. The net benefit from employing M is therefore Rs 8,000, or the area of the rectangle BEFC.

At time, D, the employee M resigns. Say, it takes three months and Rs 12,000 to select a replacement for him. The replacement, employee N, joins at time G. As it takes time for a new recruit to effectively replace an old employee, for he has to be inducted, trained and gradually made fully functional, let us plot a learning curve for N, as shown by the curve GPO. It is only after this time, that is, by time L, that he can be considered to be fully and effectively replacing M. Now, to compute the loss to the company arising from replacing M by N, let us start at time D.

1. A recruitment cost of Rs.12,000 is assumed.

2. From time G/J to time P, even the salary paid to N is not recovered fully, as he is under induction and training. (I could have ideally added induction and training cost too, but for the sake of simplicity, I have ignored it.) As such, the cost represented by the area GJPG, which amounts to Rs 8,000, has to be borne by the company.

3. The biggest element of the replacement cost is the third element represented by the area CFOPJC, that is, the net benefit that would have accrued to the company had M not resigned. This area amounts to Rs 56,000.

Adding 1, 2 and 3, it is observed that the cost of replacing M with N is Rs 76,000, or 19 months' wages of M/N. Thus we see that despite conservative assumptions, it costs as much as 1.5 times the annual wage of a knowledge worker to effectively replace him by another from the market. (Of course, this does not apply if a knowledge worker is replaced by an internal candidate who has been effectively groomed to take over. In such cases, one can and must evaluate the positive benefit accruing from the motivational energies released by a promoted employee. A discussion of this alternative is beyond the scope of this book.)

## 6. Traditional quality "control" methods are powerless

In view of the instantaneous nature of service being provided by front-line staff in geographically far-flung locations, with spontaneity and customer responsiveness being rated crucial by the market place, there is no time or possibility to use traditional methods of "controlling" quality by checking the output of the "lower echelons". Quality has to be delivered, "right, the first time ", by unsupervised, autonomous front-line staff. It is their attitude and commitment, skills and knowledge, authority and initiative, rather than managerial control systems, that have to ensure quality. Organizations can no longer be satisfied if their products merely *meet specifications*. Nor is it enough to *satisfy the customers*. The winners in corporate competition are those who constantly *delight their customers* by anticipating and exceeding customers' expectations in a consistent manner.

## 7. The autocratic manager

For reasons that will be spelt out in Chapter 2, the belief system most managers operate out of is one that suspects all human beings —other than their own exalted selves, of course—to be lazy and naturally disposed to doing shoddy, poor quality work. As such, most managers believe that their focus of activity must be to control, check and bully their "lazy" subordinates to work properly. Their approach, as well as basic belief system, will be a major stumbling block in any corporation's attempt to deal with the six elements described earlier.

## THE MANAGERIAL SOLUTION FOR THE THIRD-WAVE CORPORATION

In view of the seven elements of the new managerial problem, it appears that the only way a corporation can hope to achieve and sustain excellent performance is by having a management that has an abiding faith in the potential and willingness of their knowledge workers and front-line staff to reach perfection in their jobs. They have, of course, to back this faith with the rest of what it takes to empower front-line staff: select the right people, teach and train them, equip them with the necessary resources and authority, and permit them to take decisions on their feet, in the wider interests of the corporation and its customers. With this as the core of the solution, a management can work out the rest of what it takes to succeed in the corporate world.

## ORGANIZATIONS AS NURSERIES FOR HUMAN GROWTH

While the industrial organization of the early part of this century was primarily responsible for degrading human existence, treating Man like a cog in a wheel, the industrial organizations of the last decade of the century are poised to become "nurseries for human growth". Just as a landscape artist fights a difficult environment by carefully nurturing varieties of plants in a nursery till they are strong enough to be replanted in the open, so also will organizations have to carefully select, train and nurture human beings in a manner that will help them grow and survive in the rough and tumble of organizational reality.

For the first time in the history of economic organizations, the unfolding of human nature to its full potential of perfection has become a critical, unavoidable factor for economic success. Adam Smith's Economic Man has to be replaced by an achievable version of Abraham Maslow's Self-Actualizing Man.

While some organizations have indeed looked at themselves as nurseries for human growth, because it is the decent thing to do by the employees, all others will have to join in, if only because there is no other way to achieve healthy, bottom-line results.

Since a key element of the managerial problem is the implicit assumption of most managers that other human beings are somehow inferior to their own exalted selves, it is essential to understand how this has arisen. In the next chapter, I will trace the historical developments that have led to such a belief system, one that is centred on distrust, suspicion and negative expectations.

# 2

# A HISTORICAL PERSPECTIVE OF "THE BATTLE FOR HUMAN NATURE"

## THE EASTERN ORIGINS

On the banks of the river Saraswati, now thought to be a subterranean river flowing under the Indo-Gangetic plains of northern India, many millennia ago, wise men propounded the first ever theory on human aspiration for unfolding the species' inherent nature of perfection. According to Western historians, this was in the fourth millennium BC. However, it is claimed to have been much earlier than that by some scholars of the most ancient work that contained the philosophy of these seers, the *Rig Veda*.

This early conceptualization of Man's inherent nature of godliness grew into what came to be referred to as Hindu philosophy. As per this belief system, the life spark in every living being was a representation of godliness. Whether one was a priest, a warrior, a trader, or a labourer, it was the manner in which one lived that was held to be important. Ideally, one was to apply oneself to one's tasks without any thought of the fruits of one's effort. To give in abundance and take but a little, for one's sustenance, was the moral code one was expected to live by.

Through the centuries, different interpretations were made, populist religious practices evolved, political parties used the "Hindu" cloak for cover and the original statement of Truth got hidden, rather like the river on whose banks it was first postulated.

Buddhism, Jainism and many other offshoots of Hinduism spread, carrying similar, but modified versions of the basic faith in human nature. Many countries in the Eastern world drew their moral code for living from such and similar philosophies. Some still do.

Meanwhile, in the Western world, a different world view was developing, which, with its later military and economic success, was to influence the East considerably. The Greek philosophers, in the sixth century BC, articulated a way of life that balanced one's individual and societal role. The city state was to be the nursery for human fulfilment.

## THE ACORN AND THE OAK TREE

Aristotle said it was as natural for a human being to achieve his full potential as it was for an acorn to grow into an oak tree. He also said that just as an acorn required the right physical conditions, such as soil, heat and moisture for its growth, so also does Man require a conducive, enabling atmosphere to attain his full growth. While Aristotle saw nature as a system of capacities or forces of growth directed by an inherent aspect of itself towards characteristic ends, he also saw constraints for growth. This led him to his identification and description of the crucial role of a statesman. He saw the statesman as one who needed to understand both what was possible and what was actual. Like an artist, his role was to blend form, matter and movement to bring out the full potential. It is worth noting, at this stage, that there is a remarkable resemblance between Aristotle's Greek city state and its statesmen and the modern day's organization and its human resources specialists respectively. To stretch the similarity further, the ideal Greek city state was to have a maximum population of 5,000 while most organizational specialists today would agree that when employee force grows beyond such a size, it is necessary to restructure into smaller sized, profit centres. Schumacher, of course, had suggested a much smaller size for effectiveness.

To get back to history, it is sad to record, however, that Aristotle did not accord the right of citizenship to slaves. Their lot, apparently, was not to question, but to do and die. In India, the caste system by which a vast majority were denied similar rights, including entry into temples of worship, began a similar perpetuation of double standards. Since then, both in the East and in the West, social structures have continued to allow the existence of double standards in affording opportunities for full growth. Industrial organizations were also to fall into this trap later, "workmen" being treated differently from management and owners.

## THE COPERNICAN REVOLUTION

The birth and spread of Christianity, its central concepts and the moral conditioning that people across the globe went through is too well known to require any restatement in this book. However, a few aspects central to the theme of the book need to be emphasized. The moral teachings, and the religious content of Christianity were set in the then accepted assumption that Man, and his abode, the Earth, were the centres of the entire universe.

When Nicolaus Copernicus's book, *On the Revolution of the Celestial Spheres* was published in the year of his death, 1543, questioning the assumption that the earth was the centre of the universe, official Christendom unfortunately reacted in a violent manner. It was possibly in expectation of such a reaction that Copernicus had held back what was clearly known to him and his close friends for over 30 years. It took well over 100 years after the death of Copernicus for the world at large to accept the unavoidable astronomical truth. Giants like Kepler, Galileo and Newton had to add to and substantiate Copernicus' theory. The rigour and discipline of science had to overcome prejudices and resistance from the officials of Christendom. During this period, several people were burnt at the stake for daring to mouth the "scientific heresy" about Man's abode not being the centre of the universe.

## IMPACT ON CHRISTENDOM'S INFLUENCE

Unfortunately, however, as this astronomical fact was sought to be tied in with the unquestionable, moral force of Christianity, the hold of the latter began to get loosened. This was to be a major reason why philosophical enquiry in the West was to start following two distinctly separate lines of thought. The majority turned their attention to an exploration of the physical universe, while a small minority continued to focus on the nature and purpose of human existence.

While the laws of physics were at the forefront in identifying the place of the earth as a minute, far from prominent planet in space, they also spawned many applications by which Man could control and use physical bodies for his day-to-day living. Applications in the field of engineering accelerated the process of the industrial revolution. Manufacturing industries built around machines and machineries transformed the nature of human activity, the structure of society, relationships among and between people. Toffler refers to these changes as the second wave, which moved millions of people out of their traditional roles of prosumption (meaning the agrarian way of producing for one's own consumption) to playing the split roles of both a producer of goods (in a central place, i.e. a factory) for others as well as a consumer of goods produced by others in other, similar factories.

## ADAM SMITH'S PRESCRIPTION AND THE UNDERLYING BELIEFS

A further acceleration of the process towards this new way of life came with Adam Smith's prescription for economic action. His major work, *The Wealth of Nations*, published in 1776, was to prove a veritable blueprint for human activity for the next two centuries and more. Free market, and the implied law of the "survival of the fittest" became the concept by which most of humanity would choose to live. Within the context of our current discussion, it would be relevant to highlight what Smith had to say about the human being.

While advocating specialization of labour, in the interest of enhanced productivity, he also warned what its effect on the human being so employed would be:

The man whose life is spent in performing a few simple operations has no occasion to exert his understanding, or to exercise his invention in finding out expedients for difficulties which never occur. He naturally loses, therefore the habit of such exertion and generally becomes as stupid and ignorant as it is possible for a human creature to become.

This apparently did not worry many of those who put Smith's ideas into action. Smith had also been quite candid about his assessment of the intrinsic nature of Man, for he said:

It is in the inherent interest of every man to live as much at his ease as he can; and if his emoluments are to be precisely the same whether he does or does not perform some very laborious duty, to perform it in as careless and slovenly a manner that authority will permit.

## THE IMPACT OF INDUSTRIAL REVOLUTION ON MAN

Taking a historical perspective, and viewing the advantages of free markets over controlled economies, there can be hardly any doubt as to the advantages of the former. With the experience of what is happening in Eastern Europe, and most parts of the erstwhile USSR and its ideological allies, there can be no arguments on the subject either. But Man is not restricted to a choice between the two extreme systems. In fact, most countries that chose the path of free markets have had to temper the purity of Smith's prescription with humanistic counterweights.

Without belittling the advantages of the free market system, especially the entrepreneurial energies it releases, or questioning the far superior quality of life that it can eventually lead to—depending on the design and choice of humanistic counterweights—for the purposes of this book, it is important to dispassionately look at what the implementation of the free market system did to the common man in the West, and eventually in the East too. That Smith's basic assumption on human nature was incorrect, I will endeavour to prove later in the book. For the present, let it suffice for it to be stated that, like many before and after him, he was equating observed human behaviour under peculiar conditions to the intrinsic nature itself. The observations may have been right, but the conditions were not viewed as they should have been—they were not universal, unchangeable ones. Under different conditions, which the modern organization can provide, human behaviour can be vastly different from Smith's observations. In fact, the objective of this book is to not only prove that it is so, but also suggest how to bring about such conditions.

As the Industrial Revolution swept the world, what followed was this.

Technological improvements in farming reduced the number of people required to produce the food required by society. From about 80% of the people being gainfully employed in agrarian pursuits, including men and women, the figure began to come down rapidly. In many economically developed countries today, as little as 3% of the people are employed in agricultural production, while in less economically developed countries, it ranges all the way up to the original figure of 80%.

There was an exodus of human beings from rural, community oriented joint families, to urban ghettos or slums located near the new centres of human activity. Major compromises had to be made on the quality of life while doing so. Those employed were mainly men, who had to either bring their immediate family, or more often, leave them behind in the villages, while accepting to live alone in an urban slum.

The urban centres of production, at first very small manufacturing sheds, gradually became gigantic, mass-manufacturing complexes whose major characteristics were:

- *Standardization* of goods, processes and procedures of work, restricting the activity of thinking to those who designed the production process and the machines, while the rest were to do menial, unskilled or semiskilled jobs.

- *Specialization* , which meant that a worker was to do repetitive tasks day in and day out. By the time Henry Ford started manufacturing Model T's in 1908, it took 7,882 operations to make one car. In his autobiography, Ford notes that close to 50% of those operations were of a type that "women or older children" could perform. He also says, "We found that 670 could be filled by legless men, 2,637 by one-legged men, two by armless men, 715 by one-armed men and 10 by blind men".

- *Synchronization:* To make the machines run for 24 hours and thus increase production, it was necessary for all human beings associated with mass manufacturing to adjust their living, not around the traditional rhythm of the season or one's natural, circadian cycle, but around artificial shift timings and other production patterns. It is not at all surprising that schools began, around this time, to place a high priority on punctuality, learning by rote and blind acceptance of authority and command.

- *Maximization:* On the grounds of economies of scale, the concept of "the larger the better" took hold of all organizations. Tall pyramidal structures arose within organizations, with supposedly crisp and clear lines of command stretching across wider and wider gaps between those who took decisions and those who executed them. To ensure that the "intrinsically lazy" worker did not slacken, layers of supervisors, charge-hands and shop superintendents were employed. Productivity norms, incentives for higher production and penalties for failure completed the setting.

- *Concentration and centralization* of information, command, money and power in the hands of powerful Government and corporations: The concepts of central planning, permits, quotas, grants, and so on, are direct consequences of a small minority deciding that they have to decide how others shall live.

- *The marginalization of women:* In an agrarian setting, as it exists in many parts of India still, a woman played several roles simultaneously, such as a mother, a wife, a part-time farm hand, a teacher of children, a transmitter of culture and traditions, a craftswoman who made handicraft and household objects, an organizer, and so on. As some of her roles were location-specific and time-specific, she could time her activities in a manner that was perfectly acceptable as per the prosuming ethic of a farming community. Taking the time to give birth to and bring up children did not make her a less useful member of the community. In every sense of the term, she enjoyed equal status with men.

  When she was forced to move to an urban ghetto and reduced to doing just a fraction of what she was accustomed to do in the rural setting, her own sense of importance as an equal member of her community diminished, let alone others' assessment of her utility.

Barring a few exceptionally enlightened societies, down-town areas of most major cities of the world are close approximations to this picture even today.

23

## THE JUSTIFICATION OF RICARDO AND MALTHUS

Let us now turn our attention to how those in authority tried to justify to themselves that this was an acceptable state of affairs. The requisite social conditioning was sought to be accomplished by several people. It is best exampled by David Ricardo (1772–1823) and Thomas Malthus (1766–1834), contemporaries and friends, who united in attributing even low wages and resulting inequality to the prodigious and devastating fertility of the working classes. It was the workmen's uninhibited breeding that was said to be the cause of their poverty. This kept wages at subsistence levels—the equilibrium to which from the force of numbers, they tended. Ricardo called this the iron law of wages. Not the system, or the principles which had spawned it, but the worker himself was supposed to be the main reason for his own misery.

## DARWIN'S THESIS IN SUPPORT OF SMITH'S

As stated earlier, the implied belief in Smith's framework was that only the fittest would survive, and that it should be viewed as an inevitable way of life and a necessary cost to bear in the interest of overall efficiencies. His belief was to be reinforced by a major development in another field of science, with Charles Darwin's publication of *On the Origin of Species* in 1859.

Until Darwin, whenever any species was observed to demonstrate a marvellous ability or skill, like the giraffe's long neck, a wolf's cunning, or the chameleon's ability to change its colour to merge with the surroundings, one attributed it to God's grand design, concern, or blessing. The giraffe was believed to have been given a long neck as part of God's design so that it could reach out to the tallest of trees and at the same time, not overbalance and fall down. A wolf was believed to have been blessed with the intelligence to cope with its smaller body, as compared to, say, the lion.

In one fell swoop, Darwin disproved all of this and shook the Western Man's faith in God and his prowess. For, what Darwin proved was this:

Within all species, there are small, but significant variations in the characteristics of its members, mainly in their structure and behaviour. Those members whose variations most suited the environment they inhabited, survived and reproduced, while others gradually became extinct. Thus, among giraffes, those with shorter necks became extinct, while those with longer necks mated to produce offspring with even longer necks. Over many cycles of reproduction, the giraffe came to look as it now does.

*Likewise, Man had descended, or evolved from the Ape. He was not the special creation in the image of God who suddenly appeared in the Garden of Eden.*

Throughout history, religion had been an important force that controlled selfish and greedy behaviour among men. The moral purpose of life, the code for everyday living, the attitude to work and duty and a spirit of giving rather than taking, are central features of all religions.

Unfortunately, in the west, two major scientific discoveries—Copernicus' and Darwin's—sandwiched the creation of Adam Smith's economic, rational man. While the officials of the most influential religion fought and lost the battle against the scientific discoveries, they stood by helplessly, like everyone else in the world, as the industrial revolution reduced most people to a state when their only chance for survival was to forget about concepts such as the *protestant ethic* and to behave in a greedy, selfish manner as they traded their time and skills for money. What made it worse was the fact that Darwin's thesis lent tremendous strength to those who had advocated the principle of "survival of the fittest" for conduct of human affairs, like Smith, Ricardo and Malthus.

## THE CASE FOR HUMAN ASPIRATION AND GOODNESS

While all this was happening, the minority who concerned themselves with enquiries into human aspiration, morality, goodness and so on, were slowly being marginalized. Lone voices were raised now and then, but their impact on arresting the juggernaut of the industrial revolution was negligible. Unfortunately, many of those who were urging moral restraint, and humanistic treatment, were caught in the war between official christendom and scientists on the truth of stories and legends, a factor that need never have been allowed into the ambit of debates on human conduct. However, that was how history developed.

The one who was to have the most major impact on tilting the balance back, in favour of the exploited common man, was Karl Marx. Again, as people in the last decade of the twentieth century are still quoting Karl Marx and attempting to force-fit his theories in a vastly different context with telling negative effects, it would be important to dwell on the rise and influence of Marx on industrial establishments. Both his early relevance, and latter-day irrelevance, will be discussed at different places in the book. For the present, let me recall some essential details of his early impact.

As organizations grew in size, larger numbers of people were brought to work together, and thus share the problems together too. Their numbers, and the fact that they were pretty well driven to the wall by the abominable conditions, made it a natural setting for someone with organizing ability to suggest that they stand up and make a fight for a better deal. That is exactly what Marx did. Together with Friedrich Engels, he created the Working Men's Association (also referred to as The First International) in 1864, and united workmen, by trade and industry. Karl Marx's *Das Kapital* had far greater appeal for the working man than, obviously, the thesis put forward by Ricardo and Malthus. As the democratic wave swept the world meanwhile, in the aftermath of the French Revolution in 1789, governments and societal bodies began to take up the cause of the common man, for he now had a voice in the electoral process too. Legislations were passed, courts were set up, and systems designed, to regulate the actions of employers vis-a-vis the employees.

These developments led to the common employee perceiving his employer as an evil exploiter who, left to himself, would give him a raw deal. The unions, on the other hand, were perceived to be the saviours, but for whom, the raw deal would have been perpetuated. Unfortunately, about the only point of agreement between management and unions was the view that Man's ability and desire to work were to be treated as a commodity for trade. The underlying, unstated assumption, was a ratification of Smith's stated view that Man will work only if he is extrinsically induced to do so. Since then, till today, the world has been led to believe that this has always been the case. That the best of people had enjoyed their work or activity throughout history, in all countries, was to be forgotten or cast aside as a ludicrous concept that only idealists would waste time talking about. The protestant ethic was to be left behind as a relic of history.

New terms and words were introduced, which had not existed till then. "Rate busters" and "workaholics" were the kind of terms used to control those who relapsed into the habit of enjoying what they were doing, for "enjoyment of work" was henceforth to be treated on par with drugs and alcohol, as a bad habit to get into. Whenever organizations took care to make work interesting, and gave freedom and space for employees to think for themselves and to innovate, the more entrenched union leaders felt threatened. There have been many occasions when my advocating of humanistic policies in corporations have led me into confrontations with entrenched union leaders, for they were afraid that their popularity, and need, would be eroded. The higher the stakes for their continuing in leadership positions, the happier they were to let some amount of unhappiness and unrest continue among their members. Not only human labour, but also human misery, has become a commodity for trade.

## THE SPREAD OF WESTERN TECHNOLOGICAL DEVELOPMENT AND "BELIEF SYSTEMS" TO THE EAST

By the end of nineteenth century, improved shipping and mastery of the world's waterways and seas had already allowed the more powerful nations of the West to colonize large parts of Asia, Africa, America, Australia and the islands of the South Seas.

As it was economic might that had enabled the West to conquer the rest of the world, even the conquered grudgingly admired the economic system that was behind it all. This in turn led to importation of the belief systems behind the economic miracle—that Man was a self-seeking, greedy person whose skills, abilities and miseries at work were to be dealt with as commodities to be supervised, checked, evaluated and traded. Within a short time, cities like Bombay, Mexico City and Jakarta bore greater scars of industrialization than London and Birmingham. There are more man-days lost due to industrial unrest in these countries than Karl Marx could ever have imagined possible.

Meanwhile, there were several in the West who had pursued the trail of human nature. Soren Kierkegaard, Spinoza, Schweitzer, and many others warned of the consequences of overemphasis on the physical and material side of life. They were gradually sidelined, and each lived the life of a recluse towards their later years, limiting their influence to small communities around them, and to writing their thoughts down for later generations to hopefully pay more attention to. Spinoza was excommunicated, and even changed his name as he lived alone in a foreign country. Albert Schweitzer sought interior Africa and a jungle hospital to live in. The East caught up soon, in the global march towards the obliteration of all who dared talk of human virtues. Mahatma Gandhi was assassinated within a few months of winning freedom for India. That he was killed by a fanatic in the name of the Hindu religion—one that believes in the inherent godliness of all living beings—should be viewed historically as another indication of the direction the world was taking.

## DIMINISHING INFLUENCE OF RELIGIONS

Thus, the influence of religion on morality and modes of life was altered from a positive force to a frighteningly negative, destablisizing one. Communities that had lived together in peace for centuries, in a spirit of "live and let live", were converted through classical manoeuvres to national and electoral constituencies. Religious, ethnic and racial communities became sociopolitical groups, whose memberships were to be obtained and retained by the extent of damage one could do to those belonging to another group. This created an alternative to Marxist class wars. It is interesting to note that while those who sought to implement Marxist theories banned religious worship in their countries, the converse was true as well.In those countries where religious groups acquired political power, Marxism had little appeal. One of the original purposes of religions was to provide a system of beliefs that would allow human development within strict codes of moral and social behaviour. This was cast aside slowly but surely. Just as attendance in churches declined drastically, mosques, temples and other places of worship began to lose their moral hold on the communities they were to serve. Religious festivals lost their meaning, giving place to drunken revelries, gambling and other forms for release of social tension. In the name of religion, wars were fought and countries destroyed.

Across the globe, all events seemed to conspire to convince Man that there was really no purpose in life other than giving in to economic realities and political pressures. As Man's behaviour drastically changed under these conditions, those who chose to study his actions and behaviour were emboldened to postulate that his true nature was warped and manipulable. In the West, Freud, the behavioural scientists and evolutionary biologists led the fold, and were to have the greatest impact. Let me highlight some of their studies and conclusions.(For a more detailed analysis of this phase of development, I refer the reader to Barry Schwartz's *The Battle for Human Nature*.)

## FREUDIAN STUDIES AND CONCLUSIONS

Sigmund Freud studied the statements, behaviours and dreams of people who had come to him for cure. By definition, they were people who had faced problems in finding a balance in life, and exhibited abnormal behaviour. From his studies, he concluded that their problems arose from repression of sexual desires. His explanations, and many cures, were truly brilliant, given the fact that he had a pre-selected sample of people exhibiting deviant behaviour in societies that had not loosened the Victorian shackles of sexual prudery. That sexual repression must have caused a great many problems in such a society is obvious today, from a historical perspective. Again, Freudian theories, like the Marxist, have been extended far beyond their context with university professors, psychologists and psychiatrists still quoting him as if the world had been at a standstill for most of a century.

At the height of the industrial revolution, with one World War over and another looming ahead, the behavioural scientists entered the scene, of whom B F Skinner was one of the most influential. Before discussing the conclusions of behavioural scientists, it might help if I were to describe the type of experiments they relied upon to arrive at conclusions about human behaviour, and implicitly, human nature:

## FROM PIGEONS TO MEN: THE BEHAVIOURAL SCIENTISTS

A pigeon deprived of food is confined to a small space, bereft of anything but dim illumination, an illuminated disk at the level of its eye and a hole for grains to be introduced. By exposing food through the opening, the pigeon is excited; but before it can eat a single grain, the food is removed. Gradually, and by an accident that is bound to occur in such a small space, the pigeon's beak touches the disc. A resounding click is produced, and immediately food is introduced and allowed to remain long enough for the pigeon to grab a few grains. Then, the food is taken out, and not introduced again till the pigeon's beak touches the disc. By this process, the pigeon learns that if it wants food, it should peck at the disc first. The experimenter then lets the pigeon get a little more hungry, making it peck at the disc desperately. After say, ten pecks, the food is introduced, and the same sequence repeated, till the pigeon learns that the cost of food is ten pecks at the disc. Similarly, the cost of food is increased to fifty, seventy-five and even a hundred pecks at the disc.

This sort of experiment, among other things, is supposed to prove a major point of the behavioural scientists, *the principle of reinforcement*—people will continue to engage only in those activities that get them what they want.

Applied to the kind of conditions that obtained in most industrial settings, where Man had been conditioned by factors such as mass production technology, standardization, gross under utilization of his cognitive powers, and so on, it was observed that what was true for pigeons was true for human beings too. Industrial engineers developed incentive schemes that would have Man paid for the number of goods he produced, exactly as a pigeon earned food by pecking at illuminated discs.

## THE EVOLUTIONARY BIOLOGIST AND THE SELFISH GENE

Meanwhile, another development took place, which was to complement the events described so far. Evolutionary biologists supported the economists and behavioural scientists that all organisms were primarily maximizers of self-interest. All behaviour, including falling in love, getting married, having children, protecting one's family, and so on, were reduced to the simple explanation that the selfish gene is only interested in the proliferation and preservation of itself. Though it has been proven that the influence of culture and environment on determining human behaviour is of much greater significance, this aspect has been accorded scant regard by many evolutionary biologists.

By taking limited views of economic theory, Marxism, Darwinism, behavioural sciences and evolutionary biology, it is possible to paint a picture of Man as a greedy, self-serving, petty and manipulable being. This distorted picture has become an easy excuse to fall upon, whenever a human being wants to explain away why he is treating another of his own species in a dehumanizing manner.

## THE EVIDENCE FROM SHOP-FLOORS SUPPORTS HUMANISTS

However, there has been compelling evidence from the shop-floors of all countries that whenever such a view of Man is sought to be translated into the work situation, the results are woefully lacking in quality. Starting with the famous Hawthorne experiments in the Western Electric Company near Chicago in the late '20s, the current century has been witness to the work of several people who have attempted to change the tide of history in the battle for human nature.

The Hawthorne studies of Elton Mayo and Rothlisberger proved that human concern and attention leads to much greater impact on productivity and quality than any other factor. From the '40s, humanists led by Abraham Maslow and management theorists like Drucker, McGregor and Herzberg produced great models and theories to support the same. The successful implementation of the humanistic, Japanese system in the West, was nothing but an assertion of what the best of both Western and Eastern thinkers, philosophers and management specialists had been saying. Yet, the impact on industrial organizations of such views have, at best, been marginal. The historically evolved, impoverished view of Man has been too compelling a force to fight against and overcome. Konosuke Matsushita summed up the impasse when he said in 1988:

> We will win and you will lose. You cannot do anything about it because your failure is an internal disease. Your companies are based on Taylor's principles. Worse, your heads are Taylorized too. You firmly believe that sound management means executives on the one side and workers on the other, on the one side men who think and on the other side men who only work. For you, management is the art of smoothly transferring the executives' ideas to the workers' hands.

> We have passed the Taylorian stage. We are aware that business has
> become terribly complex. Survival is very uncertain in an
> environment filled with risk, the unexpected, and competition ...
> We know that the intelligence of a few technocrats—even very bright
> ones—has become totally inadequate to face these challenges. Only
> the intellects of all employees can permit a company to live with the
> ups and downs and the requirements of the new environment. Yes,
> we will win and you will lose. For you are not able to rid your
> minds of obsolete Taylorisms that we never had.

Whatever Matsushita might have meant by the word, "you", it would be advisable for all industrialists of the world—both in the East and the West—to take it that he meant to include all those who still have doubts in their mind about the intrinsic capacity of human nature to reach perfection. As explained in the previous chapter, the radical changes occurring in the nature of industrial activity, and their consequent impact on the role of front-line employees and knowledge workers, leave little choice for a line manager but to accept Matsushita's advice.

## THE NEED FOR A GLOBAL, NON-PARTISAN VIEW

While accepting Matsushita's advice, it is also essential that one avoids falling a prey to classical schisms like "we" v. "you", "West" v. "East", or "capitalism" v. "socialism". To believe that everything that has come out of Western economic success has been negative is as ridiculous as to believe that the only solution is to go back to the purity of Adam Smith's free markets, with no humanistic counter-weights. At the same time, adopting Eastern mysticism without subjecting it to the rigour of logical analysis will be as unwarranted as discarding its virtues because of the relative economic failure of the East. It is essential that everyone drop petty, partisan attitudes and adopt a truly global view of the problem. We need to seek solutions that will adapt meritorious ideas and suggestions from all schools, isms, regions and religions.

Global developments in diverse fields appear to help support Willis Harman's optimistic view that a major paradigm shift is taking place that will revolutionize the way Man perceives his place and purpose in the universe. Harman calls this the second Copernican revolution, for physicists, neurophysicians, psychologists, management theorists and Environmentalists are beginning to converge towards the mutually supportive view that the true potential of human nature is exactly what almost all religions have claimed it to be: Pure Quality and Perfection are inherent, rather than acquired. And life and living is entirely about how to reach and reveal it.

A fundamental aspect of the new paradigm has to be a model of human nature that is consistent with such a mutually supportive view, which is trans-racial, a-national and global. In an attempt to build and present such a model, let me start with a humanist who led the way in the West, Abraham Maslow.

# MASLOW REVISITED: WEST MEETS EAST

Abraham Maslow was born in 1908. His early years, as the eldest child of a poor, Jewish immigrant family, were spent in the slum districts of Brooklyn in New York city. His father, who had immigrated from Kiev in Ukraine, was a cooper by trade. At the age of 18, Maslow entered New York City College—which was free—and began studies in law, a subject considered to have been a sensible choice by his father. Within a year, Maslow decided to quit, for very interesting reasons. In his biographical account, Colin Wilson quotes Maslow: "The cases seemed to deal only with evil men, and with sins of mankind."

Later, Maslow studied psychology at the University of Wisconsin, which he enjoyed. As the focus of psychology was at that time on behavioural science, Maslow was to spend his student days and early working life in that field. Even as an undergraduate, he had published several papers based on experiments with dogs, rats and monkeys. Outside his working life, however, there were other passions that he developed. He married his cousin and childhood sweetheart, Bertha. He also found great comfort and enjoyment through a newfound love for classical music. Beethoven, Bach and Mozart were constant reminders to him that Man's inherent potential for perfection was real.

After moving to Brooklyn college, where he was to teach and do research for 14 years, Maslow began to move out of the influence of behavioural scientists. People like Max Wertheimer—the founder member of the gestalt school—and Erich Fromm influenced him as much as the works of European psychologists, Kurt Goldstein and Kurt Lewin. Goldstein's key concept about human behaviour was that of *self-actualization*. This was to become the cornerstone for the brilliant edifice Maslow was to build later on, redefining self-actualization as Man's "desire to become more and more what one idiosyncratically is, to become everything that one is capable of becoming".

## A THEORY OF HUMAN MOTIVATION

In 1943, he published his classic, *A Theory of Human Motivation*, where for the first time, he introduced the concept of a hierarchy of needs. He possibly had no idea as to the impact that paper was to have on the field of psychology. Within a decade thereafter, psychologists who had accepted the thesis of that paper were already so different from classical Freudians and behaviourists that they came to be termed, the "third force", or the "humanists". Maslow continued in his efforts to help build a superstructure on the foundation he had laid right till his death in June 1970. A month before he died, he noted in his journal that what the world needed was 'an ethos, a scientific value system and way of life, and humanistic politics, with the theory, the facts, etc, all set forth soberly,' and concluded—with what are probably his last recorded words—'So again I must say to myself: to work!'

## PHYSIOLOGICAL NEEDS ARE PRIMARY

Maslow postulated that while a human being has an instinctive motivation to satisfy several needs, there is a definite sequence or hierarchy, through which these needs arise. The first need level he termed, *physiological,* the most typical of which are the need for food, water, sleep and sex. In a human being who is missing everything in life in an extreme fashion, it is most likely that the major motivation would be the physiological needs rather than any other. A person who is lacking food, safety, love and esteem would most probably hunger for food more strongly than anything else.

If all the needs are unsatisfied, and the organism is then dominated by the physiological needs, all other needs may become simply non-existent or be pushed into the background. It is then fair to characterize the whole organism by saying simply that it is hungry, for consciousness is almost completely preempted by hunger. All capacities are put into the service of the satisfaction of hunger, and the organization of these capacities is almost entirely determined by the one purpose of satisfying hunger. The receptors and effecters, the intelligence, memory, habits, all may now be defined simply as hunger satisfying tools. Capacities that are not useful for this purpose lie dormant, the desire to acquire an automobile, the interest in history, the desire for a new pair of shoes are, in the extreme case, forgotten or get to be of secondary importance. For the man who is extremely and dangerously hungry, no other interests exist but food. He dreams food, he thinks about food, he emotes only about food, he perceives only food, and he wants only food.

## LIVING BY BREAD ALONE

To understand this emotionally, rather than merely intellectually, let us consider a few examples:

First, take the situation that actually exists in many of the less developed countries today. There is rampant unemployment and no social security program worth the name. There are millions of jobless people who literally throw themselves at the feet of anybody and everybody who may be in a position to offer them hourly jobs or just food in exchange for any type of labour. With heads bowed and backs bent, in the body posture of the beggars they have been reduced to, they seek out any solution to their hunger. In Maslow's own words,

> For our chronically and extremely hungry man, Utopia can be
> defined simply as a place where there is plenty of food. He tends to

think that, if only he is guaranteed food for the rest of his life, he will be perfectly happy and will never want anything more. Life itself tends to be defined in terms of eating. Anything else will be defined as unimportant. Freedom, love, community feeling, respect, philosophy, may all be waved aside as fripperies that are useless, since they fail to fill the stomach. Such a man may fairly be said to live by bread alone.

## REQUIRING JUST PARTS OF A HUMAN BEING

In the early decades of the current century, when scientific management was making its impact on the industrialized Western world, such a hungry man was the ideal recruit. He was willing to accept the most boring and routine of tasks, even if it was one of just tightening nuts and bolts in an assembly line. Immigrant labour, landless rural folk escaping famine conditions in the less developed countries and chronically unemployed blacks in the USA were, in the Maslovian scale, at a stage when only physiological needs mattered. To them, job content, quality of work life, participation and so on would have appeared to be unimportant "fripperies".

Having the image of such a man in mind, it was tempting for industrial psychologists to conclude that management could "motivate" workmen by monetary incentives alone. What was left unstated by most of them was, of course, the ability of management to threaten dismissal when faced with undesirable behaviour, backed by the power to carry out the threat whenever it was deemed appropriate by them. Besides, much of the work they had in mind did not require any prior knowledge or training. As elaborated in Chapter 2, corporate giants like Henry Ford even saw work as being done by parts of human beings . . . of the jobs required to make Model T , '670 could be filled by legless men, 2,637 by one-legged men, two by armless men, 715 by one-armed men and ten by blind men'.

Not even whole men were required, but just parts of a human being. Far from paying heed to Adam Smith's statement (referred to in Chapter 2) as to the effect on a human being of such and similar work, theories and practices were being refined to heighten this dehumanizing effect.

## GRATIFICATION AS IMPORTANT AS DEPRIVATION

It was at such a point that Freudian psychology was making its impact, based as it was on the premise that the prime objective of the libidinal (creative) energies in Man is sexual. Abnormality, by this system of belief, is viewed as resulting from suppression or inadequate satisfaction of this natural, sexual instinct. Given the general conditions most common folk in urban centres had been reduced to, it is not at all surprising that this system of belief became a popular one.

Maslow not only clubbed sexual needs together with other physiological needs but also went further to suggest that far from being the only need, they represented just the beginning of a sequence of needs. When physiological needs are satisfied, other (and higher) needs immediately emerge and these, rather than physiological needs, dominate the organism. And when these in turn are satisfied, again new (and still higher) needs emerge, and so on. This is what Maslow meant when he said that 'the basic human needs are organized into a hierarchy of relative prepotency.'

A major implication of this concept of an hierarchy of needs is that gratification becomes as important a factor as deprivation in understanding motivation. For gratification releases the organism from the domination of lower needs, permitting thereby the emergence of other and higher goals. This is a major point of difference between the Freudian model and that of Maslow. In Maslow's words,

> The physiological needs, along with their partial goals, when
> chronically gratified, cease to exist as active determinants or
> organizers of behaviour. They now exist only in a potential fashion
> in the sense that they may emerge again to dominate the organism if
> they are thwarted. But a want that is satisfied is no longer a want.
> The organism is dominated and its behaviour organized only by
> unsatisfied needs. If hunger is satisfied, it becomes unimportant in
> the current dynamics of the individual.

## SAFETY NEEDS COME NEXT

Once the physiological needs are satisfied, a human being begins to experience the stirrings of what Maslow termed, "safety needs". Typical of these are the need for security, stability, dependency, protection, structure, order, law and boundaries. Freedom from fear, anxiety and chaos is what is sought through satisfaction of these needs. In Maslow's words,

"All that has been said of the physiological needs is equally true, although in less degree, of these desires. The organism may equally well be wholly dominated by them. They may serve as the most exclusive organizers of behaviour, recruiting all the capacities of the organism in their service, and we may then fairly describe the whole organism as a safety-seeking mechanism. Again we may say of the receptors, the effecters, of the intellect, and of the other capacities that they are primarily safety-seeking tools. Again, as in the hungry man, we find that the dominating goal is a strong determinant not only of his current world outlook and philosophy but also of his philosophy of the future and of values. Practically everything looks less important than safety and protection (even sometimes, the physiological needs, which being satisfied, are now underesti-mated). A man in this state, if it is extreme enough and chronic enough, may be characterized as living almost for safety alone".

Most of us have a preference for some kind of routine or rhythm in our day-to-day life. We like to take the same route to work. We feel safe catching the same tube or train, preferably with a fair number of co-passengers we can recognize and greet. The familiar smells and sounds of our home and neighborhood seem to provide us as much security as Linus' blanket. These are but a few examples of how we experience and satisfy our safety needs every day. Safety needs assume a longer-term perspective too. The common pref-erence for a job that is permanent or has a tenure, for a reasonable bank balance, for a house one can call one's own, for insurance policies and for sound retirement plans are some other expressions of the second Maslovian level of needs.

## SHIFTING NEEDS AND SHIFTING LOYALTIES

To demonstrate better how a human being's needs shift from the physiological level to the safety level, once again consider the jobless person in an underdeveloped country. Let us assume that he lands a temporary job after many months of trying. He feels extremely happy and shows every inclination of remaining so. It is quite likely that he swears his total and undying loyalty to the benefactor who has been kind enough to employ him. However, if he continues in that temporary job for a sufficient length of time, he will find himself worrying about how to convert that job into a permanent one. If his erstwhile benefactor shows no inclination towards making his job status permanent, he will go to the closest union steward who is willing to help him out. With little or no qualms, he will be willing to shift his "total and undying" loyalty to the union, if they would meet his new need for safety.

Employers and management often express disgust at the manner in which such "ungrateful" people shift their loyalties! According to the Maslovian concept of the hierarchy of needs, employers should anticipate that their employees will experience the compelling influence of safety needs once their basic physiological needs are reasonably satisfied. The smart employer would offer the permanent status voluntarily, rather than appear to be giving in to external pressures under duress.

## TRADE UNIONISM OFFERED A SAFETY BELT

In Chapter 2, when tracing the historical developments that led to the birth of trade unions, it was shown that trade unionism was born when large numbers of people were congregated in dense, urban centres. Using Maslow's model, one can interpret this development by the observation that a critical mass of people were made to feel threatened simultaneously, their safety needs being inadequately met.

When people began to organize themselves, many in management reacted in the worst possible manner. Far from realizing that such an attempt to organize was an expression for the need of safety, they actually threatened employees with further deprivation of the same safety needs. Let us discuss two examples to elaborate this point.

In 1884, workers in the USA united in their attempt to have an eight-hour working day legalized. 500,000 of them struck work on May 1, 1886 in support of this demand, as many of them were being forced then to put in 12-to-14 hour workdays. Within four days, the strike was broken and the leaders arrested. Four of them, Parsons, Fischer, Engels and Spies were charged with treason, found guilty and hanged. In his last address to the court during the year long trial, Fischer prophetically said, 'The more the believers in a just cause are persecuted, the quicker will their ideas be realized'. By the turn of the century, the trade union movement had taken firm root in the USA and May 1 was being celebrated as International Labour Day across the world in memory of the four martyrs.

In 1874, across the globe, in Bombay, India, a British Inspector of Factories, Redgrave visited the city's textile mills and reported that the working conditions were appalling. He suggested immediate remedial measures, but was ignored. Soon thereafter, in 1884, the first ever trade union in India was formed, by Narayan Lokhande, in the same textile mills. Lokhande and his colleagues were hounded but not hanged. The first ever industrial strike in India was to take place later in the same industry.

Not all employers reacted in such a manner. There were notable exceptions in the very same countries and at about the same time, who chose to deal with employees differently.

In the USA, Eli Lilly, the giant pharmaceutical corporation that employs over 30,000 in several units located in the mid-western part of the USA, between Detroit and Chicago, has an impeccable record of industrial peace. While the automobile corporations with their headquarters in Detroit have had exactly the opposite reputation, it is useful to identify what Eli Lilly has done differently.

In personal interviews conducted among the staff and executives of Eli Lilly, I learnt that the founder of the corporation, Mr Lilly himself, had prioritized fair treatment of employees from the very beginning. One of his sons remained personally in charge of personnel for several decades. To questions asked of over 100 people in Indiana, as to who the best employer in the state was, over 80 % responded without hesitation, " Eli Lilly ".

In India, in the same textile industry, Jamsetji Tata proved how corporate success and employee wellbeing were mutually supportive. His first textile mill, the Empress Mills, was opened on Jan 1, 1877, almost exactly when Redgrave's report was probably being shelved. By the turn of the century, employees of the Empress Mills were already beneficiaries of a free medical scheme, provident fund program, creches for children of women employees, night school for employees who wished to develop themselves further, perfect ventilation and humidified air, and hosts of awards for performance, pension schemes and special allowances to help those who were disabled during employment. All of this had been voluntarily implemented, several decades before laws were contemplated, let alone passed.

In all countries, wherever employers took pains to adequately satisfy the physiological and safety needs of their employees, and thereafter created a feeling of belongingness between the employees and their corporation, tensions eased and quality of work improved. To understand this better, let me continue with Maslow's hierarchy of needs.

## THIRD COME THE BELONGINGNESS AND LOVE NEEDS

Maslow explained that if both physiological and the safety needs are fairly well gratified, there will emerge the love and affection and belongingness needs, and the whole cycle already described will repeat itself with this new centre. Now the person will feel keenly, as never before, the absence of friends, or a sweetheart, or a wife, or children. He will hunger for affectionate relations with people in general, namely for a place in his group or family, and he will strive with great intensity to achieve this goal. He will want to attain such a place more than anything else in the world and may even forget that once, when he was hungry, he sneered at love as unreal or unnecessary or unimportant. Now he will feel sharply the pangs of loneliness, of ostracism, of rejection, of friendlessness, of rootlessness.

To illustrate how Maslow's arguments apply to current-day reality as well, let us see what happens, in our example, to the worker who has a secure, permanent job. He begins to seek the companionship of those who have something in common with him. In the underdeveloped and developing countries, where there are many first-generation urban immigrants, it is normal for an industrial worker to seek the company of his *gaon-wallas*, or people who originally belonged to the same village. He manages to find lodgings in the same slum or *chawl* as his ethnic folk and begins a search for a wife to start a family.

That he was once a starving individual whose concept of utopia was lots of food is but a distant memory for him, as he spends his wakeful hours figuring out how to satisfy his belongingness needs. Unconsciously, he even subordinates the already satiated lower needs, to the conscious satisfaction of his new need. The evening meal, or the Sunday lunch becomes a social affair with its own rites and rituals. He likes to have his family and friends around while having the meal. It is their company, and a feeling of belonging, that is the motivation, rather than the food *per se*. A burnt dish or a spilt drink could even become a matter for laughter, as the family revels in its togetherness.

## A COMMUNITY THAT INCLUDES RATHER THAN SUBMERGES

Other expressions of this need are the old school tie, the urge for membership in clubs, associations such as the Freemasons, Rotary and the Lions, festivals, family gatherings and reunions and the fraternities in university campuses. When physiological and safety needs are reasonably satisfied, a human being's predominant need is to belong to a community of fellow beings in a manner that includes rather than submerges him. E F Schumacher, in his book, *Small is Beautiful*, has dwelt at length on how organizational designs that cater to this need for belonging prove to be very successful. Many modern-day work group concepts, including Japanese style "quality circles," are built around the satisfaction of this need in Man.

Even children begin to exhibit this tendency at a very early age. While a baby initially concentrates on satisfying her physiological needs—getting her fill of milk and sleep, at the same time freely wetting her nappies and bed—she very soon demonstrates her instinctive ability to climb the Maslovian hierarchy. Proximity of parents, visibility of familiar objects and habitual sounds and smells constitute her safety needs while the need for parental love, stroking, petting and inclusion in the activities of home life are a clear demonstration that she has reached the third level of needs.

## THE REBELLION OF YOUTH AS A SYMPTOM

Maslow believed that the tremendous and rapid increase in T-Groups and other personal growth groups and intentional communities may have been motivated by an unsatisfied hunger for contact, for intimacy, for belongingness and by the need to overcome the widespread feeling of alienation, strangeness and loneliness. Our mobility, the breakdown of traditional groupings, the scattering of families, the generation gap, the steady urbanization and disappearance of village "face-to-faceness", and the resulting shallowness of friendships have together led to many people feeling deprived at this Maslovian level. Some proportion of youth rebellion groups could also be motivated by the profound hunger for groupiness, for contact, for real togetherness in the face of the common enemy, any enemy that can serve to form an amity group by simply posing an external threat. The same kind of thing was observed in groups of soldiers who were pushed into an unwanted brotherliness and intimacy by their common external danger, and who may stick together throughout a lifetime as a consequence. 'Any good society,' Maslow concluded, ' must satisfy this need, one way or another, if it is to survive and be healthy.'

## THE DISAPPEARANCE OF THE BELONGINGNESS NEED

That this need arises only if the lower two needs are reasonably satisfied may be verified quite easily by considering a common enough example. Let us consider a child of five, who is in her element at home, an image of total happiness. Imagine her being taken by her parents to visit new neighbours. The child immediately subsides and withdraws into a shell, holds fast to her mother, and replaces her smile with a frown. She refuses to greet the neighbours, including the new kid next door. She takes her time to satisfy herself that her safety is not going to be threatened. Only when a sense of security returns does she start making overtures to the neighbours, initially venturing a smile, then moving within an arc of a few yards from her parents and eventually daring to go outside the visible range of the parents. Within the hour, she could be so happily adjusted to the new neighbours' presence that she may even resent the fact that the visit is over. The fact, however, remains that the affectionate side of her personality—which gives and receives love —would have temporarily taken a back seat while she was testing out the satisfaction of her safety needs.

It is much easier to observe the Maslovian hierarchy operating among children rather than among adults as infants do not inhibit their reactions while adults have learnt to inhibit natural instincts as part of cultural and social conditioning. Only under extreme conditions is it equally self-evident among adults. We will revert to this while discussing the concept of threshold limits in Chapter 5.

## FOURTH COME THE ESTEEM NEEDS

According to Maslow's model, when one's physiological, safety and belongingness needs are satisfied, one is faced with a new set of higher needs. He termed them "esteem needs". Maslow said, "All people in our society (with a few pathological exceptions) have a need or desire for a stable, firmly based, usually high evaluation of themselves, for self-respect, or self-esteem, and for the esteem of others. These needs may therefore be classified into two subsidiary sets. These are, first, the desire for strength, for achievement, for adequacy, for mastery and competence, for confidence in the face of the world, and for independence and freedom. Second, we have what we may call the desire for reputation and prestige (defining it as respect or esteem from other people), status, fame and glory, dominance, recognition, attention, importance, dignity, or appreciation." While Maslow appreciated the "dangers of basing self-esteem on the opinion of others rather than on real capacity, competence and adequacy to the task," he surprisingly concluded that the "most healthy self-esteem is based on deserved respect from others". To fully appreciate the chasm between "respect from others" and "self respect", let me go back eleven centuries and refer to a classical piece of work, Rajasekhara's *Kavyamimamsa*.

It is believed that Rajasekhara must have lived in the period between A D 880 to 920. Like Aristotle, Rajasekhara was a teacher of kings. King Nirbhaya Mahendrapala, who ruled over the country of Madhyadesa (now, part of central India), with his capital in Kannauj, and his son and successor were both Rajasekhara's pupils. While *Kavyamimamsa* originally contained 18 *adhikaranas*, or volumes, only the first adhikarana has been found. The rest are lost to us.

In *Kavyamimamsa*, Rajasekhara addresses himself to the rules, methods and processes by which a poet can reach self-actualization. He distinguishes three specific stages in the development of the creative faculty amongst artists, namely, *aupadeshika, aharya* and *sahaja*. Translated, the three words respectively mean 'learnt', 'gotten' and 'innate'. To highlight the nature of this classification, without losing its aesthetic essence, let me relate a real-life incident that occurred about twenty years ago:

A professor of oriental art had obtained a grant to revive the art of miniature paintings. He went to a village on the slopes of the Himalayas that was once known as the centre of this art form. He soon found out that no artists remained in the village, as they had also joined the exodus to the plains, in search of a better livelihood. Aware that craftsmanship was normally handed down from father to son, he looked around the village and located the house where the greatest master of them all had lived. He began his search for the descendants and finally located a grandson of the great master in a town in the plains. The poor man was eking out a livelihood as a painter of road signs, as that was the only use society had for his painting skills. The professor found out that he had been painting miniatures till a few years earlier, and had come down to the plains when his materials and equipment had run out. When the professor offered to support him in reverting to the traditional work back in the village, the painter agreed immediately.

Within a month, the painter was settled in his old home in the village, with all the tools, paints and brushes. The professor left him to his task for about two months. When he returned to check on the progress, he saw the painter totally engrossed in his task, quite oblivious to what was happening around him. Not wishing to disturb him, the professor left after checking with the family that the painter had all that he required. When the professor returned after a few weeks, he found the miniature completed. It was a superb creation, far better than he had hoped for. As he was looking at it with a magnifying glass, he noticed that there was no signature of the painter. When he pointed this out, the painter nodded and said, 'That's as it should be, for I did not paint it . The professor was flabbergasted: 'I saw you painting it myself a few weeks ago when I was here. How can you say now that you didn't paint it?' The painter, very agitated now, pleaded with the professor not to make such statements, all the while looking fearfully at the miniature painting. After a heated discussion, the professor began to understand.

## The level of *aupadeshika*: Nurturing of a student

The painter's education had started at an early age. He first received instructions' from his father-cum-guru on the maintenance of brushes, paints and tools, on the nature of colour and its hues, and on the details of the craftsmanship that went into the painting of miniatures. He initially worked like an apprentice, learning from what he observed. When his father thought he was ready for it, he

MASLOW'S HIERARCHY OF NEEDS

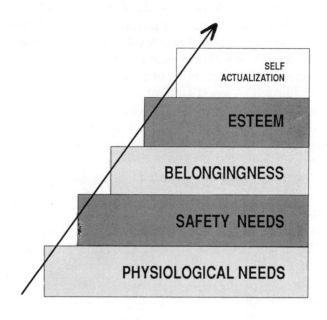

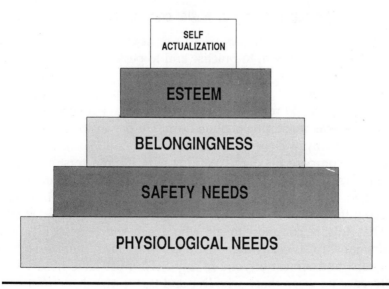

*Figure 3.1*

was allowed to try his hand at painting. He was corrected as he progressed and gradually reached a stage when all he required to do was *abhyasa,* or practice. The one quality considered most important for a student at this stage of development was considered to be, *anusila,* meaning "devoted application" or "obedience".

This was Rajasekhara's first level of creative development, *aupadeshika.* The student's objective, at this level, is to constantly make use of the master's "recognition" of his progress and thereby continually correct himself. A good student, having been accepted by the right master, wastes no time in questioning the merit of what the master has to say about his work. Feedback on performance, in other words, "recognition by (respected) others" is the only recognition that matters.

There is another important element to this stage. Before the painter and his father had begun their daily lesson, it was customary for them to pray together. As a child, the painter could not make sense out of this, but he had nevertheless gone ahead with the ritual till it became an automatic habit. As he progressed further, he began to realize that there was a distinct correlation between the state of his mind and the quality of what emerged during the lesson. But he could not quite understand why or how.

## Aharya: The self-esteem of a master craftsman

The painter then progressed to the next stage, *aharya.* He was basically left to himself, to practise and to perfect. Ananda Coomaraswamy explains in *Transformation of Nature in Art*: 'The fruit of *anusila* , or devoted application, is *slistatva,* or "habitus", meaning "second nature".' Progressing towards this stage, the painter began to feel he was mastering the medium. He began to experiment, to try out new approaches, to take short cuts and to improvise. He began to compare his own creations with the masters' and started a self-correcting course for himself. However much others praised him and his work, he knew that he was his own best critic. "Recognition by one's own standards", was the level he had reached.

That this is common to all who reach the levels of "master-craftsmanship" is easily demonstrated. Musicians, chefs, executives, teachers, and almost anyone in any field must have observed the difference between those who live and thrive on others' praise, and those who have absolute standards by which they evaluate the quality of what they do. 'I could have done better', 'I am capable of much better quality', and 'Oh ! This is nothing. I was at my best on . . .' are some of the standard expressions of people who have reached this stage of development.

## *Sahaja*: Merger of the doer and done

To get back to the tale of the painter, as he struggled and prayed, for several years, to reach perfection, he began to slowly reach the final stage. The automatic habit of starting his activity with prayers began to assume a different order of importance altogether. He found a sense of peace, quiet and total relaxation in him, when the theme of the painting would unravel itself quite naturally. He learnt to give free rein to his faculties and let the painting take shape. As a master craftsman, in the earlier stage, he had been conscious of himself as being different from the craft that he was trying to master. Now, he and the art-form had coalesced into a unity. The Doer and the Done had merged. He had reached Rajasekhara's final stage of *sahaja*. Even today, many Indian languages use the word, *sahaja* to mean "confluence" and "natural, easy flow". This is also close to Maslow's definition of self actualization, for what Maslow said was this:

> Even if all these (the physiological, safety, belongingness and esteem) needs are satisfied, we may still often (if not always) expect that a new discontent and restlessness will soon develop, unless the individual is doing what he, individually, is fitted for. A musician must make music, a poet must write, if he is to be ultimately at peace with himself. What a man *can* be, he *must* be.

The painter had explained why he objected to the professor even suggesting that it was he, the painter, who had created the painting: Just as water does not feel proud of its ability to transform itself into vapour, a man who has reached the stage of *sahaja* or self-actualization feels no pride in a natural expression of his full potential. The painter had understood that the quality that was missing earlier in his works was due to the contamination caused by his personal ego. That was why he was so agitated when the professor kept pressing him to specifically acknowledge his personal role in the creation of the painting.

## OWN AND OTHERS' DOMAINS

It should be obvious by now that the fit between Rajasekhara's model and the last two levels of Maslow's hierarchy, albeit split into three, is indeed striking:

- *Aupadeshika* corresponds with "recognition by others";
- *Aharya* corresponds with "self-esteem"; and
- *Sahaja* corresponds with "self-actualization".

The difference between "recognition by others" and "self-esteem" is far greater than what in fact Maslow realized. Up to the level of "recognition by others", one's need satisfaction is greatly dependent on others:

- At the physiological level, for satisfaction of the need for sex and food,one is dependent on other beings and outside forces adequately responding to one's needs. As for sleep, sufficient comfort and lack of disturbance from others are normally necessary prerequisites.
- At the safety level, one seeks the protection of a group of people like a union, or is attempting to save for the future to cope with imagined and real danger. One is conscious at this need level of attempting to protect oneself from the threat of outside, rather than internal, forces.
- At the belongingness level, which by definition is a function of acceptance by others, one's needs are satisfied only when another human being is willing to play his or her role.
- "Recognition by others" is again, by definition, a function of others' power over us. To grant recognition, or not, is another person's decision, and not under one's control.

Maslow's first three levels and part of the fourth level can thus be said to exist in *others' domain*.

When one moves up the hierarchy to *aharya* ( self-esteem ), where one is seeking to master one's chosen vocation, task or field of endeavour, one could be viewed as having moved into *one's own domain*.

STAGE 1 OF EAST-WEST MODEL

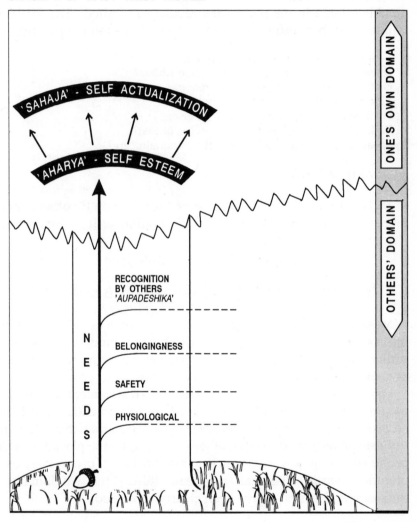

*Figure* 3.2

## "WHAT'S A HEAVEN FOR?"

Great thinkers have recognized the significance of this difference, and have echoed the same thoughts. In his elegiac poem, *Lycidas*, Milton calls "recognition by others" or fame, "the last infirmity of a noble mind". In the poem, *Andrea del Sarto* (called "The Faultless Painter"), Robert Browning speaks through Morello, a painter:

I, painting from myself and to myself,
Know what I do, am unmoved by men's blame
Or their praise either. Somebody remarks
Morello's outline there is wrongly traced,
His line mistaken—what of that? or else,
Rightly traced and well ordered—what of that?
Speak as they please, what does the mountain care?
Ah, but a man's reach should exceed his grasp,
Or what's a Heaven for?

Victor Hugo dismissed the level of "recognition by others" even more contemptuously when he said, 'Popularity? It's Glory's small change'.

## THE EAST-WEST MODEL OF MOTIVATION: A FIRST STEP

Maslow's hierarchy of needs is normally shown as in Fig. 3.1. If we incorporate the implications of Rajasekhara's model, as discussed earlier in the chapter, we can view human motivation and development as shown in Fig. 3.2. Some explanations may be in order:

First, I have incorporated the Aristotelian statement that it is as natural for a human being to achieve his full potential as it is for an acorn to grow into an oak tree; secondly, rather than showing self-esteem as a need like the others below it, I have placed it as the prime objective towards which a human being progresses, as a prelude towards self-actualization; and, thirdly, the two domains— *one's own* and *others'*—have been clearly separated.

## CONCLUSION: INTENSE ACTIVITY IS THE FOCUS

Man is born with the instinctive need to thrust himself all the way towards self-actualization. The path towards self-actualization runs initially through satisfaction of a series of needs—which order themselves hierarchically—and later, through intense activity in his own chosen area of endeavour.

The way in which this model applies to all varieties of activities in all walks of life will be demonstrated throughout this book. For the moment though, I have mainly applied the model to poets and painters. Like children, artists express themselves more candidly and are, therefore, easier to use as examples. To illustrate the motivation and behaviour of the more reticent, global businessman, I shall start by investigating the *bottom-line* connection between the hierarchy of needs and the quality of one's endeavour.

# THE QUALITY OF ENDEAVOUR—INTRINSIC VERSUS EXTRINSIC MOTIVATION

## ON BEING A MASTER CRAFTSMAN IN A "LIMITED" JOB

Some years ago, in Pune, India, four tired executives were being driven back home from work at the end of a long day. The driver was Laxman, a 58-year old man with less than two years to go before retirement. He had been on the company's rolls for many years, one among many drivers employed by a giant Indian corporation that had over 30,000 employees. Each time the car stopped for an executive to alight, Laxman would hop out, holding the door open for the executive to alight and, thereafter, gently close the door. I was the fourth and last executive to be dropped, and had observed Laxman's agile behaviour. When it came to my turn, I got out fast, but not fast enough. Laxman had come running around and caught the door just before I could bang it shut. In a friendly manner, I told him that he need not have bothered to extend the courtesy to me too, a young executive still in his twenties. Laxman gave a sweet, toothless smile and murmured something unintelligible. To ensure that he would not feel obliged to repeat his actions the next day, I made the same point again. Laxman replied by saying that it gave him pleasure to extend such courtesies. When I held my ground, indicating that it did not give me pleasure at all, and that it actually made me feel distinctly uncomfortable, he gave me this remarkable explanation for his behaviour:

'Sir, I have been driving this car ever since the company bought it four years ago. I look after it myself. So far, the car has had no problems at all. There is not even a single scratch on the body, the brake linings have not been replaced, the door linings are the original ones that came with the car, the engine purrs healthily, there is no rattling . . . . The company had neither the management information system to record such data nor the practice of assessing drivers on such performance indices. In fact, the policy was to replace cars every three years with new ones. That did not, however, stop Laxman from seeking perfection in his limited job, even going to the extent of camouflaging his protection of door linings with old world courtesy!

As Laxman spoke, there was a quiet pride in his voice and his sweet, toothless smile became broader and broader. Had I not provoked him, he would have probably never revealed his outlook on his job, and quietly retired within two years. He had obviously transcended *others' domain* and was working in his *own domain*. Acquiring self-esteem through mastering his job, with its potential for self-actualization, was what drove him on, in an apparently instinctive manner.

## THE CHINESE PARALLEL, LINKING QUALITY OF OUTPUT WITH MOTIVATION

That there is a distinct correlation between the need level one has reached, and the quality of one's endeavour was known to the ancient Chinese long ago. Dating from the T'ang period, there exists a threefold classification of painting, namely divine (*shen*), profound or mysterious (*miao*) and accomplished (*neng*).

- The first of these implies an absolute perfection, the product of a painter who seems to make no effort of his own, "his hands

55

appearing to move spontaneously". From the last chapter's analysis, it should be clear that the miniature painter had finally reached this level of quality, when he himself had moved up the hierarchy of needs to self-actualization, or *sahaja*. The correlation between the East-West model developed so far, and the Chinese classification of quality is indeed striking. A product that can be truly classified as divine, or *shen* is the result of a self-actualizing individual's efforts.

- The second level implies mastery and perfection that are typical of a master craftsman. Chang Hao ascribes such a level of perfection to a master who "works in a style appropriate to his subject", implying both a conscious deliberateness as well as a definite separation of the artist from his painting. As such, this level is obviously short of the point where the doer and the done naturally coalesce. This level clearly corresponds to the level of "self-esteem" or *aharya*.

- The third level refers merely to dexterity, achieved by an adept pupil, corresponding to the level of "recognition by others", or *aupadeshika*.

## INTRINSIC MOTIVATION AND CORPORATE EXCELLENCE

The qualitative result of people's activities would be extremely high if they were primarily motivated by the interest, enjoyment, satisfaction and challenge of the endeavour itself. This is what psychologists refer to as "intrinsic motivation". Conversely, if they are applying themselves to a task due to any "extrinsic motivation" in that they perceive the possibility of achieving other goals through accomplishment of a task—like the satisfaction of physiological, safety, belongingness or recognition needs—the quality of performance can be expected to be of a relatively inferior level.

This is something that most managers refuse to acknowledge, in practice, even if they are willing to pay lip service to it. Yet there is abundant research data to support the conclusion that intrinsic motivation leads to relatively superior performance as against extrinsic motivation. Here is a brief summary of research data gathered since Maslow's death in 1970:

- Lepper, Greene and Nisbett (1973) demonstrated this through a simple exercise conducted with nursery school children. First, the children were given felt-tipped pens to play with, an activity that most children enjoy. Observers unobtrusively measured the amount of time for which each child played with the pens. The children were then taken to a separate room where they were given clean, white paper and asked to draw pictures with the pens. Some of the children were selectively told they would receive "good player" awards (or, to use our language, offered "recognition by others") if they did the drawing well; others were not.

A week later, back in the nursery school setting, the children were again given felt pens, with no statement at all being made about "good player" awards to anyone. The children who had received awards previously were *less* likely than others to draw with the pens at all. If they did draw, they spent less time at it than other children and drew pictures that were judged to be less complex, interesting and creative.

- Beth Hennessey and Teresa Amabile (1988), while discussing the effect of social and environmental influences on intrinsic motivation, claim that 'the impact of monetary rewards has received the greatest amount of attention, and the evidence is clear. The experience of performing a task for money significantly decreases subjects' intrinsic motivation for that activity (Calder & Staw, 1975; Deci, 1972; Pinder, 1976; Pritchard, Campbell & Campbell, 1977). Yet monetary payment is not the only type of reward that has been observed to have such deleterious effects. Widely ranging varieties of reward forms have now been tested, with everything from good player awards to marshmallows producing the expected decreases in intrinsic motivation (Greene & Lepper, 1974; Harackiewicz, 1979; Kernoodle-Loveland & Olley, 1979; Ross, 1975).'

The significance of these experiments is three-fold:
1. They prove the hypothesis that intrinsic motivation leads to relatively superior performance, as compared with extrinsic motivation;
2. They have demonstrated that the introduction of extrinsic motivation negatively affects the level of intrinsic motivation previously present; and
3. They also highlight, in a simple manner, what has actually happened to Man and his attitude to work over the past 300 years, as was elaborated in Chapter 2.

From the time man's ability and skills at work were used as a commodity to be bought through extrinsic rewards, and management practices were built around such a trade, intrinsic motivation for work began to be eroded. It is not at all surprising, then, that managements of industrial enterprises are grappling with the problem of *quality* all the time. After all, what quality can be expected from people who are never allowed to grow beyond the level of "recognition by others". The corresponding Chinese level of product quality—dexterity, or *neng*—is all that can be obtained. To achieve quality of output that can be described as profound (*miao*) or divine (*shen*), one has to rely on intrinsic motivation of a human being to reach out towards "self-esteem" and "self-actualization". As we have seen earlier, true quality, of perfection, can be reached only when the doer and the done merge. It can never be achieved when the doer is consciously trying to trade with what he can do.

## THE GIGANTIC OAK AND THE GNARLED TREE

To better appreciate what has been said so far, let me use the Aristotelian example of the acorn and the oak. If a gardener had made the mistake of planting an acorn under a ledge, or a roof, the acorn would grow up crooked, seeking light. If the mistake is spotted in time by the gardener, he will replant it elsewhere, tie the plant to an erect stick, and wait for the plant to redirect itself. The gardener would have no doubts as to the plant's ability to do so, for that is the plant's *nature*. As soon as the plant has redirected itself, he will remove the stick, for he knows that the stick's role is over. Retention of the stick will, the gardener knows, inhibit further growth of the plant into a gigantic, erect oak tree.

This analogy may be a useful one to keep in mind, while contemplating the deleterious effect of extrinsic motivation on the natural, intrinsic motivation. For, if the gardener had not spotted the mistake in time, and the plant had continued to grow crooked and become a gnarled caricature of an oak tree, he would have found that the intrinsic motivation for the plant to grow erect and large had been killed altogether. We will revert to this example later. In Fig 4.1, I have drawn the analogy in a manner that will hopefully set a train of thought within the right brain of the viewer.

GNARLED TREE

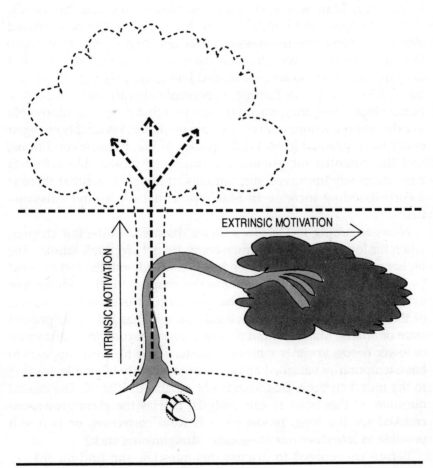

EXTRINSIC MOTIVATION

INTRINSIC MOTIVATION

*Figure 4.1*

It is ironic that we witness true quality whenever people are engaged in what is referred to as, hobbies, rather than when they are working. We respect those who get fully absorbed in sports, bullfights, cuisine, wines, pop music, theater, fashion, and so on, calling them fans, aficionados, gourmets and connoisseurs. Barry Schwartz sums it up well by pointing out that by converting Man's daily activity into a tradable commodity, what must have once been like "play" to him has been converted into "work", the underlying presumption being that play is more enjoyable than work.

Simultaneously, through aggressive marketing, and improved advertising skills, strengthened by the rapid growth of information technology, Man was also being tempted to increase his needs. Within the space of a hundred years, Man's "needs" have increased almost in a geometric progression. Take his needs for transportation. His mode of travel has changed from horse-drawn carriages and slow moving trains to air-conditioned limousines, high-speed, luxury trains like the TGV in Europe, supersonic aircraft and Concordes. In developed countries, most families will find it next to impossible to exist without a minimum of two cars per home, preferably changed every three years at least. While quality of life, hygiene conditions, and the potential for pursuing a variety of pleasurable activities have definitely improved substantially, it is also a fact that there is a corresponding increase in Man's potential for feeling "dissatisfied".

Now, according to Maslow's thesis, discussed in the last chapter, when the lower needs of a human being are not *adequately satisfied*, the higher needs disappear. This tendency, coupled with the fact (proved by the experiments quoted earlier in this chapter) that introduction of extrinsic motivation results in the reduction, or even disappearance, of the intrinsic motivation previously present, has led to the present state of affairs: Man's natural ability to reach beyond the satisfaction of lower needs, towards achieving mastery over his work, appears to have temporarily vanished among a large majority of people, leading to the mistaken belief that Man is not capable of it at all. The crucial question, at this point in the analysis, is: Has the plant grown too crooked for too long, rendering it beyond correction, or is it still possible to introduce our allegorical, straightening stick?

Before we proceed to discuss this question and find an answer as to how to get out of this seeming impasse, it is necessary to familiarize ourselves with another major stumbling block. This is best described through an exercise that I have conducted over the past five years, covering over 3000 people, in different countries. The reader may wish to subject himself or herself to it too, or conduct the exercise on any randomly assembled group of 20 to 24 members. A typical procedure for conducting the exercise is as follows:

*Step 1*  Assemble a group of 20 to 24 supervisors/ managers/ teachers and seat them in sub groups of seven or eight;

*Step 2*  Ask them to individually fill out the questionnaire given alongside in Fig. 4.2.

*Step 3*  Ask them to add the numbers circled and fill the resultant figure in Box A;

*Step 4*  Ask each group to give the average of the totals filled in Box A by its members;

*Step 5*  .Ask the individuals to now answer the same questionnaire again by drawing a square against their choice, with one difference: Instead of giving their views about other human beings, let them give their views on how they would rate themselves;

*Step 6*  Ask them to add the numbers they have drawn a square around and fill the resultant in Box B;

*Step 7*  Again, ask the groups to give the group average score for Step 6.

*Step 8*  Ask them to subtract the figure in Box A from that in Box B and fill the resultant in Box C.;

*Step 9*  Ask them to write beside Boxes A, B and C, the group average scores too;

*Step 10*  On an overhead projector, or a chart, display the group average scores for the three or four groups.

## THE EXPLANATION: BETTER THAN THE REST OF HUMANITY?

It has been found, as may be expected, that while the score for A is around 15 to 22, the score for B is around 27 to 31, and C is around 8 to 10. The three alternative explanations for the scores is then given to all the participants to decide which explanation is most likely to be the right one:

## QUESTIONNAIRE

The following pairs of statements represent assumptions about how people behave in relation to their work. Consider each pair of statements for a few minutes and, in each case, circle the number on the scale that most accurately represents your view.

**Example:** On considering the pair numbered I,
if you agree with the statement given on the left, you will circle the number ❶;
conversely if you agree with the statement given on the right, you will circle the number ❹.
If your view is between the two extremes, you will choose to circle the number ❷ if your view is closer to the statement on the left and circle the number ❸ if your view is closer to the statement on the right.

| | | | | | | |
|---|---|---|---|---|---|---|
| I | Most people have no real interest in their work | ❶ | ❷ | ❸ | ❹ | People enjoy work and achievement |
| II | People are interested only in their own benefit | ❶ | ❷ | ❸ | ❹ | People like to help each other |
| III | Fear of punishment makes people work more efficiently | ❶ | ❷ | ❸ | ❹ | Punishment leads to fall in results |
| IV | People are basically dishonest | ❶ | ❷ | ❸ | ❹ | People are basically honest |
| V | People avoid responsibility | ❶ | ❷ | ❸ | ❹ | People enjoy responsibility |
| VI | People are basically not open in their dealings with others | ❶ | ❷ | ❸ | ❹ | People are basically open in their dealings with others |
| VII | Total authority and control produce best results | ❶ | ❷ | ❸ | ❹ | People respond best when given freedom of action |
| VIII | People are not interested in the objectives of their organization | ❶ | ❷ | ❸ | ❹ | People are interested in the objectives of their organization |

A     B     C

☐   ☐   ☐

*Figure 4.2*

*Alternative 1*  By a singular coincidence, the participants are indeed about 50% superior to the rest of humanity;

*Alternative 2*  The participants are overestimating themselves;

*Alternative 3*  The participants are underestimating the rest of humanity.

Without much persuasion, alternative 3 is normally accepted as the true explanation. The effect of such underestimation of others is almost as devastating as the other two reasons for the current impasse, i.e. the Maslovian tendency for higher needs disappearing when a lower need is chronically threatened and the fact that extrinsic motivation undermines intrinsic motivation. The reason for all of this lies in what is commonly referred to as the Pygmalion effect, or the self-fulfilling prophecy.

## THE PYGMALION EFFECT OR THE SELF-FULFILLING PROPHECY

This effect is best understood by a real-life example. A researcher went to a school in a midwestern state of the USA, seeking permission from the principal to ratify a test he had designed. He explained that he had developed a test which would identify the two students who were most likely to progress most in any class, and he wished to try it out in the school. The principal agreed and the researcher went to each class in the school and had his test conducted. He came back a week later with the evaluations and met the teachers of each class. He confidentially told each teacher which two in their class were likely to progress most in the next six months. He also requested the teachers not to divulge this information to anyone, least of all to the students concerned. When the researcher came back after six months, over 90% of the teachers confirmed that his predictions were correct. The two he had picked in each class had indeed shown the maximum progress.

He then called all the teachers and the principal together and revealed that the test had actually been a hoax, in that he had picked two students in each class at random. The reason for the identified students actually showing the maximum progress was the teachers' expectation of such a progress, he explained. While the teachers had not verbally divulged their expectation to the students concerned, their non-verbal communication, including their body language, had been powerful enough.

This is really the essence of the Pygmalion effect—the expectation of a result most often leads to that result actually being achieved.

## The statue that came alive

The term, "Pygmalion effect" owes its origin to ancient Greek mythology, concerning a king of Cyprus, Pygmalion. The king, who was also an accomplished sculptor, once carved a beautiful figure of a woman in stone. He fell in love with his creation, and through the strength of his own will, aided by the grace of Venus, the Goddess of Love, brought the statue to life. (For those who feel cheated when a story is not completed, the King married her and lived happily ever after.)

George Bernard Shaw's play, *Pygmalion* is also based on this concept. Professor Henry Higgins's confidence that he can convert a flower girl into a personable society lady who can pass off for a duchess, eventually transforms Eliza Doolittle. Without belittling Prof Higgins's skills as an expert on languages and dialects, Shaw attributed Eliza's transformation to his infectious enthusiasm and conviction of success. The Pygmalion effect has been tested repeatedly in different conditions and among different people, and has been found to be true. In factory settings, where poor performers were transferred from one place of work to another, and introduced as "above average performers" to the new supervisor, remarkable results ensued. Not only did they outperform the average employee, but they also were assessed by peers as the most sought after team-members.

At a US Army Command training centre, 105 soldiers were tested for aptitude and randomly assigned to three expectancy categories: high, regular and "unknown command potential". Eight instructors were given these contrived expectancy ratings for those in their courses. Trainees of whom instructors expected better performance scored significantly higher on objective achievement tests and exhibited more positive attitudes and greater motivation. They also perceived their instructors to be better leaders.

Summing up the findings of more than 300 such studies, Robert W Goddard (1985) claimed justifiably that the findings had proved the following:

1.  What managers expect of their subordinates and the way they treat them largely determine their performance and career progress;

2. A unique characteristic of superior managers is their ability to create high-performance expectations that subordinates can fulfil;

3. Less effective managers fail to develop similar expectations and, as a consequence, the productivity of their subordinates suffers;

4. Subordinates, more often than not, appear to do what they believe is expected of them; and

5. The highest output is achieved by jobholders whose supervisors expect—and insist upon—high performance. ('Come on, I know you have it in you to do better than that!')

Knowledge of the Pygmalion effect has existed for some years now, inviting managers to first correct their attitudes and beliefs about others and then worry about what else needs to be done to ensure great performance from them. Most line managers have at best responded with lip service and continued in their scientific way, with greater automation, standardization, better human engineering and so on, the basic intention being, "How do I eliminate errors that are bound to come up due to the human factor?" As explained in Chapter 2, many events and findings, such as Social Darwinism, behavioural science, the *selfish gene* and Adam Smith's *Economic Man* have combined to strengthen Man's disbelief in the potential for greatness and perfection among his fellow beings.

## THE NEW MANAGERIAL PROBLEM OF FRONT-LINE SERVICE PEOPLE AND KNOWLEDGE WORKERS

As was discussed in Chapter 1, the nature of industrial activity has undergone such a major change that the so-called lowest echelons of all organizations will only have either of two types of employees: *a front-line service deliverer* or a *knowledge worker*. It was also pointed out that while over 90% of the former's interactions with guests cannot be *seen, heard, or even heard of,* the latter have to function at faster speeds, in increasingly remote locations. As such, both these categories cannot be supervised and "managed" like before. Hence, the managements of Third-Wave organizations have no option but to not only believe that their employees will score as well in the exercise as their own exalted selves, but also, like good Pygmalion managers, communicate that high expectation strongly and well.

## CONCLUSION

To sum up the conclusions reached so far, we find that

1. Quality of performance is best when an individual is intrinsically motivated towards self-actualization through achievement of mastery and self esteem in his chosen field of endeavour;

2. The Chinese classification of paintings by their quality has an exact correlation with the East-West model developed in the last chapter, substantiating the thesis that the higher a human being has reached in his hierarchy of needs, the better is the quality of whatever he does;

3. Introduction of extrinsic motivation negatively affects quality, and also undermines the intrinsic motivation previously present; a plant can grow either straight up into a beautiful, large and well spread out tree, or grow crooked, to become a gnarled tree ... the crooked growth eventually destroying the original capacity for actualizing its gigantic potential;

4. "Work" has been reduced from a noble task that man could have been happily and intrinsically motivated to engage himself in, to an economic commodity that is negotiated for in the market place through extrinsic motivation, thus leading to two mistaken beliefs,

    (a) man will and should work only if such work can be utilized to gain satisfaction of some other need, and

    (b) man is actually incapable of intrinsic motivation for work.

This has resulted in the managerial problem of *quality assurance*, for such a belief system does not allow a human being to grow beyond *others' domain* into his *own domain*, when the need for self esteem and self actualization will produce *profound* and *divine* quality of output.

5. With increasing proliferation of goods, and higher deemed comfort levels, most men feel that their lower needs are inadequately satisfied. This has led to the temporary disappearance of Man's higher needs, and consequently his desire to reach out towards them;

6. The self-fulfilling prophecy, or the Pygmalion effect, has been playing itself out, not so much like the original, romantic story of the Greek King and his love, but rather like a Greek tragedy. The historical developments discussed in Chapter 2 have led to most people harbouring a cynical view of the rest of humanity, and this view has acquired a self-fulfilling, negative force; and

## STAGE 2 OF EAST-WEST MODEL

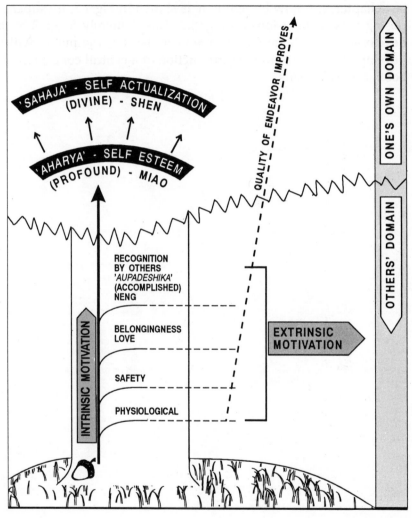

*Figure 4.3*

7. The first step towards enabling Man to reach his full potential, when all his endeavour will be marked by authentic quality, is for those in authority to convince themselves that Man does have that potential in him.

The East-West model of motivation, which reached stage 1 in the last chapter, can now be redrawn as shown in Fig.4.3, by superimposing these conclusions on Fig. 3.2. This is merely Stage 2 in the development of the model. In the next chapter, the model will be developed further with the introduction of a central concept of this book, *threshold limits*.

# 5

# THRESHOLD LIMITS: OF SPRINGS, STRINGS AND VISION

## DEFINING "WILL", "APPETITE" AND "DESIRE"

In the third part of his seminal work, *Ethics*, where he deals with the origins and nature of emotions, Spinoza suggests that Man should differentiate between *will*, *appetite* and *desire*. Relating Spinoza's work to the East-West motivation model developed so far in the book, we see that

- *will* corresponds with a force that guides Man's instinctive thrust upwards to self-esteem and self-actualization;
- *appetite* corresponds with that part of each hierarchical level of need, the non-satisfaction of which can be expected to normally inhibit or deter Man's progress up the hierarchy; and
- *desire* corresponds with the greedy, relatively unjustified part of each hierarchical level of need, the satisfaction of which should

not be viewed as a necessary prerequisite for one's upward movement.

## INTRODUCING THE CONCEPT OF "THRESHOLD LIMITS"

A wise person who has a strong *will* to climb up the hierarchy towards self-actualization will impose upon his needs, a "threshold limit" for satisfaction. Further, he will set this threshold limit as close as possible to the point of separation between his justifiable "appetite" and greedy "desire" for each of the need levels. Let me illustrate with an example:

A healthy person's physical appetite amounts to some 2000 calories of food intake per day. Similarly, appetite at the "safety need" level may warrant a roof over your head that you can call your own by the time you are 30 years old. However, if you spend your energies satisfying physical "desires" for another 1000 calories per day, in the form of chocolates, alcohol and caviar, and insist on worrying yourself sick till you have a fully paid up palace that you can call your own before you reach the age of 25, I would say that you have set too high a threshold limit for yourself. This will result in your energies being diverted away from progressing towards higher needs.

While intrinsic motivation will thrust upwards as soon as one's appetite needs are satisfied, the effect of extrinsic motivation will be to increase threshold limits and draw energies towards the satisfaction of desires.

## NOT CHRONIC, BUT REASONABLE GRATIFICATION OF THRESHOLD LIMITS

Maslow believed that 'strength and health have been ordinarily produced in our society by early *chronic gratifications* of safety, love, belongingness and esteem needs'. This statement has been quoted by many as the weakness in the humanists' point of view. By introducing the concept of threshold limits, Maslow's statement can be corrected thus:

Psychological strength and health in our societies have been ordinarily produced by those who had imposed upon themselves adequately low threshold limits for satisfaction of physiological, safety, belongingness/love and recognition (by others) needs, such limits being met in a relatively easy manner in the society to which they belonged.

Now, by superimposing the concept of threshold limits over Stage 2 of the East-West motivation model described in Fig.4.3, we arrive at Stage 3 of the model, as shown in Fig. 5.1.

## THE *SPRINGS* AND *STRINGS* OF THRESHOLD LIMITS

The figure requires some explanation. First, I have represented threshold limits by a spring, with one side fixed firmly at the point where appetites transform themselves to desires. The other end of the spring is stretched by desires. The spring will be strong, and short in length, for those who intend to grow up towards self-actualization, governed by intrinsic motivation. The spring will be like an endless string for those who have given up, and are wallowing in the desires that are satisfiable only in *others' domain*. Their actions will be controlled by extrinsic motivation offered by others. It is such people who have been studied by behaviourists for most of this century and found to show a remarkable resemblance to their laboratory rats and pigeons. It is not at all surprising that industrial engineers found that their incentive schemes worked well on such people, whose springs had been replaced by strings. They could, literally be played with like so many puppets on strings.

To appreciate and accept the correlation between low threshold limits and self-actualization, let us consider an extreme case—the code of conduct prescribed by most religions of the world for those who wish to be priests. They are startlingly similar in that all of them prescribe low to very low threshold limits, with Catholics and some sects of Hindus, Jains and Buddhists prescribing the lowest of all:

At the *physiological* needs level, celibacy, constant fasting, minimum physical comforts, simple and limited food and sleep are not uncommon features; at the *safety* needs level, the would-be priests are expected to relinquish personal wealth, home and possessions; at the *belongingness/love* level, one is expected to give up attachment to one's immediate family and society, replacing it with an attitude of universal love for friend and foe alike; and at the *recognition by others* level, the Catholic priests and Hindu swamis even give up

71

## STAGE 3 OF EAST-WEST MODEL

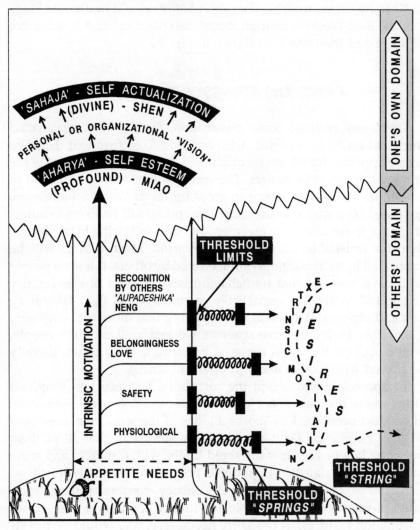

*Figure 5.1*

their names and personal identity, with no medals, ribbons or shoulder stripes to show for their status. These are all replaced by a simple cross or a smearing of ash.

The Buddha's call to give up desires, the Jewish concept of a "good, moral life of moderation" and the Muslim practice of Ramadaan fasts each year, are all indicative of the fact that low threshold levels have historically been considered a necessary prerequisite for those who wished to seek godliness, whether in themselves, others, or elsewhere in the cosmos.

## THE CORPORATE EXECUTIVE: BETWEEN GOD AND CRIMINALS

This book does not aim to make priests out of corporate executives. Rather, it is intended to illustrate how corporate executives can help themselves, and others for whom they are responsible, grow up towards self-actualization through their normal tasks. Nevertheless, it is necessary to know that the model that is being developed in this book can explain the behaviour of the most virtuous among men as also the most abnormal of criminals. While a discussion on criminal behaviour will have to wait till Chapter 7, for the moment, let it suffice to be said that as corporate executives fall somewhere between gods and criminals, the model's ability to include, and explain the behaviour of, both extremes of humanity should be comforting for the reader.

Great religions of the world, both in the West and the East, had projected a *Vision* of what a good human being would look like and behave. With the decline of religious influence, this "Vision" also got blurred, leaving Man with no alternative Vision but that of Adam Smith's Economic Man—one who lived by, and for extrinsic motivation. Regrettably, this alternative Vision is being actualized everywhere. As a result, most of us have managed to equip ourselves with very long threshold springs, our threshold limits being set much farther right (in Fig. 5.1) than they ought to have been. As our desires multiply, with more and more attractive products flooding the market place, we also sometimes forget the existence of the spring altogether, with the moving, right end of the spring being mistaken for the fixed, left end of the spring. For, by habit and custom, yesterday's desires become today's appetite.

We seem to have gradually perpetuated the self-fulfilling prophecy of the Economic Man, becoming greedy, self-serving, petty and manipulable. For such a being, threshold springs can be said to have been replaced by endless strings, manipulable by those in the *others' domain* who have the puppeteer's power to pull the strings. It is interesting to note that this distorted Vision is almost exactly the opposite of what the great religions had projected as the ideal human being.

That being the regrettable picture of reality, it is left for institutions such as the family, the school, the university and the corporation to recreate a Vision that will be powerful enough to redirect human beings towards a life of low threshold limits and high intrinsic motivational thrust for achievement of excellence.

To understand the very critical nature of a Vision, and its relationship with low threshold limits and achievement of high quality end results, it will be useful to consider an example.

## THE EFFECT OF HIGH THRESHOLD LIMITS ON YOUNG MBAs

Let us look at two fresh MBAs who have been recruited by a corporation in a consumer goods industry, as management trainees in sales and marketing. Let us assume that they are about equal in their intelligence, qualifications, pleasantness of disposition under ordinary circumstances and personality profile. Moreover, through a similar kind of upbringing, they have both got used to having high threshold limits, i.e. mistaking some desires for legitimate appetites.

It is normal for most corporations in India to put such fresh recruits through an intensive program of familiarization. During this phase, the MBAs travel from city to city, market to market, shop to shop, following the corporation's products from the wholesale dealer to the retail outlets. This means living in different, dubious hotels each night, putting up with great physical discomfort, eating and drinking whatever is available—sometimes of doubtful, hygienic standards—walking miles in hot, uncomfortable and crowded markets, and so on. They normally lose sleep and weight, develop minor ailments and allergies, and have long evenings to spend, far from social centres of activity.

If one of the young men has a strong, personal Vision of himself as a top grade sales and marketing professional ten years hence, he will have no problem in temporarily setting for himself low threshold limits–in that he will be content with any bed to sleep on, will eat the simplest of food and drink the commonest of beverages. He will look at this phase as a great learning experience and will quickly move up the hierarchy of needs. He will concentrate on picking up adequate knowledge of the markets, and thereafter, sending in a good training report that will justify his recruitment and later progress as a marketing executive.

If the other young man is unable to even temporarily lower his threshold limits, he is likely to spend his time complaining, about the food, the accommodation, the heat, the discomfort of travel, and of everything around. As suggested by Maslow, his higher needs, for knowledge or career progress will appear to be mere "fripperies". Like many before him, he is likely, then and there, to start planning for a change in his job.

While the first young man, by maintaining low threshold limits, rises to the *aupadeshika* or "recognition (by the executive to whom he has to submit a report after each phase of training) level" immediately, the second young man flounders at the lowest of the needs! Their lives will take different paths altogether.

Having counselled several hundreds of people who initially resembled the second young man in the case, I have learnt that one of the best methods of helping such people is to enable them to develop a strong, personal Vision of themselves ten, or fifteen years hence. They are then able to intelligently reason out, and thereby develop the wisdom, as to why they ought to impose low threshold limits on themselves, albeit for a limited time.

A young chef, who was to replace another, in a hotel located in one of the remotest places in India, was reported to be dragging his feet about the transfer. I was told he would go only if a proper, air-conditioned car was available for his transportation to the new location, and also that he wished to have an assurance that the transfer would be only for two or three months. After a half-hour discussion, when we discussed what bus routes he had used as a student, the career paths of the most successful chefs which almost always included stints in green-field sites, the organization's bias for willing, committed chefs who wouldn't shy away from such challenges, and so on, the young chef not only accepted the transfer, but also took an overnight inter-state bus so as to take up his new responsibilities from the next morning till whenever the corporation wanted him to be there!

## EDUCATION IN THE SETTING OF THRESHOLD LIMITS

Let me now turn to the issue of how we learn to set threshold limits, and the effect of individual and group Vision on our ability to do so. At this stage in the book, I will be merely touching on the influence of parents, schools, colleges and corporations, to the extent it is required to explain the connection between Vision and threshold limits. An elaborate treatment of the topic, covering details of Human Resources Management, as well as education and training of parents and teachers, the importance of Aesthetics in early education, etc. is reserved for later chapters.

## PARENTAL INFLUENCE ON THRESHOLD LIMITS

During early childhood, parental discipline, or lack of it, is the prime influence. Wise parents use a mixture of persuasion, counselling, logic and discipline to help a child learn how to voluntarily adhere to a regular schedule of sleep, food and physical exercise. This way, a child gets to know what are acceptable threshold limits at the physiological level. If a child is pampered, through excessive supply of chocolates, little or no insistence on physical exercise and improper sleeping habits—with every minor wish for gratification of desires being met immediately—high threshold limits become the norm. A child with unduly high threshold limits is normally referred to as a "spoilt" child. The presence of a good role model, especially if either of the parents can fill the role, also works as a powerful Vision, for the child often makes fantasy decisions of what he or she would like to become based on the influence of such a role model. Hero worship of sports stars has a similar effect too. When a Carl Lewis appears on the television screen, extolling the virtues of a drug-free life, a child appreciates why drugs are bad.

## A GOOD SCHOOL TEACHES THE WISDOM OF LOW THRESHOLDS

The next major influence on the child is the school. The child begins to learn that much greater effort is required to satisfy his or her needs. At home, well-meaning parents quite often anticipate and gratify their children's needs voluntarily and willingly. In school though, other children with similar needs are not only competing with you, but are also the source for satisfying, or denying the satisfaction of, your needs. For example, to satisfy your safety needs, from the bullying of older and bigger children, you learn to team up with others and also to become physically strong enough to cope with, or deter, threatening behaviour. To satisfy your belongingness needs, you learn the basic ground rules of teamwork, and the spirit of "give and take". To satisfy your recognition needs, from other children as well as teachers, you learn exactly how much effort has to be applied! In other words, the *wisdom of setting socially acceptable, rather than inflated, threshold limits begins to dawn on the child.*

## REDUCING THRESHOLD LIMITS: THE HEROIC ACT

Another very important aspect of threshold limits is also learnt while still in school. You learn how to apply the springs of threshold limits ever so often, which helps you move up and down the hierarchy of needs at will, rather than in a fatalistic manner. In other words, you learn that you have to sometimes give up the satisfaction of one need for another. For example, to gain recognition as a brave person, if you take on the class bully, your physiological and safety needs are threatened considerably. At the same time, if you play for safety all the time, you get to become unpopular. Gradually, *the very important lesson is learnt that nobility is ascribed, and respect given, to those who are able to sacrifice a lower need for a higher one.*

All forms of literature abound with examples of heroic figures who exhibit this very ability, and children are exposed to them all the time. Indeed, heroism can be reduced to this one common factor, the ability to drastically reduce threshold limits of a lower need for the sake of a personal or group Vision. Here are some examples:

Sydney Carton, in *The Tale of Two Cities* displays this ability as he decides to do a "far, far nobler" deed than he had ever done before, offering himself to the guillotine in place of another; Hector, as he battles Achilles at the gates of Troy for a lost cause, is doing much the same thing. Mahatma Gandhi, every time he started a satyagraha for a noble cause, was sacrificing food and water intake for days on end. Mother Teresa has been living on almost minimum threshold levels, to bring succour to the most destitute of the aged people in Calcutta.

### Even light fiction characters do the heroic act

This act of "heroism" has been used in light fiction and humorous literature too. P. G. Wodehouse has employed it repeatedly. Here is a familiar scene from his *Joy in the Morning*, in which Nobby Hopwood and Boko Fittleworth are appealing to the higher needs of Bertie Wooster. They persuade Bertie to risk more than mere physical assault and arrest by getting him to assist in a burglary at Steeple Bumpleigh. He is asked to risk the wrath of not only his uncle, Lord Worplesdon but also that of the indomitable Lady Worplesdon, his infamous Aunt Agatha:

'Then everything depends on Bertie.'
'Everything.'
'You don't think he will object?'
'I wish you wouldn't say things like that. You'll hurt his feelings.'
'You don't realize the sort of fellow Bertie is. His nerve is like chilled steel, and when it is a question of helping a pal, he sticks at nothing.'
Nobby drew a deep breath.
'He's wonderful, isn't he?'
'He stands alone.'
'I've always been devoted to Bertie. When I was a child, he once gave me a twopennyworth of acid drops.'
'Generous to a fault. These splendid fellows always are.'
'How I admired him!'
'Me too. I don't know a man I admire more.'
'Doesn't he remind you rather of Sir Galahad?'
'The name was on the tip of my tongue.'
'Of course, he wouldn't dream of not doing his bit.'
'Of course not. All settled, eh, Bertie?'
It's odd what a few kind words will do (writes Bertie). Until now, I had, as I say, been all ready with the *nolle prosequi*, and had indeed opened my lips to shoot it across with all the emphasis at my disposal. But as I caught Nobby's eye, fixed on me in a devout sort of way, and at the same time was conscious of Boko shaking my hand and kneading my shoulder, something seemed to check me. I mean, there really didn't seem to be any way of *nolle proseqing* without spoiling the spirit of the party.
'Oh, rather,' I said. 'Absolutely.'

From history to classics to P. G. Wodehouse (which is not to imply that the works of the late PGW are not likely to be rated as classics in the years to come), heroism has almost always implied the ability to reduce the threshold limits of one's lower needs for the sake of higher, nobler ones.

## VILLAINY INVOLVES EXCESSIVELY HIGH THRESHOLD LIMITS

Conversely, villainy has almost always been associated with over indulgence of lower needs, and the inability to reach up towards higher needs. Debauchery, rape, murder, greed—all at the expense of others not satisfying even their appetite needs—are standard representations of villainous behaviour in history, literature and films.

When children are not able to reduce threshold limits temporarily, abnormal behaviour arises. The battle between expectations and ability, 'will' and 'desire' starts and complex problems develop. For a discussion of this, we have to wait till Chapters 6 and 8.

## EXTRINSIC MOTIVATION GRABS THE SCHOOL LEAVER

The transition from school to college, or university, or directly to work, is the next major factor that influences threshold limits. Barring a small percentage, the vast majority make this transition without much knowledge of career opportunities existing in the external world. Extrinsic motivation, for gratification of safety (through qualifications that will get them a job, and a living), belonging (through societal and family expectations and pressures) and recognition (through admission to the most sought after course of studies, universities or job) become the main factors that effectively and, in many cases, permanently grab the springs of threshold limits, replacing them with easily manipulable strings.

## THE SMALL MINORITY OF POTENTIAL LEADERS RETAIN CONTROL OF THE SPRINGS OF THRESHOLD LIMITS

A small minority, the potential leaders and high achievers of tomorrow, decide quietly to do what intrinsically makes sense to them, irrespective of external factors. They retain control of the springs, keeping them both strong and short. They stand out by their non-conformist behaviour, original thoughts and unconventional views. All of them share the twin virtues of a strong, personal Vision and the ability to set low threshold limits for lower needs. Their energies gush towards achievement of their personal Vision.

A useful image we can use to understand such people is that of a river with strong, unbreachable banks. Low and fixed threshold limits serve the same function as the banks of a river, in that they help channel the flow to the end objective. Flexible, easy to relax threshold limits are like weak banks that allow for unnecessary flooding *en route*, with no water reaching the sea. Energies of people with such threshold limits get dissipated in the satisfaction of unnecessary desires at lower levels, leaving no scope for surging upwards.

## THE CORPORATION'S INFLUENCE ON INDIVIDUAL THRESHOLD LIMITS

By the time young people are ready to join a corporation to start their working life, they have had many years of working with their threshold limits. Yet they are mostly uncertain as to whether to trust their intrinsic urges, or to respond to extrinsic ones. In Indian institutions offering MBA programmes, most students who passed out in the 1970s and 1980s swore allegiance to the functions of marketing, finance and management information systems. However, as these were the very functions that supposedly had the maximum career scope for advancement up organizational hierarchies during these decades, one is tempted to guess that for some of them, extrinsic rather than intrinsic motivation was behind the professed love for these functional areas of specialization.

When corporations meet students in campuses at the time of selection interviews, the main problem facing them is how to sift the intrinsically motivated from the rest. As we saw in Chapter 4, superior quality of performance will come from the former, and not the latter. Those corporations that have a culture and tradition of fair play in treating quality performance, irrespective of the functional areas of work, will find it easier to do this important sifting at the time of selection. Let me explain this point with an example from the Taj Group of Hotels.

## SIFTING THE INTRINSICALLY MOTIVATED FROM OTHERS

We used to visit all the major hotel management institutions in India, recruiting an average of around 150 young graduates each year. In the normal address to the prospective candidates, we appealed to the students to candidly tell the interview panel what functional areas of the hotel's operations actually interested them most, rather than focus on those areas which were rumoured to be the best ones to "get into" for later advancement. A typical example we used to try and convince them was this:

'Sunil Gavaskar, among the greatest cricketers of all times, stands at around 5' 4" and is clearly not the fastest on his feet. However, he was blessed with a natural instinct for batting, a keen eye, a sense of timing, patience, strong wrists and everything that a batsman needed to make it to the top grade. Let us assume he had been persuaded, when still in school, to opt for tennis instead. For even those who are ranked 300 in world tennis make more money than the world's best cricketer. We would have lost a cricketing genius, Gavaskar would have lost a brilliant career, and the world would have got another club-class tennis buff, at best. So, for Heaven's sake, and your own, please tell us what excites you intrinsically and allow us to start your career in an area in which you are bound to do well. You will then be able to build confidence in yourself and your abilities. We can rotate you around other functional areas later, and build your career up the organizational hierarchy gradually; but, first, let us concentrate on helping you (go up your own hierarchy of needs and) achieve mastery over what comes naturally to you.'

## THREAT TO SAFETY KILLS INTRINSIC THRUST

Despite this appeal, quite a few professed their love for "general management", rather than for culinary skills, or other such areas, as the societal and family pressures have had the effect of making a person mistrust his or her instincts. Thus, they "played safe" by opting for supposedly prestigious career routes. Threshold limit springs appear to get replaced by strings controlled by extrinsic motivation, leading to a kind of "herd mentality". En masse, whole groups of youngsters kill their personal Vision and intrinsic urges as they move towards occupations that will land them, for life, in *others' domain*.

Corporations have, therefore, a major role to play in convincing young recruits that their prime concern should be to master intrinsically appealing functional areas of specialization. The only way this can be done is by the corporation demonstrating that adequate organizational systems exist to enable everyone to gratify reasonable threshold limits, irrespective of their functional area of specialization, and that the best in all areas can hope to get rewarded in a reasonably fair and equitable manner. This is easier said than done. Let me explain the difficulties, as well as the hard and soft options from which management have to choose, by quoting another example from the Taj Group.

## THE HARD BUT NECESSARY OPTION FOR HUMAN GROWTH

From the 150 graduate recruits a year, after they had spent about three years in the corporation, we had to select the best for speedy promotion and advancement. This is a hard, but necessary option that corporations have to exercise if they wish to retain the best and the brightest of youngsters. Even in Japanese corporations, where seniority-based promotions have been the rule, a different kind of recognition system appears to be working powerfully. A Japanese executive told me that the most challenging assignments and tasks are given to the best, and special care is taken for their growth and development. Organizational members know quite well who are considered to be the best. Honour and prestige are attached to this, and the Japanese culture sets a high value by it.

This decision by which a few get picked as the best from a peer group, whether for promotion, or for special assignments and tasks, is a very hard one to make as it disturbs the threshold levels of the entire cohort. During the three years separating their joining, and the time this first formal selection is made, the belongingness need threshold limits are raised considerably for the entire group, the satisfaction of which is primarily dependent on peer group relationships. Many youngsters stay together, sharing accommodation; they also have common friends and belongings like music systems and vehicles. At the "recognition by others" level, they would have got used to being recognized as a member of the batch of 1985 or whatever, thus sharing group recognition. Now, when only a select few get identified for promotion, advancement, or assignment to prestigious tasks, all the others in the group get affected adversely, for

- Some of their colleagues are obviously being "recognized" as superior, and by implication, their own recognition is denied;
- Their cozy peer group gets disturbed, tension rising between the chosen few and others, with jealousy and charges of favouritism spoiling the closeness of the group; and
- The long-term safety of an advancing career appears to be threatened.

Yet, this has to be done.

## THE SOFT OPTION OF ALLOWING HIGH THRESHOLD LIMITS

Many organizations, especially in government and quasi-government sectors, have tried to avoid these problems by sticking to seniority-based promotions, thus committing an error tantamount to throwing the baby out with the bath water. For, such policies encourage abnormally high threshold limits for safety and belongingness of the majority. They ignore the need for recognition by the best and the brightest, let alone their later need for mastery, self-esteem and self-actualization. That such organizations the world over are known for their inefficiencies, lack of quality and perfection should not be surprising at all. As we have seen in Chapter 4, quality of endeavour is directly related to an individual's place in the hierarchical, motivational level. Pampering to high threshold limits at lower needs leads to individual abnormality and organizational inefficiency. I will deal with what happens when human beings transgress reasonable threshold limits, individually or *en masse*, in the next chapter.

## CORPORATE VISION AND ITS IMPACT ON
## ORGANIZATIONAL MEMBERS

The ability of corporations to effectively influence their employees' threshold limits, as a necessary step towards corporate excellence, is crucially dependent on the answers to these three questions:

1. Does the corporate "Vision" have the capacity to excite the intrinsic motivation of its employees, and make them feel part of a larger, nobler cause that they fully identify themselves with?

2. What sort of threshold limits does the corporation, as an entity, set for itself?

3. Do the Chief Executive Officer (CEO) and the rest of the top management practise what they preach, particularly in the setting of personal threshold limits?

This intricate relationship is best described through a real-life example, one I was fortunate enough to have experienced personally for almost a full decade.

## A MODEL FOR EMULATION: THE VISION AND STORY OF TELCO (PUNE)

By 1965, the Tata Engineering & Locomotive Company (TELCO) had already made a name for itself by virtue of the reliability and popularity of its range of vehicles. It had, in fact, cornered over 70% of the domestic market for heavy vehicles. Its only manufacturing plant set up in collaboration with Daimler Benz, AG, was in Jamshedpur, Bihar, a township that had been created from scratch by the Tatas at the turn of the century. The visionary CEO of the corporation, the late Sumant Moolgaokar, took a series of decisions, which surprised many then, but have been lauded since:

- He bought almost 1000 acres of rocky, grassless, dry land about 20 miles from the University town of Poona (now Pune), right across the Indian peninsula from Jamshedpur; the place was referred to as Moolgaokar's folly in the early days.
- He then engaged a team of horticulturists and landscape specialists to plan the conversion of this arid land into an oasis, as a setting for his vision of a modern, integrated engineering complex. His Vision was to indigenously design, manufacture and assemble sophisticated machine tools, press tools, material handling equipment, castings, and, of course, a range of automobiles.
- He set up an indigenous engineering research and development centre, with funds and facilities for experimentation, prototype building and testing;
- He created a world standard training facility that could nurture young, uninitiated men, many in their teens, into becoming top-grade technicians, special tradesmen, master craftsmen, engin-

eers and designers; residential accommodation for the students and the teachers was built to make it a self-contained mini-university.

He saw to it that the *nurseries for plants, people and ideas were in place* as a first step towards actualizing his grand Vision.

## THE MAGICAL TRANSFORMATION

In the next 15 years, a magical transformation took place in the physical environment, in the type of people who were attracted to and worked in the place, in the quality of ideas that were generated, and in the excellent standard of its products.

1.  The soil was replaced, the natural contour of the land was used to form a lake, trees grew to cover the 1000 acres, and migratory birds began to use the site as a stop-over in their journey from one hemisphere to another.
2.  Young men, in their teens and early twenties, joined by the thousands, attracted by the vision of what was being attempted, and they grew in confidence as they were helped to acquire mastery in those fields of engineering and management which they were intrinsically motivated towards.
3.  The collaboration with Daimler Benz was not extended when the term expired in 1969, as Moolgaokar, the Pygmalion manager he was, believed that his research and development engineers would be able to *go it alone.*
4.  Design engineers graduated from making column drilling machines to sophisticated transfer lines that would automatically transform a raw casting into a machined cylinder head.
5.  The hardware for management information systems was changed from the old IBM 1401 to an on-line, third generation system.
6.  The top management of the plant set for themselves Spartan threshold limits, as everybody from the General Manager downwards plunged into a frenzy of activity, sharing the same canteen food, factory tea and the long, arduous working hours of a six-day week.

By 1978, the first automobile rolled out, designed by TELCO engineers and manufactured by locally trained people, using machines that were by and large the creation of TELCO engineers. There was magic in the air, as over 10,000 Indians joined in the task of leapfrogging several decades of engineering advancement. By the turn of the decade, TELCO products were successfully competing with world leaders for a niche in the export market.

### Threshold limits voluntarily set low

During this decade of transformation, I learnt how a corporation and its top management can powerfully influence their employees to *voluntarily* set low threshold limits in a joint effort to actualize a compelling Vision. For example, whenever a transferee from the more comfortable, Jamshedpur plant complained about the lack of physical amenities, the harsh physical environment, lack of time for socializing, the long and difficult daily journey to the plant, the fact that the position of peons had altogether been abolished, and so on, the then GM of the plant, Sharad Jakatdar, advised me to offer them a transfer back to Jamshedpur. To the best of my knowledge, nobody accepted the offer: all of them wished to be a part of the team which seemed to be on a definite course to actualizing Sumant Moolgaokar's Vision, and low threshold limits were accepted as part of team norms.

## GREAT LEADERS HAVE KNOWN THE EFFECT OF A "VISION" ON THRESHOLD LIMITS

That people can, and voluntarily will, reduce threshold limits if they are excited enough by a joint Vision, is a fact that most great leaders seem to have known.

At the battle of Agincourt, on Saint Crispin's Day, King Henry V made an unparalleled statement of Vision which is worth looking at closely from our perspective. In Act IV, Scene III of Shakespeare's play, *Henry V*, the Earl of Westmoreland verbalizes a wish "that we now had here but one ten thousand of those men in England that do no work today". The King, in immediate response, says,

> I pray thee wish not one man more. If it be a sin to covet honour, I am the most offending soul alive. . . I would not lose so great an honour, as one man more methinks would share from me. He today that sheds his blood with me shall be my brother; be he ne'er so vile,

this day shall gentle his condition: And gentlemen in England, now a-bed, shall think themselves accursed they were not here, and hold their manhoods cheap, while any speaks that fought with us upon Saint Crispin's Day.

The English fought and won the battle of Agincourt, for the King had no doubt whatsoever of the outcome and how the credit for it would be shared among his men and himself. He was sharing the same, low threshold limits as his men, he was risking his life and safety, and he was showing how a joint act of heroism could be accomplished through such a sacrifice.

Another example of this was when John Kennedy articulated his Vision for the American space programme. Rather than set the normal type of time-bound, dry targets, John Kennedy simply said that *the first man on the moon would be an American*. Almost overnight, the American space organization, NASA was transformed into a living force, galvanized into a frenzied pace of action by the young President's vision. As against the then US average of 23 % turnover of manpower per year, experienced by the average organization, the turnover in NASA almost disappeared for four years. A researcher was told by a janitor in NASA that there was no way he would leave NASA till an American landed on the moon. It is worth noting that there was no doubt in the mind of the janitor that the first man to land on the moon would indeed be an American.

## MAJORITY OF US REQUIRE A *GROUP VISION* LIKE THE ALLEGORICAL STICK TO REDIRECT US

A good and strong *group Vision*, articulated in a manner that is understood by all members of an organization has the same effect on its members as a personal vision has on a few great people who are able to visualize it for themselves. Only a few individuals have the innate ability to develop strong visions that galvanize their intrinsic motivation to a hyperactive state. The rest of us are dependent on those leaders who have the ability to include us in their wider vision. Without such a strong vision to divert us from giving up our habitual thirst for "desires", it is all too tempting to let down our defenses, loosen the springs, and fall a prey to extrinsic motivation. *Such compelling Visions act like the stick a gardener uses to redirect a plant growing crooked.*

Returning to the TELCO (Pune) example, one aspect which I

believe was crucial to the success achieved was the fact that the top management shared the problems of all members by applying similar threshold limits on themselves. It was difficult for visitors to tell an executive from a worker. Sharad Jakatdar and his management team quite often had more machine dust on them than the machinists themselves.

Some years later, I heard a personnel manager relate an incident that is just the opposite of TELCO (Pune) of the 1970s:

Wage negotiations had been in progress at an establishment, between the local management and the union. The management team had been reiterating the company's poor financial state, and the need to settle for a low wage increase. The union had bargained hard for several days, and seemed to have finally been convinced by the copious financial information and arguments of the management representatives. They stopped the discussions for a lunch break, and reassembled for what the personnel manager had believed was going to be the final session when an agreement would be reached. However, he was shocked to observe, on resumption, that the attitude of the union had undergone a significant change. They took a hard stand, and began to insist on a big hike in wages. What had happened during the break was this: The President of the Union, a driver by trade, had observed a new Mercedes Benz in the executive parking lot and on enquiry, had learnt that it had been bought by the corporation for the Vice President overseeing the operations of that particular establishment. The Union President had naturally decided that he was not going to respond to the management's "crocodile tears" any longer.

In March 1991, when world recession was compelling major corporations to declare large numbers of employees as being redundant, this is what a major, international bank did. While the management announced that 5000 employees were being declared redundant in 1991, and another 13;000 were proposed to be made redundant in the next five years, the news also got around that the Chairman of the Bank had received a 21% pay increase. That the particular bank is known for its poor service should surprise no one.

The fact of the matter is that when it comes to appealing to employees to settle for low threshold limits, there must appear to be a sense of fairness and equity in the manner in which senior management set threshold limits for themselves. I am not suggesting a communist, or socialist solution. These have failed too many times, and too recently, in the former USSR, Eastern Europe, and elsewhere for anyone in his right mind to make such a suggestion. I am merely suggesting that everyone should be reminded of the famous test of fairness prescribed by British Common Law: *'What would be the opinion of the common man on the Clapham omnibus?'*

## ROLE MODELLING BY TOP MANAGEMENT, A MUST

When a whole organization has to rise upwards to make a joint Vision come alive, the top management have to show the way by a visible readiness to lower their threshold limits as well:

1.  At the physiological level, by empathizing and sharing the physical discomforts of the "troops";
2.  At the safety level, by demonstrating that when things go wrong, it is their heads which will be on the chopping block first;
3.  At the belongingness level, by playing their roles as team members, in the "give and take" of everyday life and by ensuring a caring atmosphere for people to work in;
4.  At the recognition level, by shunning personal credit, and insisting on open-handed sharing of praise, if and when it becomes legitimately due; and
5.  At the self-esteem level, by concentrating on achievement of group mastery and group-esteem through actualization of the joint Vision.

To reach that stage, you have to, like the late Sumant Moolgaokar, first build a nursery for developing a critical mass of human beings who have the intrinsic motivation to jointly strive for the actualization of a common Vision. Such a critical mass will generate and maintain the heroic spirit required to reduce threshold limits of lower needs. Thoughts of physical discomfort, insecurity, deprivation of sufficient time for social revelries, games and hobbies, ego gratification and self aggrandizement will be voluntarily sacrificed for the group achievement of a common Vision.

## CONCLUSION

We have reached the following conclusions in this chapter:
1.  To move up the hierarchy of needs, you should not expect

"chronic" satisfaction of lower needs; you should be ready to settle for adequate satisfaction of reasonably low threshold limits.

2.  Ideally, these threshold limits should be set as close as possible to the point separating "appetite" and "desire" at each level of need.

3.  People who have a strong personal Vision find it easy to thrust themselves upwards towards self-actualization, by voluntarily imposing upon themselves low and strongly held threshold limits, rather like the firm banks of a river that allow the directed flow of the river into the sea.

4.  When the springs of threshold limits are weak and long, and behave like an endless string, extrinsic motivation for the satisfaction of desires effectively redirects energies away from intrinsic motivation for mastery, self-esteem and self-actualization.

5.  Even children, by instinct as well as through exposure to history, literature and films, learn that personal nobility is a function of one's ability to reduce one's threshold limits at lower needs for the sake of gratifying higher needs.

6.  Much of what has been discussed in this chapter is an indirect confirmation of Maslow's assumption that there is a hierarchy in which Man's needs order themselves, as we have observed that it requires tremendous effort, even heroism, to give up a lower need for a higher one; and it requires no effort whatsoever to give in to a lower need instead of reaching a higher one.

7.  Parents, schools, colleges, society and corporations have their respective roles to play in influencing your ability to set threshold limits, and to effectively operate the springs of thresholds.

8.  Government and quasi-government organizations have failed to produce excellence in their products and services because they have settled for unduly high threshold limits for safety and belonging needs, thus blocking the growth of their organizational members towards higher needs, a prerequisite for high quality of endeavour.

9.  Organizations that wish to influence their members in setting low threshold limits and thus reach up towards mastery over their respective work, must first evaluate themselves on these

three key issues:

9.1 Can their "vision" excite the intrinsic motivation of their members?

9.2 Are the threshold limits of the corporation, as an entity, fair?

9.3 Are the top management, including the CEO, the right role models?

10. Barring a few who are intrinsically motivated by their personal vision, the majority of human beings require a leader, or a corporate leadership, to articulate a larger "Vision" of which they can be a part, to develop the direction and *will* that is required for setting low threshold limits.

# 6

# TRANSGRESSING THRESHOLD LIMITS

In the absence of a strong, personal or group Vision, it was observed that it is all too easy to let go of threshold springs, and wallow in *others' domain*. Though threshold limits vary from one community to another, from the less developed countries to the more developed, and from one decade to another, it is surprising how common the universal feeling of discomfort is when faced with human beings who have unnaturally high threshold limits. In fact, very similar common language terms are used to describe such people, as we will see later in this chapter when we look at what happens to people who transgress reasonable threshold limits.

At the *physiological* level, terms such as glutton, "sleepy Tom" and sex maniac are commonly used to describe those who are seen to have an excessive need for food, sleep and sex respectively. Such people tend to spend much of their wakeful time on seeking gratification of *desires* at the physiological level. Rather than progress up the hierarchy after satisfying their appetite, they announce to the world by their actions that they have an endless threshold string at the lowest of Maslovian levels. Anyone with knowledge of the work of behavioural scientists can manipulate such people with relative ease. One can understand them by either thinking of the rats and pigeons behavioural scientists work with, or of a crooked tree, as shown in Fig. 6.1.

Important work with high quality standards are never assigned to them, for it is quite beyond them. They can be employed, at best, for routine work that can be inspected, checked, closely supervised and controlled.

## EXECUTIVES WITH HIGH SAFETY THRESHOLDS SAY, "YES ... BUT ... "

Similarly, unduly high threshold limits at the *safety* level would be ascribed to those who refuse to take risks, hoard money in a miserly fashion, resist any and all change, or avoid stating any opinion definitely by using "Yes ... but ... " kind of phrases all the time. Corporations abound with such people, especially in countries and industries where job mobility is low. What makes the problem acute is the fact that in many countries, corporations own almost everything that an executive appears to possess—his accommodation, furniture, car, club membership, social status, credit cards for entertainment, and so on. The *safety* stakes are so high for executives to continue in their employment that it is not at all surprising that everything they say, or do, is from the perspective of protecting themselves and their high safety threshold limits.

Young and vigorous MBAs who join a corporation with grand ideas for bringing about change sometimes get surprised at not only the extent, but also the nature of resistance they face whenever they suggest the smallest of changes. Senior executives with high safety threshold limits will be found extremely non-committal, refusing to either openly support, or oppose, any suggestion for change.

One such senior executive used to amaze everyone with his consummate skill in both agreeing and disagreeing with any proposal whatsoever. Once, when a young executive had come to him with a brilliant idea, he had this to say to the young man: "Very good idea. Its worth considering, but have you considered 'so and so' and 'such and such' implication? If I were you, I would proceed

93

## GNARLED TREE

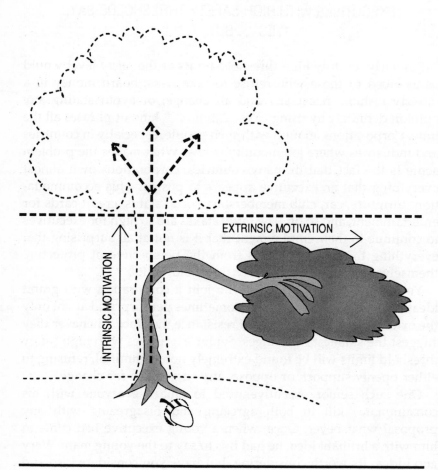

*Figure 6.1*

94

carefully. That is not to say that I am telling you to give up the idea. I like young people with ideas, but be cautious. My advise to you is to hasten slowly . . . And, feel free to come to me any time. My door is always open to young, energetic people like you."

The cleverness of the man ensured he was *safe* irrespective of what the young executive chose to do:

- If the young man implemented his idea, and it succeeded, the senior executive could take credit for success, as he had specifically said, 'Very good idea. Its worth considering . . . . I like young people with ideas' and had also pointed out a few implications to be considered.

- If the young man implemented the idea and it failed, he could truthfully say that he had warned him to be careful as he had indeed said, 'If I were you, I would proceed carefully . . . hasten slowly;'

- If the young man chose to give up the idea, but the CEO later thought it ought to have been implemented if and when he heard about the idea having been mooted, the senior executive could pretend to be surprised why the young man had not implemented the idea for he had specifically told him, 'Very good idea. It is worth considering;'

- If the young man gave up the idea, and the CEO later thought it would have been disastrous had he implemented it, the senior executive could truthfully say that he had discouraged the young man by raising relevant objections and pointing out certain implications.

The danger of such people to corporations is quite obvious, but they survive in reasonably large numbers for various reasons. Let me elaborate the two most important reasons. First, they are considered to be excellent subordinates by those who are authoritarian in their style of management. There are some excellent short stories by P.G. Wodehouse dealing with a few variations of such people, termed "yes men" and "nodders". The job of the former is to say, "yes" whenever the boss expresses an opinion, while that of the latter, who is one step lower in the hierarchy and hence is not to be heard but only seen, is to nod his head in agreement with the boss.

A second reason for their survival lies in what they do when they get found out. In one case, when a senior executive was appointed in a large private sector corporation from outside, this is what happened.

The newcomer, when faced with "double speak" communication, responded by insisting on clear "yes" or "no" answers. This was tantamount to a serious confrontation, for it could lead to loss of the best safety shield. All old executives with high safety thresholds began a mutually supportive action by which the newcomer was effectively made nonfunctional. Withholding of information, blatant lies, misinformation, misallocation of resources, rumours, gang warfare and other similar arsenal was used to make the newcomer understand that he had a simple choice before him: either join the gang by swearing allegiance to *status quo*, or quit. The newcomer quit.

Many large corporations have, in the past, managed to survive despite the presence of large numbers of executives with high safety threshold limits, essentially because they enjoyed monopolistic control of markets, or because an even business climate allowed bureaucratic decision making based on past practices, policies and traditions. However, in view of the rapidity with which everything is changing in the world, corporations that do not weed out executives with high safety thresholds will join the list of those who go bankrupt. The logic is quite simple. A changing environment needs rapid responses based on clear, but chancy, decisions being taken in time. That is exactly what executives with high safety threshold limits will never do. Besides, they will also stand in the way of others who might be capable of doing so, for the very existence of the latter threatens them by the obvious contrast that becomes evident to the rest of the organization. As was highlighted in the example, the "high safety threshold limit" group, for their own survival, pressurize everyone else to either join the group, or get out.

## COMMUNISTS AND SOCIALISTS EMPHASIZE HIGH SAFETY THRESHOLDS

At a macro level, one can argue that communist and socialist block countries are facing great problems today because they catered to raising threshold limits at *physiological* and *safety* levels unduly. In the erstwhile USSR, before the recent changes, an organizational study of a hotel revealed the following.

An electrician was the best paid employee at a monthly salary of 275 roubles. While the general manager received 260 roubles, a departmental head received 240 roubles. The salaries of the rest of about 500 employees in that organization ranged between 240 and 275 roubles per month. As against this, for a total expenditure of 23 roubles a month, the State provided them with living accommodation, transportation, electricity, water and subsidized food. The normal working pattern for most people was to work one day and take off for the next three days. It was explained that as each person worked for 24 hours at a stretch (supposedly), giving three days off after each work day was mandatory as per Union rules. The actual fact was that hardly anyone worked more than eight hours even during the work day: the general manager of the hotel took some visitors for dinner at one of the restaurants run by his hotel. The restaurant had the capacity to serve 400 guests at a time. At the time they entered, there were about 200 guests and over 25 waiters in the restaurant, but he had to abandon the idea of dinner after waiting for 15 minutes because the dirty plates in front of the other 200 empty chairs had not yet been cleared.

In a well-run hotel, no restaurant manager would allow more than a minute for removal of soiled crockery and cutlery, replacement of table linen and relaying of the covers. Nor would he allow guests to walk away with the restaurant half empty, let alone risk it with his General Manager as the accompanying host for the party. A similar occurrence in any society that did not allow high threshold limits at the safety level, would have resulted in a few people losing their jobs, and rightly so. For, they would then have had more efficiently run hotels, attracted more tourists and earned considerably more in convertible currencies of value.

With physiological and safety levels abundantly satisfied, and with no system for the recognition of work performance or reward, people in communist and socialist societies have grown like the allegorical, crooked tree as shown in Fig. 6.1. As discussed in Chapter 4, the quality of effort that ensues from people who have levelled off at the safety level has to be very low too. Such societies therefore produce goods of shoddy quality that have no market, leading to a permanent balance of trade problem.

In countries where unions have outlived their essential usefulness by trying to justify absurdly high threshold limits at the safety level, similar results have been observed. In an engineering company in India, a union steward assaulted a personnel officer in front of four other executives, because someone recommended by him had not been selected in an interview. Some months later, the personnel officer and his manager had resigned from the company, but the particular union steward continued to make his presence felt. Incentive schemes designed two decades earlier on the principles of "pigeon pecks and food" (discussed in Chapter 2) were still in operation in the company. During the intervening period of twenty years, the Union had used its strength to successfully disallow incorporation of technological reduction of operation time in productivity calculations. This had led to employees completing their "quota" of work in about four hours each day. Resistance to change of any kind, particularly for productivity and quality improvement almost always results when people collectively plateau at any lower need level, and this was evident in the company. Examples of this type can be found in the thousands in countries where the trade union movement has shifted its role from ensuring reasonable safety of employees to one of maximizing threshold limits at the safety level.

Many affluent people who have come up the hard way bemoan the fact that their children are being denied the lessons of hardship. In his recently published autobiography, *The Ragman's Son*, Kirk Douglas talks about bringing up children in Beverly Hills, where some of the richest and most successful Hollywood stars live:

> In this environment, children do not thrive. These children, surfeited with every indulgence, seeing stars and limousines and Rolls-Royces coming up and down, depositing other stars and famous directors for dinners, are having miserable childhoods. . . To the rest of the world, it looks as if these kids were brought up with everything.

Born Issur Danielovitch Demsky, the son of an illiterate immigrant Russian–Jewish ragman, Kirk Douglas should know the difference between growing up with bare *appetite* needs being satisfied, and a Beverly Hills childhood. Without trying to extol the virtues of poverty, Kirk Douglas sums it up well: 'It's difficult to overcome affluence'. Yes. *When threshold springs are stretched beyond their elastic limit, they lose the ability to spring back to their original shape and length.* Then, high threshold limits become the norm, one from which it is extremely difficult to retract. Kirk Douglas gives a few hints as to how he brought up his four sons without spoiling them. Of his eldest son, Michael, he says,

> Michael was supposed to join us (the rest of the family) in Hawaii, but I
> was mad at him. He was almost flunking out of the University of
> California at Santa Barbara, so I wouldn't let him come. Michael got his
> act together, even got a job in a gas station, and became Attendant of
> the Month.

Michael indeed got his act together, for he went on to become a top
grade actor himself, winning Oscar awards both as an actor and as a
producer. In this remarkable autobiography, Kirk Douglas gives
another important clue as to how to avoid being trapped by high safety
threshold levels. Talking of his own college days, he says,

> I made another crucial decision—not to take any more courses in
> education. I had been advised to get a teaching credential so that I
> would have *something to fall back on*. But I didn't want to have
> something to fall back on. I didn't want a trap to fall into if getting
> an acting job was difficult. I was one course—one easy course—away
> from the credential. I didn't take it. I totally cut off that avenue,
> deliberately boxed myself in.

By deliberately setting low threshold limits at the safety level, he
was ensuring that his energies would be channelled according to
the direction that his intrinsic motivation was urging him to proceed along. Despite many ups and downs in the early stages of his
career, he kept trying to make a success of his acting career as he
had provided no escape route for himself. That he eventually
succeeded well, both as an actor and as a father, could be traced
back to his apparently instinctive knowledge of the relationship
between low threshold limits, hard work and quality of endeavour.

## THE LEVELLING OFF AT THE *"BELONGINGNESS"* LEVEL

When people set high threshold limits at the 'belongingness' level,
they face and create even more complex problems. The classic case
that immediately leaps to one's mind is a character from one of
Somerset Maugham's novels. Elliot Templeton, in *The Razor's Edge*
spends most, if not all his wakeful time in being part of the *elite
society*. The proper attire, manners, etiquette, the right conversation,
the right exchange of gifts, being seen at the right party with the
right people . . . in fact, *to belong* was the driving force of his life.

Even on his death bed, his only worry was that he had not received an invitation for a major social event that was scheduled to take place later that week.

While individuals might form themselves into groups, originally to satisfy their own safety or belongingness needs, groups begin to develop a culture and force of their own very soon. The group culture then begins to impose new demands on members, initially subtly but later with brute force. Crowds become mobs, religious groups become killers, and associations become dangerous cults. Individuals who initially seek membership for good reasons—to satisfy their appetite needs of safety and belongingness—find themselves drawn into committing actions they might have never imagined themselves capable of.

To demonstrate the positive and negative influences of a group on its members, we organized a series of planned events at a "leadership development workshop" for young managers of the Taj Group of Hotels. In the first part of the workshop, lasting a week, the participants had been formed into four groups. By the time the week ended, the members of each group had got close to each other, and were observed going out together, eating together and sharing a lot more with each other than with those outside the group. When they reassembled for the second part of the workshop, conducted two months later, they were allowed to form themselves into four groups in any way they wished. Without exception, all 32 broke up into the same four groups as before.

## FIERCE GROUP LOYALTY LEADS TO HATRED OF OTHERS

On the next day, the participants were told the groups had to be reassembled in a different manner, the membership for each group having been decided with a view to having complementary personality types in each group. There was much resentment and groaning, but they were forced to comply with the trainers' decision. In the next four days, a series of inter-group competitions were arranged, designed to heighten intra-group participation. Skits, music competition, fancy dress, redesign of group space, group uniform and many other activities got each group developing an identity and culture of its own. By the end of the third day, the new groups were so closely knit and possessive of their group membership that many apparently strange events took place:

- When a member of one group entered the group space belonging to another, to borrow a felt pen, he was called a spy and was physically pushed out;
- One participant, who was sharing a room with another who had been part of his group in the first part of the workshop but was now a member of another group, stopped talking to his erstwhile friend, looking suspiciously whenever he entered or left the room;
- The groups moved *en masse* wherever they went, arranging to have breakfast, lunch and dinner at synchronized times in prearranged places, and sought to avoid other groups as far as was possible within the confines of the resort where the workshop was being held.

Among other lessons learnt through these experiential learning exercises were the following two important, negative aspects of a feeling of excessive belongingness:

1. When you are fiercely loyal to a group, you unconsciously begin to distrust and dislike all those who are not members of your group: racists, religious bigots and Nazis have drawn much of their energy by sharing group hatred of common enemies.
2. You begin to behave with outsiders in a manner that you would not have normally done, even to the extent of severing relationships that had been healthy and mutually supportive earlier.

## INTER-DEPARTMENTAL FRICTION AND RIVALRY A RESULT OF HIGH INTRA-GROUP BELONGINGNESS

With this background, it should be relatively easy to appreciate why many corporations get torn apart by internecine warfare waged by people owing allegiance to their functions, departments, units, and bosses. Classical schisms between line and staff executives, between Production and Quality, between Accountants and the rest and between Marketing and Production owe their origins to this phenomenon.

In a large corporation, a Production Head began to enjoy his reputation as a man who could pulverize all Service functions, especially in joint meetings. His witticisms, rude and rough behaviour and openly insulting language became the talk of the corporation. He was held in awe by his subordinates, and hated by everyone in the Service functions. Overnight, a marvellous solution was implemented, which worked wonders. In an organizational change, the particular executive was transferred as Head of Services. Within six months, he was a different man, for he had seen the problems from the other side, as head of a new group. By the time he retired, he was playing the role of an elder statesman to whom executives would go for counselling.

By careful job rotation, broad-based training, cross-functional exposure and planned transfers, corporations can effectively counter the ill effects of high belongingness needs. By making an employee feel that he belongs to a larger whole, rather than a subculture, the human need for belongingness can be used as stepping stone for growth up the hierarchy of needs, rather than a plateau to level off at.

## THE ARCHETYPAL HIGH-PROFILE EXECUTIVE HAS HIGH THRESHOLD LIMITS FOR RECOGNITION BY OTHERS

Those who follow the Maslovian hierarchy of needs right up to the need for "recognition by others", by achieving satisfaction of reasonable threshold limits of lower needs, are but one step away from entering their *own domain*, but it is the most difficult step of them all. As the poet said, this level does indeed prove to be "the last infirmity of noble minds", particularly in corporations.

At the *appetite* level, if this level is understood as *aupadeshika*, or the legitimate need of a student to be recognized and corrected by his master, we have seen that an individual can move up to the *self-esteem* level on the satisfaction of such an appetite. However, what does happen for most of us is that we begin to enjoy the feeling of being recognized to such an extent that we become addicted to it. You want to stand "first" in class, you want to become the star sportsman who outshines everybody else and you want to *stand out* in any activity you take up. To do all this, you need to beat somebody else, and you understand that there is a major difference between your desire for recognition and all the other needs you have experienced.

Your feeling of satisfaction, in the three previous levels of needs, was not at all dependent on others being denied the satisfaction of *that need*. In the case of the *desire* for recognition by others, you learn that it is primarily dependent on others being denied the recognition that is accorded to you. Everyone can't come first, everyone can't be a sports star and everyone can't be the boss's favourite. By definition, it appears that you are dependent on others forming a backdrop to heighten your achievements.

## THE OPTION APPARENTLY IS TO BE A PUPPET
## OR A PUPPETEER

In this distorted view of recognition, you see executives losing sleep over such issues as not being allotted as big an office as a colleague, not being chosen by the boss for the most sought after assignment, not being able to afford the visibly expensive holiday that another is reported to have had, not being received by a sufficient number of lackeys on arrival in an airport, not being given the largest suite in the best hotel and not receiving a standing ovation after every public address. Such insufferable people crowd corporate corridors. Short of announcing that they have permanently packed up their threshold springs at this level, and that they have replaced them with strings that puppeteers with power can manipulate at will, they do everything else. Gradually, it dawns on them that in such a distorted world, one is either a puppet or a puppeteer. Puppets accord recognition to puppeteers, and the latter begin to wonder if it is not possible to use a similar method to pull the strings of *desires* at other lower needs too. They begin to experiment with this concept and arrive at a new learning: whoever takes control of the strings, assumes power. The power over the extrinsic motivation of people, or the power to reward and punish, as exercised in most large organizations, is indeed an interesting phenomenon to study. Let us consider a real life example from a multi-unit corporation.

## IT ALSO APPEARS THAT ONLY ONE PUPPETEER CAN EXIST

A unit manager in this organization assumed control over the extrinsic motivation of staff by introducing non-standard rewards and punishments. Grant of a holiday, expenses paid by the unit ostensibly for work, foreign trips and assignments, entertainment expenses used as a cover for approving personal entertainment of the family, and a host of other methods were used by the unit manager to take control. The CEO at the corporate headquarters did not like this, as he had taken enormous pains to ensure that all staff knew that he was in complete, unitary control of their fate. He even used to insist on signing all communication to staff involving promotions and salary increases. Faced by the sudden challenge, the CEO now responded by resorting to a new practice. All correspondence from him began to go directly to staff, rather than being routed through the unit head, as had been the practice earlier. When the unit head objected to this new practice, the CEO used a classical counter manoeuvre.

Aware that other unit heads might also resent his assumption of such unitary power, he decided to use the incident to reassert his power. He let the unit head raise the issue at a meeting when there were a sufficient number of senior executives with *high safety threshold limits* to say "yes" and appropriately nod, in agreement with the view—put forward helpfully by one of the group—that staff in units would actually feel honoured if they received communication directly from the big boss himself. The unit head lost the round, but learnt an important lesson:

*In most corporations, it appears that there is space for just one major puppeteer to perform. When some of those who are supposed to be puppets suddenly start acting free of the puppeteer they appear very threatening to the major puppeteer. Threatening, because other puppets could also get similar ideas. Such people are therefore either made to resume their puppet roles, or forced to leave the organization.*

If all of this sounds familiar, it is not surprising. History is full of puppeteers getting surprised, and wrathful, at any of their human puppets getting out of control. Spartacus was a puppet who tried to become free of his puppeteer, and was killed. Thomas Becket was one who had appeared to be the ideal puppet till he suddenly realized that 'there was a hollow in me where honour ought to be'. He began to exhibit signs of replacing his strings with springs, and there was a murder in the cathedral.

## A MANAGER CAN BE LIKE A GARDENER OR A PUPPETEER

As discussed in Chapters 4 and 5, the quality of output that ensues from people who are extrinsically motivated is vastly inferior to that produced by intrinsically motivated people. Senior managers who resemble puppeteers, or puppets, will therefore never be able to either produce, or enable the production of, quality and perfection. Their work will at best reach what the Chinese classified as *neng*, whether the work is accomplished by themselves, or by their subordinates.

To clarify this point further, consider a common enough observation.

> Several senior executives appear to have no problems when it comes to getting high quality output from young, intrinsically motivated subordinates several rungs below them in the organizational hierarchy. However, they tend to face major problems while interacting with mature subordinates who have reached very close to them in the hierarchy.

A possible explanation is that a young subordinate's appetite needs at the first four levels—up to "recognition by others"—require a minimum number of years to be satiated. By carefully spacing out the rewards program, a clever senior executive can control the energies of the younger person. A flat or a house in a posh locality, membership in a costly club, international travel and exposure, bigger and better offices, professional recognition at a peer level through press and other publicity are some of the rewards that could be given in recognition of high quality work. If these are acceptable "appetite" needs among corporate youth, and they are seen to be achieved meritoriously, the young men who work hard and enjoy themselves while doing so look at these rewards as bonuses for their efforts.

During these initial years, most young people also need to be guided by a master; therefore, very strong attachments are formed which permit the exercise of a master's seemingly autocratic power over the pupil. It is when the young man shows signs of naturally moving one step ahead—into achieving self esteem in his *own domain*—that the master shows his true colours. If he is one who models himself after a gardener, rather than a puppeteer, he will be delighted that his "pupil" has graduated to the level from where outstanding work of great quality will spew forth. He will accordingly let go of his controls, at least as much as is possible within the context of the larger goals of their organization, and watch with pleasure as the erstwhile pupil blossoms into a master himself.

If the master is one who models himself after a puppeteer, he will react by denying appetite needs of lower levels and force the pupil back into a dependency relationship. Some of the usual manoeuvres that are resorted to are exclusion of the pupil from important meetings (to show that the pupil no longer belongs), refusal to approve or clear even routine decisions concerning the pupil (to deny "recognition" accorded even to the lowliest and also to reduce the pupil's feeling of safety), withholding of information and access to resources essential for the pupil attaining mastery over his work area (thus throttling upward growth to self-esteem and self-actualization) and initiation of direct communication with the pupil's subordinates (thus making the pupil feel like an outcast, threatened and unrecognized).

Within the confines of a corporation, news spreads very fast. From being a high-flying young executive to an outcast, the journey can be made in as little time as a day. Smiling secretaries who earlier encouraged your barging in without appointments will suddenly find plausible reasons for keeping you out. Central services, such as mailing, printing, security, accounts and personnel, will suddenly begin to quote rules, procedure and policies from manuals that had never been referred to when you were a rising star. In no time at all, you realize that if you want to have your appetite needs satisfied at the four lower levels, you must make an important decision : either forget about letting your instincts and intrinsic motivation govern your natural progression towards self-esteem and self-actualization, and become a puppet for the corporate puppeteer to play with; or recognize that the *master* has feet of clay, refuse to play ball and take control of your threshold springs, and life.

The first option is one which the majority of people exercise, to end up as mediocre hacks resembling the allegorical, gnarled tree. To exercise the second option, you require more than mere resolve. It requires that a strange lesson be learnt first, one by which you develop the ability, like Beethoven, "to take Fate by the throat".

# 7

# Taking Fate by the Throat: Freudian "Sublimation" by Individuals and Organizations

If you are enmeshed in a world of high threshold limits, driven by extrinsic motivation, and find yourself in the unenviable position of a puppet, is it possible to escape from the situation, and if so, how? Before seeking an answer to this question, consider the results of the following exercise. You might wish to subject yourself to the exercise too; as this will make it possible for you to relate your own experiences with what follows in this chapter.

## AN EXERCISE FOR YOU TO TEST YOURSELF AGAINST 3,000 OTHERS

In the past ten years, I have conducted this exercise with over 3,000 people. Men and women, in the age group of 18 to 60, with nationalities ranging from Indian, Sri Lankan, and Mexican to American and British, have done the exercise. The results have been remarkably uniform, with over 90% reporting identical answers. The typical procedure for the exercise starts with assembling about 25 participants. They are then taken through the following steps:

- *Step 1:* The participants are asked to write down on a sheet of paper, their answer to the question,"What has been your single greatest learning experience in life?"

Before letting anyone answer the question, I explain:

1. By a "single" experience is meant a one-time event that has occurred, and not a lifelong experience. Answers like "Knowing my mother has been my greatest learning experience" are therefore to be avoided, even if they be true.
2. To identify the greatest of the many learning experiences you may have had, pick that experience but for which you would not be "as wise" as you have become.
3. The answer to this question is not meant for sharing. You can therefore be quite honest and brutally frank.

- *Step 2*: After ensuring that each participant has picked his single, greatest learning experience, they are asked to write down, in a separate sheet of paper, their answer to the next question, "What were your feelings or emotions at the time this greatest of learning experiences had just started?"

Again, before the participants begin to answer the second question, I explain:

1. It is essential that you identify the feeling or emotion you experienced *at the start* of the experience, and not what you felt halfway through the experience, or at the end of it.
2. In describing your feeling, try to use single words rather than sentences, such as 'high'/'low', 'happy'/'unhappy', 'confident'/'unsure' and 'enthusiastic'/'despondent'.
3. You will later be sharing your answers to the second question in groups of seven or eight people. I suggest you leave out autobiographical statements and just write down six or seven words, each word describing your feeling.

- *Step 3:* After ensuring that each participant has completed Step 2, they are asked to form groups of seven or eight. After the groups are formed, volunteers are called for, to act as coordinators for each group. The volunteers are told to have the group members share their answers to the second question, and to observe if any pattern emerges.

- *Step 4*: The volunteers are asked to report on the pattern, if any, that they have observed.
- *Step 5*: *As the volunteers report, they are asked to give the words that were found to be common in the members' lists, and these words are noted on a board or projected on a screen.*

Without exception, all the groups in all countries have reported that the greatest of learning experiences begin to the accompaniment of feelings such as

*hurt, upset, denied, rejected, insecure, lost, unhappy, lonely, shocked, frustrated, angry, scared, nervous and dejected.*

Typical examples of experiences some participants shared with the rest of the group members were:

- I failed in an examination that was important, and I felt that the sky had fallen on me; my life appeared ruined and I regretted not having taken life seriously enough before. I had to salvage my life from nothingness. . .
- My father died when I was in college, with three younger brothers and sisters still in school; my mother and I found we had no one to turn to. . . we economized, lived frugally and I dropped out of college to start earning. . .
- My boss dumped me for no apparent reason, began to deal with my subordinates and everyone in the organization treated me like an outcast. From the heights of professional security, I crashed. I developed ulcer, lost all self-confidence . . . till I made up my mind, "To hell with them, I'll show them what I am made of . . . "

## THE LEARNING IS THAT WE WERE MEANT TO BE HEROES

My explanation for this universal phenomenon is this:

Even though we are aware, from our schooldays, that heroism and great achievements are possible only through the sacrifice of lower needs for the sake of higher ones, many of us fall into the trap of getting used to high threshold limits for lower needs. We are not quite conscious that this leads us to assume roles as puppets in the hands of puppeteers who pull our threshold *strings*, which in turn inhibits our ability to reach upwards to higher need levels. When an event takes place suddenly, which forces lowering of threshold limits—at the *physiological, safety, belongingness/love* or *recognition by others levels*—drastically, and we find that we do have the inherent capacity to cope with such an experience, we identify such an experience as our *greatest learning experience*. It is through such apparently accidental experiences that we learn what our true capacities are. While animals and plants do not have the capacity to control their needs, and apply threshold springs, human beings appear to have such a capacity. Identifying that capacity, and being aware of it within ourselves, leads us to the knowledge that we were meant to be heroes, rather than greedy, self-serving, petty and manipulable beings. Instinctively, all human beings recognize the discovery of this knowledge as the most valuable learning.

The fact that over 90 % of more than 3,000 men and women from various countries were able to jointly identify such an experience as their greatest learning experience should strengthen the hope that it is not too late for redirecting our energies towards self-actualization. We have not yet become too gnarled and old for the allegorical stick to be used, provided we appreciate the fact that many apparent punishments happen to contain within them an opportunity for us to learn how to live a life of low threshold limits.

## STARTLING SUPPORT FROM OTHER RESEARCH DATA

History is replete with data to support the explanation that has just been offered. In studies of eminent personalities conducted by many researchers, a startlingly similar pattern has been observed. A good summary of such findings has been presented by R. Ochse (1990), which the reader might wish to refer to. Given below are some highlights of the findings.

Goertzel and Goertzel (1962) observed that 25% of a group of 400 eminent historical figures had been physically handicapped, almost 50% had been subjected to financial ups and downs and as much as 75% had been troubled by broken homes, rejecting, over-possessive, estranged or domineering parents. In a subsequent analysis, Goertzel, Goertzel and Goertzel (1978) found that 85% of 400 eminent people of the twentieth century had come from markedly troubled homes.

Another finding in studies of the early life experiences of eminent people is that a disproportionate number of them were bereaved of at least one parent in early childhood. The only other subgroup with approximately the same proportion of childhood bereavement are delinquents and suicidal depressives, which fact will be explained later in this chapter, while demonstrating how abnormal psychology can be included within the ambit of the model.

Figure 7.1, which is adapted from Albert (1980), shows the percentage of individuals in various groups who lost a parent before the age of sixteen. It will be observed that while less than 10% of the average population have had such bereavements, it ranges between 25 and 55 % among eminent achievers in different groups and between 15.5 and 49% among psychologically depressed people.

To avoid any misapprehension, let me hasten to say that I am not at all suggesting that people should be deliberately made to suffer the pains of losing a parent, or lose an arm or a leg, so that they may learn how to cope with low threshold limits. Far be it from my objective to suggest that. In the past, and present, for that matter, people have learnt from accidents and grown, while an equal number , if not more, have developed enormous abnormalities from similar accidents. In Chapters 8 and 9, I will deal with how the more fortunately placed people can help others, through counselling, teaching, visioning, etc, such that life's accidental blows could be converted into great learning experiences.

What is worth noting, from the research findings quoted, is the fact that the most eminent of historical figures, as also their twentieth century counterparts, will also report that their greatest learning experiences had also been similar to my research sample.

## BEETHOVEN AS A CLASSIC CASE IN POINT

A classic case of a human being who coped with a series of life's blows, and drastic lowering of threshold limits at almost every level, is Beethoven, whose music has brought fulfilment and joy to so many countless millions across the globe, generation after generation. Let us consider his life and works briefly, from this perspective:

PERCENTAGE OF SUBJECTS WHO LOST
A PARENT BEFORE SIXTEEN YEARS OF
AGE - ADAPTED FROM ALBERT (1980)

| GROUP | n | % Bereaved |
|---|---|---|
| **Politicians** | | |
| American Presidents | 39 | 34% |
| British Prime Ministers | 48 | 35% |
| **Creative people** | | |
| Cox's historical geniuses | 135 | 30% |
| Eminent Scientists (Roe, 1953) | 64 | 26% |
| Eminent French and English poets (lost father — Martindale) | 33 | 24% |
| Eminent English poets and writers (Brown, 1968) | 57 | 55% |
| **Psychologically disturbed** | | |
| Highly distressed | 100 | 27% |
| Medium depressed | 97 | 15.5% |
| Non-depressed (Beck et al, 1963) | 100 | 12% |
| Outpatient depressives | 216 | 49% |
| Outpatient Controls | 267 | 21% |
| **Control groups** | | |
| College students (Gregory, '65) | 1696 | 6% |
| Adolescents, general population (Hathaway & Monchesi, '63) | 11329 | 8% |
| General British population (Ferri, '76) | 17000 | 9% |

*Figure 7.1*

Ludwig van Beethoven was born in 1770. His father Johannes Beethoven was also a musician, but of limited talent. He was violent man given to alcoholism and bouts of uncontrollable temper. The father also disapproved of his son's attempts to create his own music, and showed his displeasure by forcing him to practise other people's compositions. Visitors to the Beethoven home reported having witnessed young Ludwig being woken up in the middle of the night, *to practise*. It was also known that the father often used to physically assault the son. In modern parlance, Ludwig was, in every sense of the term, a battered child.

At the age of 16, Beethoven's mother died, and he lost the only person who seemed to have had genuine affection for him. In his mid-twenties, when his musical prowess was just beginning to blossom, he was afflicted with a crippling hearing impairment. By the age of 32, he knew he was deaf.

Fate appeared to have chosen Beethoven as an example, for she reduced his threshold limits to the bare minimum, or even less. At physiological, safety and belongingness level, he had been subjected to the most severe denial of need satisfaction. History records how Beethoven dealt with Fate, for this is what happened.

In October 1802, Beethoven retreated to a place near Vienna, Heiligenstadt, where he was to write a heart-rending document addressed to his brothers:

> For the last six years, I have been afflicted with an incurable
> complaint which has been made worse by incompetent doctors.
> From year to year, my hopes of being cured have been gradually
> shattered and finally I have been forced to accept the prospect of a
> permanent infirmity . . . obliged to seclude myself and live in
> solitude . . . could not bring myself to say to people: Speak up, shout,
> for I am deaf. Alas! how could I possibly refer to the impairment of a
> *sense* which in me should be more perfectly developed than in other
> people, a sense which at one time I possessed in the greatest
> perfection . . . on the point of putting an end to my life.

## BEETHOVEN'S DECISION "TO TAKE FATE BY THE THROAT"

Yet, Beethoven did not give up. He overcame what was the lowest point in his life by vowing *"to take Fate by the throat"*, and entered a phenomenally purple patch of his creative life. In the six years that followed the Heiligenstadt testament, Beethoven composed some of his best music—The Violin Concerto, and the Third, Fifth and Sixth symphonies. He was a master craftsman who could not be denied. His works during this period can only be described as profound, or *miao* according to the Chinese classification mentioned in Chapter 4.

After this burst of energy, which lasted till about 1809, Beethoven was surprisingly withdrawn. He was increasingly drawn into his own inner world, and appeared to be quite completely oblivious to the rest of the world. He was quite clearly out of "others' domain", and was in his "own domain." It was to take almost a full decade before Beethoven's musical genius again burst out. This time, however, his music was to take on a different quality altogether. Both the Ninth Symphony and the Missa Solemnis were composed by him during this period. In describing these two compositions, most music critics use words like, "mystic", "divine", "other-worldly" and "immortal". To listen to the Missa Solemnis in a Church with a good pipe organ in place is an ethereal experience indeed. To witness the majestic march of the Ninth symphony into its fourth movement, and hear Schiller's "Ode to Joy" is another experience that transports audiences to dizzy heights. Beethoven was clearly self-actualizing at this last stage of his life. Whatever music was composed by him during these years was indeed *shen,* or divine. It had to be.

## CORRELATION WITH FREUD'S PSYCHO-ANALYTIC EXPLANATION

Not all of us are aware that each of us has, within himself, the intrinsic ability to respond to Fate's arrows in such a strong manner as Beethoven. We require expert help and guidance to identify, and thereafter build upon, our intrinsic ability to do so. Without such help, many of us mistakenly feel that it is Fate who has caught us by the throat. That is why, in the statistics quoted earlier in the chapter, it was found that there were as many delinquents and suicidal depressives as eminent men among those who had been bereaved of at least one parent in early childhood.

To better understand how this happens, and what may be done to help those who are not able to help themselves, let me present an explanation based on Sigmund Freud's own words, albeit with a few modifications and extensions. In September 1909, Freud delivered five lectures on psychoanalysis at the Clark University in Worcester, Massachusetts. I have taken excerpts from the fifth and last lecture of this series, and in the explanation after each excerpt I have elaborated how Freud's description of psychoanalysis can be extended beyond the sexual impulse, to cover all other human needs too:

*Freud: If a person who is at loggerheads with reality possesses an artistic gift (a thing that is still a psychological mystery to us), he can transform his fantasies into artistic creations instead of into symptoms. In this manner he can escape the doom of neurosis and by this roundabout path regain his contact with reality.*

*My explanation:* When a human being has the intrinsic capacity to seek "self-esteem" and "self-actualization" through concentrated activity in any endeavour, he has a much better chance of dealing with reality in whatever form Fate decides to present it. Far from showing neurotic symptoms, he will deal with the drastic lowering of threshold limits like a Beethoven. He will withdraw himself into his field of endeavour, or "work" in a manner and with a concentration that would be of much greater intensity than normal. Work itself becomes a cure for the worldly problem that has confronted him.

On several occasions, I have found executives responding to major, personal calamities through intense work. To suggestions that they could take time off from work if necessary, they normally respond with statements like, "It's o.k. I actually find it a relief to be back at work" and "I'll go mad if I don't immerse myself in some work that can stretch me". This reaction is typical of those who, like Beethoven, have a strong instinct to "take Fate by the throat". But crucial to this ability is a human being's state of preparedness to progress through the *aupadeshika* stage to *aharya and sahaja* . He should already have reached a stage in his involvement with his field of endeavour where he can become independent of others' recognition of his performance, for this movement is normally into one's "own domain". The "will" to become a master craftsman, or achieve satisfaction through setting and meeting one's own standards of perfection does not come easy. It requires years of toil, tutelage and *abhyasa*.

*Freud: The mental and somatic power of a wishful impulse, when once its repression has failed, is far stronger if it is unconscious than if it is conscious; so that to make it conscious can only be to weaken it. An unconscious wish cannot be influenced and it is independent of any contrary tendencies, whereas a conscious one is inhibited by whatever else is conscious and is opposed to it.*

*My extension and elaboration:* We have seen that the satisfaction of a felt need is a prerequisite for psychological growth. We have also seen that when one's appetite needs are satisfied, instead of moving up the hierarchy, human beings can also deviate towards wishing satiation of "desire" needs at the lower level itself. When either the initial impulse for the satiation of appetite needs, or the later impulse for satiation of desires, is not adequately met, a human being feels unhappy.

One who is totally ignorant of the fact that it is natural for him to seek need satisfaction in a particular sequence, or that he will feel unhappy when such satisfaction is denied, will naturally be unaware why he is unhappy. As a first step towards improving his lot, Freud suggests that he should be made conscious of the fact that his unhappiness stems from the nonsatisfaction of a natural impulse. While Freud restricted himself to the sexual impulse, it is suggested that it applies to all levels of needs.

What makes this first step crucial is the fact that human beings who are denied satiation of their needs react to such repression in varying degrees of destructive manner. Either it is self-destructive, or it is directed externally. A major study of this subject has been carried out by Colin Wilson. I recommend his *Criminal History of Mankind* strongly. In this treatise, Wilson has correlated the Maslovian hierarchy of needs with abnormal behaviour, using criminality among Mankind as a representative indication of abnormality.

To focus on some of the moot issues concerning even a definition of what constitutes criminal behaviour, let us consider "theft" in different forms.

- A burglar who plans entry into a house and purloins money, jewellery and other valuables from a middle-class home is one who is premeditatedly committing an act that is going to affect the "security" needs of the middle-class family at a basic, "appetite" level;

- Robin Hood and his merry men stole from the rich Normans and redistributed the wealth so gained among the downtrodden, poverty stricken Saxons. By so doing, they were denying what was tantamount to the satiation of "desires" among the rich and, in turn, satisfying the "appetite" needs of the poor. In the early stages of the communist movement, and many other socialist movements, leaders of political parties promised much the same too;

- Using inter-religious and inter-caste feelings of insecurity, political leaders cause fear-psychosis with a view to capturing vote banks, loot personal property through hired thugs and eventually strengthen themselves. By so doing, they deny the "appetite" needs of unsuspecting common folk in order to satisfy the their own "desires"—for power—and that of their followers—for looted property;

- A poor boy, unable to stand the pangs of hunger, and seeing his mother and brothers starving, steals bread from a bakery. By so doing, he satisfies his and his family's "appetite" needs, but he threatens the basic fabric of trade through the denial of legitimate value for a product, namely money for bread.

While considering these cases, and assessing the extent of criminal behaviour exhibited in each, we are tempted to grade such behaviour in this manner.

The worst criminal is one who denies the satiation of others' "appetite" needs for satisfying his "desires"; the next is one who denies the satisfaction of others' "desires" for satiating his own "desires"; the third will be the category of those who deny the satisfaction of others' "appetite needs" for his own "appetite" needs. As for those who deny the satisfaction of others' "desires" for satiating their "appetite" needs, it is tempting to believe that the inherent problem of criminality is not centred in them but rather in the societal conditions that allow such disparities. The last category, i.e. those who deny the satisfaction of one group's "desires" in order to satiate the "appetite" needs of another, we laud as heroes just as Robin Hood has been revered over the centuries.

While theft as a phenomenon is relatively easy to understand, other acts that follow unconscious repression are far more difficult to comprehend and deal with. Let me highlight this with an example from corporate India:

A young executive had become irritable, unpopular with colleagues and subordinates, and a problem for the boss. His output had begun to come down, and mistakes plagued his every action and recommendation. What was surprising was the fact that he had been known to be just the opposite a mere three months ago. He had also had a brilliant track record. With a gold medal for his scholastic achievements in a prestigious management school, he had entered his vocational area of finance with instant success. He had revamped the costing and budgetary control systems, set up a management accounting procedure and created a reliable and speedy management information system. He had received awards and promotions rapidly and was seen as a "fast track" youngster who was regularly in the limelight. Two consecutive awards from the Chairman of the company had about sealed his reputation as a Young Man who was set to go places.

Yet, such a man had begun to go to pieces all of a sudden. There were several incidents that had taken place almost simultaneously, which had had this effect. His only son had turned out to be a spastic child, he had been overlooked for a promotion, with a less flamboyant, plodding chartered accountant being preferred for the No.1 slot by a management that had suddenly exhibited its classical preference to a traditional accountant, and he had fallen foul of a powerful line executive. To compound the problem further, what had been a mild flirtation with an office colleague had not only assumed the proportions of a major involvement but had also become public in an embarrassing manner.

With his emotional relationships in a mess, and worried over his son's health and his own professional future, the young man's self confidence had been rudely shaken. His threshold limits had thus been suddenly reduced at every level just about the time the lack of a classical Accounting background was threatening to block his path towards reaching greater heights in his field of endeavour.

Before we proceed to the next part of this chapter when we will discuss how such a human being could be helped, let us take a leaf from Freud's book and hold the position that the first step towards helping such a human being is to make him conscious of the individual repressions that had led to his current state. As regards the manner of doing it, we have to wait till Chapter 8 when we will discuss the art and science of counselling.

# FREUD'S THREE AVENUES FOR DEALING WITH FAILED REPRESSION

Freud goes on to talk of three avenues open to a patient, after he has become conscious of any failed repression. Let me extend Freud's analysis to cover the entire spectrum of human needs, rather than the merely sexual:

1. The first avenue, according to Freud, is to help the patient such that *Repression* is replaced by a *condemning judgment* (the italics are Freud's) carried out along the best lines.'

If a human being is talked to, and helped to identify that his impulse for need gratification was in the "desire" domain, rather than essential "appetite", he finds it possible to replace his feeling of deprivation with a self-condemning judgment. Such a self condemning judgment will help him consciously lower his threshold limits and equip himself with strong threshold springs. In the examples quoted in Chapter 5 about the two MBA marketing management trainees, as well as the young chef who was dragging his feet about a transfer to a green-field site, this was exactly what was done.

In the case of the young finance specialist referred to earlier, whose life appeared to be falling to pieces, what may be done through professional counselling is threefold:

- First, he could be helped to appreciate the fact that having a spastic son is not the end of the world; there are many who face such a situation in life. He could be made to count his blessings first—that he had a son while many do not have one at all, that he was educated and materially comfortable enough to be able to help such a handicapped child and so on—and thereafter resolve to condemn his own past, helpless approach towards the issue;

- Secondly, he could be made to consciously accept the fact that while his own MBA background had helped him steal a march over his colleagues in the initial years, his handicap of a non-CA background was one that he would have to live with. That he would have to develop a coping mechanism for it; compensating for his lack of a professional accountancy background with sufficient indepth experience in traditional accounting work must become a new and overriding concern. That his feeling of resentment against his top management, and traditional accountants as a class, was not right and would lead him nowhere but down; and

• Thirdly, he should be helped to develop a condemning judgment against his own lack of wisdom in getting involved in an office flirtation while his family—both his son and his wife—needed as much emotional support as he could give them.

That he was indulging in a series of escapist acts, as an unconscious response to unsatiated appetite needs and desires, is a fact that he must be helped to appreciate, accept and condemn.

**2.** *Freud's second avenue of psycho-analysis was to make it* 'possible for the unconscious instincts revealed by it to be employed for the useful purposes which they would have found earlier if development had not been interrupted. . . We know of a far more expedient process of development, called *sublimation*, in which the energy of the infantile wishful impulses is not cut off but remains ready for use—the unserviceable aim of the various impulses being replaced by one that is higher, and perhaps no longer sexual.'

This is a perfect explanation for the findings of the exercise on the emotions accompanying one's greatest learning experiences, and the rest of data on eminent people presented earlier in the chapter. What people did, when faced with drastic lowering of threshold limits at *any* level, is nothing but what Freud termed *sublimation*. While Freud believed sublimation was possible only for sexually repressed energy, the data presented earlier in the chapter clearly shows that sublimation is possible at all the levels: physical handicap, death of a parent, financial ups and downs, ostracism from one's community, denial of recognition and various other forms of deprivation have led to such sublimation.

To take up the case of the young finance executive further, he could be counseled to find the inner "will" to deal with his triple blow through "sublimation". Resolutions like, 'I'll make my son deal with his handicap and actualize his God-given potential as best as possible. . . it is not for nothing that I am considered to be brilliant, and I will direct my talents and energies towards helping my son', 'Okay, I am not a chartered accountant; but there are any number of MBAs who have become successful finance directors. I too will become one . . . I will prove I am as good in traditional accounting functions as any ranking chartered accountant,' and 'Let me take stock of my emotional relationships, rebuild what is of value to my well being and have the courage to break relationships that are destructive' can and must flow out of the young man if he really should make something of his life. A floundering "will", resurrected thus, could give him a new direction and purpose for life, and rebuild him towards psychosocial health.

3. *Freud went on to conclude*, 'We must not omit to consider the third of the possible outcomes of the work of psycho-analysis. A certain portion of the repressed libidinal impulses has a claim to direct satisfaction and ought to find it in life.'

Again, while Freud restricted himself to the study of satiation of sexual appetite, we can logically extend this statement to include appetite needs at all of the Maslovian levels. The human impulse to seek satisfaction of appetite needs at all levels must be considered a legitimate one, for nonsatisfaction of these appetites would normally hinder further growth of a human being towards psycho-social health. While heroism does imply voluntary sacrifice of one's appetite needs at lower levels towards reaching a "vision", one should exercise caution while doing so. In attempting to reduce one's threshold limits, one has to be careful not to eventually reach the fate that was in store for the strong horse of Schilda. Let me quote Freud on this story:

> German literature is familiar with a little town called Schilda, to whose inhabitants clever tricks of every possible sort are attributed. The citizens of Schilda, so we are told, possessed a horse with whose feats of strength they were highly pleased and against which they had only one objection—that it consumed such a large quantity of oats. They determined to break it of this bad habit very gently by reducing its ration by a few stalks every day, till they had accustomed it to complete abstinence. For a time things went excellently: the horse was weaned to the point of eating only one stalk a day, and on the succeeding day, it was to be put to work without any oats at all. On the morning of that day the spiteful animal was found dead; and the citizens of Schilda could not make out what it had died of.

> We should be inclined to think that the horse was starved and that no work at all could be expected of an animal without a certain modicum of oats.

If you happen to work for an organization that resembles the town of Schilda, which does not realize that all human beings have legitimate *appetite* needs at all levels of the hierarchy, you might have to take different, and more aggressive steps. Otherwise, like the horse of Schilda, when you have been starved to death, others in the organization might be wondering why you had failed.

## GROUP AND ORGANIZATIONAL "SUBLIMATION" IS POSSIBLE TOO

Just as individuals can respond to crises through sublimation of energy, so also can whole groups of people be guided to do. Let me give two examples to elaborate this point.

In the late 1970s, soon after the automobiles started rolling out of the TELCO plant in Pune, it was announced by the Government that major repair work required a complete shutdown of the supply of electric power for a full week. With over 10,000 employees in the plant, and a union wage settlement due, the management was loath to pass the effect of disruption to the employees. What we actually did was this.

We saw that for the first time, we were going to have the opportunity to have mass meetings of all people whose work was interconnected. During that week, day after day, in every shop, employees from the departments of production, maintenance, quality control, production engineering, industrial engineering, personnel, costing, etc met to discuss common problems, and arrived at solutions themselves. In the shop manufacturing cylinder blocks, the Engineer in charge of Quality Control provoked a heated discussion with a statement that over 90% of all rejections were due to mistakes committed by operators. In the discussions that followed, workmen, inspectors, supervisors and engineers probed every conceivable reason for rejection, and jointly arrived at what corrective steps would have to be taken. Within a few months thereafter, the Chairman of the organization was present personally on the occasion of the cylinder block line completing four consecutive weeks of zero rejection. By the early 1980s, TELCO had about the most successful record of participative shopfloor management. Line after line, month after month, there were reports of zero rejection. Arun Maira, who had pioneered and led this development, knew that the process had really succeeded when he found out one day that a strange series of events had begun in the shop that was turning out pressed sheet metal parts for the body of the truck. The semi-skilled workmen had begun to take turn to go for lunch so that production was not be interrupted; during the tea break, an inspector from the quality control department had been persuaded by the workmen to show them how to use the inspection gauges so that they could check their own work . . . and of course, rejection rates crashed to zero in no time at all.

## STAFF COMMITMENT TO "SUBLIMATE" IN A CRISIS

A more recent example was at the Taj Palace Hotel in New Delhi. With the looming Middle-East crisis, it was expected that the entire hotel industry would have a severe downturn. As the Taj Group of Hotels has a stated policy of not retrenching staff due to any business downturn, even though the wage bill is the single biggest expenditure head in most hotels, the employees of the group enjoy a high degree of security. At the same time, as internal growth has been encouraged to the extent that more than 80% of the senior positions are filled by those who had joined the organization as freshmen trainees in their teens and early twenties, the general commitment of the staff is normally quite high.

With the news of the Iraqi invasion of Kuwait as a backdrop, I conducted a one-day workshop for the departmental heads and a fair representation of their teams. The objective of the workshop was to initiate voluntary steps for cost reduction, without in any way affecting the quality of service offered to guests. By the end of the day, a worried group had become a highly charged team who had committed themselves to reducing expenditure by over 15 % of the estimated ratios. The General Manager of the hotel was flabbergasted by the energy released through sublimation of an entire group of people. He told me a few days later that there was a kind of party spirit in the hotel, with all the staff sniffing around to see how wasteful expenditure could be cut. The best example was that of a room attendant who had left a bundle of about 150 pens. Recognizing them to be of the variety that are kept with the guest stationery in rooms, the Executive Housekeeper sent for the room attendant and asked him where he had found all the pens. Came the reply, 'Well, you told us that each pen cost us Rs "X". I have observed many people from other departments taking pens from housekeeping trolleys and guest rooms for use and not returning them. Some of my colleagues and I went around after work yesterday and collected all the pens we could find all over the hotel.'

Thousands of ideas poured out from the staff, and the general manager found that he had to set up a separate coordinating group to ensure that the ideas were vetted, and implemented with care and speed.

The two examples merely highlight the fact that just as a strong "Vision" can help people voluntarily set low threshold limits for themselves, and derive immense enjoyment from applying themselves towards the actualization of the "Vision", so also can a crisis be converted through proper leadership into an opportunity for sublimation of group energies towards solving the very crisis. When Fate, whether it be in the form of a puppeteer type of boss, or as any other crisis, threatens you or your organization, you might be doing yourself an act of kindness if you were to remember Beethoven, and thereafter proceed to "take Fate by the throat". All it requires is the ability to react to the lowering of threshold limits by instinctive *sublimation*.

When parents, teachers, corporate management and others in positions of power and authority, decide that they will behave like gardeners and not puppeteers, human beings can be helped to grow rapidly and surely towards psychological health. Based on the discussions of the earlier chapters, we are now in a position to address ourselves to the question of how this model of motivation may be applied to facilitate such psychologically healthy growth. To help us do so, let me figuratively update the model by incorporating all the details that have been discussed so far. We thus arrive at Stage 4 of the model, as shown in Fig. 7.2. We will first look at what parents and teachers can do to facilitate early growth of a child in a manner that effectively guards and nurtures the child's intrinsic *will* to reach out towards self-actualization.

## STAGE 4 OF EAST-WEST MODEL

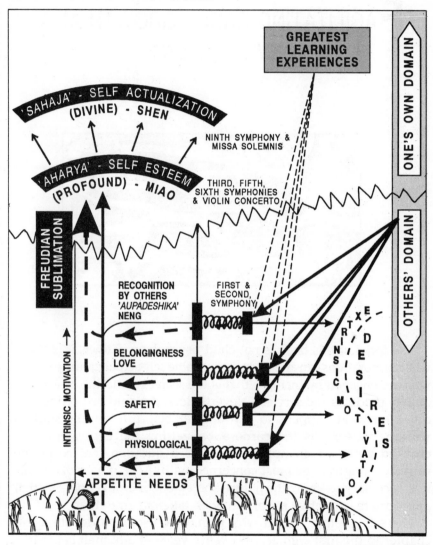

*Figure 7.2*

# 8

# FACILITATING EARLY GROWTH AND DEVELOPMENT

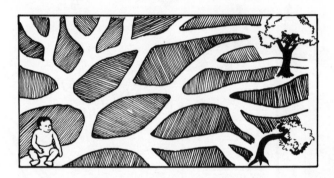

The focus of this book is not child psychology. Rather, it is about what corporations can and must do to enable self-actualization of *adults* who are engaged by them, as that is the secret behind the creation of quality products and services. Nevertheless, it would be pertinent to dwell on what happens to a youngster before he or she starts a working career. "Is the corporation getting the equivalent of a crooked plant, or an upright one," is a question that corporate recruiters ought to be most concerned with. Also, if a crooked one, it is necessary to know the nature and extent of crookedness so that appropriate corrective actions may be taken to straighten it.

There is another reason why it may be useful to devote a full chapter to the first eighteen to twenty years of a human being in a book that addresses itself to the corporate executive. While many managers believe that they are natural experts at human resources management, with God-given talents for understanding people, they begin to exercise doubts when they have to apply such natural expertise on matters concerning their own children.

# MANAGERS' CHILDREN PLAY AN IMPORTANT ROLE

At one time, in a large Indian corporation, there was a senior executive who was the archetype "closed shop" manager. He used to get visibly upset if anyone in his division approached the Personnel Department with any problem. He seemed convinced that he was not only considered an approachable executive but also well versed in the art and science of counselling. He had committed the common error of mistaking the assenting noises made by sycophants for genuine respect and affection. Immunized by such self-deception, he was often heard claiming that there was no need for a specialist Personnel Department for any purpose besides taking care of traditional welfare and administrative matters, apart from keeping the company out of labour courts. However, when it came to the question of his own 16-year-old son, he found it perfectly acceptable to approach the Head of the HR function with a request to find out "what motivated " his son and to counsel him! Apparently, the only son did not share his father's views about his own expertise in counselling, let alone his knowledge of human nature.

On another occasion, and in another corporation, an HR specialist had spent several years trying to convince shopfloor line managers that the best way to treat fresh graduates from the elite Indian Institutes of Technology (IIT) was *not* to subject them to routine, uninteresting work that challenged their physical stamina rather than their intelligence. He had met with very little success till the son of one of the most influential managers joined an IIT. One evening, when the son had invited his IIT friends over to meet his father, almost all of them casually mentioned that they were not planning to make a career as engineers. They were quite unanimous in their feedback that their seniors had expressed the view that one's intelligence was not tested at all in an engineering job. Their plan was to complete the IIT degree and proceed thereafter to get a post-graduate degree in management. According to them, jobs that demanded use of grey cells were normally reserved for those who joined as management trainees. This was like a bombshell to the hardened engineer the father was, for he could not think of anything more intellectually stimulating than an engineering career. By the time the evening was over, the father had cornered the HR specialist and was soliciting ideas about how to make a young engineer's job more intellectually challenging in his corporation.

## INTERPRETING CHILD PSYCHOLOGY THROUGH THE EAST-WEST MODEL

Thus, a full chapter on child psychology appears justified in this book, with a view to not only indicating the kind of knots and turns a youngster can develop even before completing his or her 'teens but also to kindle the interest of the most difficult of line managers. Some of the suggested methods of interacting with a child can be directly applied to adults in organizations too, like counselling, encouraging intrinsic rather than extrinsic motivation and aiding the process of sublimation when faced with a problem. With this limited perspective in mind, let me present a simplified interpretation of child psychology.

Child psychologists have, over the past century, been engaged in what is termed the *nature-nurture controversy*. Is it one's inherent nature alone that determines how intelligent one is, how affectionate one becomes, how unhappy and insecure one feels? Or, do environmental conditions have the capacity to determine them by themselves? Those who say "yes" to the first question call themselves *hereditarians* while those who support the second contention are called *environmentalists*. Thankfully, many people who were forced to take a practical view of the matter resolved the critical issue by studying how the hereditary and environmental forces jointly affected the development of a human being. To relate some of the important observations made on the subject by Child psychologists to the "East-West model" developed in this book, I will focus on the classical model of one of the most important neo-Freudian child psychologists, Erik H Erikson.

## ERIKSON'S PSYCHOSOCIAL THEORY AND THE EIGHT SETS OF CRISES

An anthropologist by training, Erikson was also a certified teacher under the Montessori system. Though he studied with Anna Freud, Erikson substantially differed with her and Sigmund Freud. While agreeing that a child had instinctive drives and a natural preoccupation with different parts of the body, he gave equal importance to the child's interactions with the environment. He replaced Freud's psychosexual theory with his psychosocial theory. As Erikson also studied those who could be described as "healthy personalities" as against the "neurotic" ones studied by Freud, a brief study of Erikson's main thesis on child development will be pertinent to our task at this time. In describing Erikson's model, I will use the terms developed in this book so far, so that the reader is able to better appreciate the consistency between a developmental, psychosocial approach to child psychology and the "East-West" model.

Erikson identified eight sets of crises that a human being faces before reaching full maturity. At each stage in life, a child faces the option of developing a trait or characteristic that will eventually enable it to reach an adulthood focussing on self-actualization. The alternative at each stage is to develop an opposite set of characteristics that will lead to an adulthood that will resemble a gnarled tree. Let me dwell on each stage separately:

## Basic trust v. basic mistrust

If a child's needs for food, sleep and physical comfort, a sense of safety and affection, are satisfied up to its appetite levels in a regular manner, without random variations and intermittent denials, the child will develop a sense of trust. That people around are predictable, have a natural interest in satisfying its appetite needs and will not withhold such satisfaction in an unreasonable manner are the convictions that get built at an early age of the child. According to Erikson, this phase is between birth and the first birthday!

As we have seen in our discussions earlier in the book, satisfaction of basic appetite needs are essential for the "will" of a human being to demonstrate its intrinsic motivation to direct itself towards psychologically healthy growth. Just as a sapling springs out of the earth, reaching upwards and straight towards sunlight, exhibiting its latent potential to actualize itself as a full-grown tree later, so also does a child show clear indications of its potential at such a tender age. Careful and sensitive "nurturing" by the parents thus allows the child's "nature" to exhibit itself in its best form.

When children are subjected to random, unreasonable behaviour of those closest to them, leading them to doubt whether or not their appetite needs will be satisfied adequately and periodically, they will naturally become mistrustful. Their young minds will be beset with doubts, fear and suspicion. Inadequately equipped as they are to satisfy their appetite needs by themselves at this age, they will suffer from such maltreatment in a helpless fashion. Their "Will", under such adverse circumstances, fails to find its early direction towards psychologically healthy growth. The sapling springs up crookedly. While it is not yet a permanent damage, and is capable of later correction—as per Erikson's and our own model—the damage must nevertheless be viewed as serious and definitely avoidable.

### Autonomy v. shame and doubt

In the next phase, from the age of one to three, children develop their motor and mental skills, providing them an opportunity to give free reign to their independence. A child who has developed a trusting nature, having no need to waste his or her energy and thoughts towards the satisfaction of lower needs, will use the newfound independence to allow further growth of the "will". Intrinsic motivation, powered by natural instincts, directs the child towards those activities that will provide the right ingredients for healthy development. Such children acquire confidence in themselves, learn to *trust their own instincts,* and develop a sense of autonomy.

On the other hand, if every attempt of the child to express its independence and natural wish to think and act autonomously is met with parental caution , disapproval and discouragement, the child reacts in one of two ways.

- The child could begin to doubt its natural instincts and passively accept its inadequacy to become autonomous. Unnecessary dependence on others' direction thwarts the natural growth of the "Will". Early signs of growing crookedly into "others' domain" may be picked up at this stage if one observes carefully.
- The other way some children react is to develop a sense of "shame" for wishing to do things that the adult world frowns upon. This could degenerate into later feelings of guilt and inadequacy, or make to the child do things secretively, lying to put up an acceptable front. An equally worse development could be one of defiant shamelessness whereby a child deliberately indulges in actions that provoke negative reactions from others.

## UNDERSTANDING THE FOUR QUADRANTS OF THE JOHARI WINDOW

To better understand this later aspect of shame, one can do no better than to reflect on a concept put forward by Joseph Luft and Harry Ingham, the *"Johari window"*. The name owes its origin to the

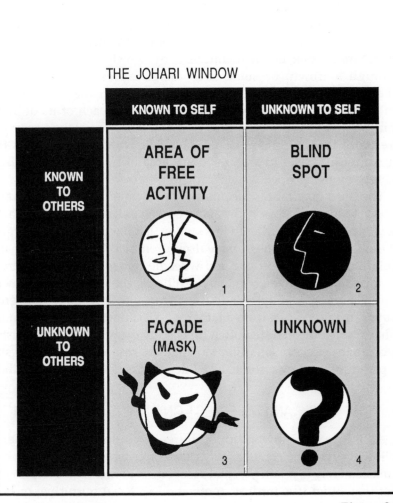

Figure 8.1

131

two first names, Joseph and Harry. The window is figuratively shown in Fig. 8.1, with four quadrants representing four distinct aspects of every personality:

The first quadrant is the "area of free activity" representing that personal space or area of oneself about which information is openly and readily shared with others. Mutual understanding between people is best in this space, and friendships blossom between people who mutually like and respect what is shared about each other in this space. Two people who dislike serious reading but enjoy pulp fiction, and who have not hidden it from each other might be able to spend hours sharing the latest M & B to have hit the stands.

The second quadrant is the "blind spot", or that aspect of ourselves which we know nothing about but which is fairly obvious to others. If one has a mannerism by which one shows disgust through a frown, or some such facial expression which one is unaware of, the only way to get to know about the effect this has on others is to be open to feedback. Likewise, each of us do many things without being conscious of them, but others who observe us are more than conscious of the fact that we do them. One's first quadrant increases in size, i.e. one's area of free activity increases, merely by being open to feedback to others.

The third quadrant is the "mask" or "facade" that we deliberately put on to hide what we know about ourselves from others. This habit, as was pointed out earlier in this section, is something that we acquire at the tender age of one to three itself prompted by a sense of shame. Children who ham, act coy and wheedle things out of their parents by a pretence of love are merely exhibiting the early signs of such a trait. As one grows up, this trait expresses itself in more dangerous ways. To gain respect from a father who is a doctor, lawyer or in any other profession, children often innocently express a childish wish to become the same in later life. Most fathers respond gleefully to such expressions for they assume the evidence of genetic influence in them.

## THE "MASK" AND ITS EFFECT ON INTRINSIC MOTIVATION

As the years go by and the children begin to have doubts about following upon their childish wish, they often hide their doubts behind a mask merely to retain parental acceptance. Rather than accepting the fact that either true intrinsic motivation or social nurturing, or both, have changed their ostensible nature to follow the footsteps of a doting father, many children grow into adulthood with their masks intact. Devoid of intrinsic motivation to pursue the career, but caught up in the need to retain parental affection and recognition (extrinsic motivation), such people enter careers which never offer them even a glimmer of a chance to be idiosyncratically what they were meant to be. They end up as mediocre hacks, wondering and lamenting over the reality of an unfulfilled life.

When the wearing of a mask becomes second nature to people, they develop relationships based on an unreal projection of their images. Such relationships rarely ever mature into true friendship or love, for proximity and familiarity pierce masks and their true selves appear. Among the exceptions are Wodehousean heroes who pretend to be teetotalers and vegetarians merely to impress their lady loves. They find their release when they find that, upon the lowering of the mask, their lady loves profess to have been disappointed with the earlier facade but to be excited by the true, cocktail loving carnivorous selves.

When one learns to disclose oneself and drops his masks, one again extends the area of the first quadrant, or the space of free activity.

The fourth quadrant is the "Unknown" space, for it is that area about which information is unknown to self and others. This is the "potential self" which is yet to be realized. When we catch ourselves responding to crises through sublimation, saying to ourselves, "Gosh! I never knew I had it in me to do that", we are merely acknowledging the existence of the fourth quadrant in ourselves. A good parent, teacher or organizational superior will trust that the fourth quadrant exists and facilitate unfolding of this hidden space.

## TWO WAYS OF INCREASING THE AREA OF "FREE ACTIVITY"

As one can observe from Fig 8.2, the first quadrant can expand to fill the entire space of the window through "openness to feedback" and "self-disclosure". The former pushes the first quadrant space to expand to the right, while the latter pushes it to expand below. The two together have the effect of helping an individual make the transition from current reality to the state of being an open, facadeless self-actualizer. What should be observed, from the context of a child, is the fact that the instinct to wear a mask is an acquired one, resulting from an inability to correctly resolve the childhood crisis of "autonomy v. shame and doubt".

## Initiative v. guilt

A closely related next step in the child's development normally occurs between the ages of three and five. A trusting child, with a sense of confidence in its own autonomy, begins to use its abundant—according to many parents, overabundant—energy to satisfy its curiosity about the immediate environment. Discoveries fill every moment of its day, and the child begins to exhibit the quality of initiative so necessary to enhance its own knowledge of the world around it. If parents and others around it—including teachers and siblings—encourage this course of self-discovery through initiative, the child learns the causal relationship between initiative and learning.

Parental restrictiveness, whatever be the rationale behind it, can only thwart the child's growth at this stage. Short of thrusting the proverbial hand to save the child from going under for the third time, the parental role at this stage must essentially be a nurturing one. The "will" of the child is busy learning to guide it to learn how to satisfy its appetite needs by itself as also to thrust upwards towards arenas of activity that provide the ingredients for the child's idiosyncratically unique growth. Whether an adult eventually self-actualizes, that is, becomes "idiosyncratically what he or she is potentially meant to be", is crucially dependent on how well this quality of initiative has been allowed to be developed between the ages of three and five.

## LEARNING TO USE THRESHOLD SPRINGS

This stage can best be described as one in which a child learns its first lessons on how to set and operate threshold springs with a view to moving up the hierarchy. When a younger sibling arrives on the scene, and a child is forced to understand that it has to share parental affection and recognition, it is nothing other than learning how to live with lower threshold limits at the belongingness and recognition levels. The child has to be helped to learn the difference between appetite and desire, and also to sublimate its energies towards its own focus of interest, whether it be drawing and sketching, or building blocks and sand houses. A parent should assure the child that there is no need to lose its sense of trust, or develop any doubts about the security of its relationship at home. By including the child in enveloping the newborn in a cloak of

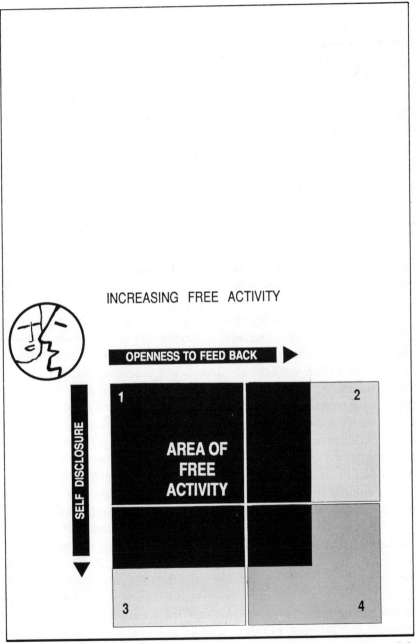

INCREASING FREE ACTIVITY

*Figure 8.2*

affection, the elder child's belongingness needs begin to get satisfied in a new way—by giving love rather than demanding it. As this is the way one's Belongingness needs are satisfied in the rest of one's life—in a two-way, sharing manner—it is important that a child learns this crucial lesson: *the most loved people are those who never demand to be loved but shower others with love.*

Children also begin to ham at about this age, in a childish attempt to satisfy their recognition needs. Rather than pander to it mindlessly, parental disapproval must be sensitively communicated, and children taught to sublimate their energies towards a focus of activity that holds genuine, intrinsic interest for them.

When parents pay inadequate attention to children at this stage, complications arise in many ways. To merely buy peace for themselves, if parents give children chocolates, comics and dolls, the lesson that children learn is that if one makes sufficient nuisance of oneself, one will receive "goodies". Worse still, love begins to be represented by "goods", rather in the manner adults learn in later life that affection should be represented in terms of gifts, garlands and "goodies". In such a society, marriages will naturally be ostentatious, wasteful and involve exchange of huge amounts of gifts, money and goods.

It should be possible for the reader to now appreciate how many children begin to grow crookedly into the "desire" domain of lower needs, and lose their intrinsic "will" to grow up towards self-actualization. When we hear children being described as "spoilt", we are merely recognizing the fact that they have been allowed to grow up with unnecessarily high threshold limits. An overfed child demanding more food, or screaming for parental attention at the drop of a hat, is a disturbing sight to most of us. Disturbing, because we see early signs of a sapling that is being allowed to grow crooked, rather than upright towards actualization of its full potential.

It is against this background that one should view the manner in which children are prepared for passing admission tests of prestigious schools. Their playing hours are drastically reduced. They are suddenly made to speak in English rather than their mother tongue, and asked to recite verses that make no sense at all. That children get completely confused, and take a dislike to such thwarting of their natural instincts should surprise no one. Many of them, having learnt to trust their parents, or at least fear their authority, give up their protests and attempt to fall in line so as to conform to the general pattern that the best school in the neighbourhood demands.

Those children who are "lucky" enough to pass this first gruelling "test" begin their long journey through the educational labyrinth with their trust intact, although at the great cost of losing a sense of their own autonomy and initiative. As they learn not to give free rein to their urge to draw and paint abstract forms, but to draw trees, engines and people—or, worse still, dab conventional colours on pre drawn, printed figures in mass produced books—true autonomy and initiative are slowly replaced by the ability to conform and be conditioned.

As for the children who "fail" the entrance test, mistrust of the adult world and/or a sense of deep shame colour their perceptions, preparing them for the next failures in the form of developing a sense of guilt and inferiority. Helpless parents, unschooled in the way of dealing with this apparently universal phenomenon, look on as their children get subjected to such absurd tensions. What the parents ought to do at this stage is very simply this:

Let the children know that it is not calamitous to fail such tests, provide them appetite level satisfaction of security and belongingness needs, and help them sublimate their energies towards recognition by seeking admission in an alternative school. Help them see positive virtues of the new school, highlighting whatever merits it may have, be they better playgrounds, more time for play, less conditioning and homework, or any other aspect. The important result to be achieved at this stage is to ensure that the child feels satiated at the appetite levels of physiological, safety and belongingness needs, and learns its first lesson as to how one can react to a sudden lowering of threshold levels through sublimation.

## Industry v. inferiority

Between the ages of six and eleven, a child's natural energy ought to direct its sense of autonomy and initiative to industriousness. According to Erikson, this phase of growth is normally marked by a child's natural desire to learn how things work in an active manner. The child's innate ability to engage itself in action, and derive joy out of it—the essence of *intrinsic motivation*—thus expresses itself in no uncertain manner at such an early age. When adults thwart such childish attempts to engage in action by dismissing and discouraging them as mischievous or troublesome, children react in different ways. They either rebel against such restrictions and silently go ahead doing whatever they feel like—

showing the natural ability to "sublimate" their energies—or give in to external pressures and judgments. The latter reaction will lead to children losing faith in their intrinsic ability to engage in action on their own, and become purely reactive in their behaviour, a veritable prey for extrinsic motivators. This cannot but lead to "inferiority" in every sense of the term.

During this phase of a child's life, there are innumerable occasions when the child faces apparent "failures". They are laughed at when they make a mistake in class. If they forget a line on stage, or sing out of tune, or fall down, or get reprimanded by a teacher, other children laugh at them. If they fail in a class test, or even do badly in relation to parental desires and expectations, parents ensure that they are made acutely aware of their failure. When most parents want their children to stand first in class, and most classes have about fifty children in crowded schools, the probability of a child "failing" to meet parental expectations is 98%.

The effect of such failures is a felt lowering of threshold limits. When one's friends and classmates laugh at one's failures, one feels insecure, alienated and small. Translated, it means lowered threshold limits at the safety, belongingness and recognition levels. Parental disappointment and reprimands lead to a similar effect.

## COUNSELLING IS AN ESSENTIAL SKILL FOR ALL

Children of this age are ill-equipped to handle too many failures by themselves. They will develop a sense of "inferiority" if they are not *counselled* appropriately, and helped to learn the crucial lesson of how to react to "failures" through sublimation. As this skill of "counselling" is one that parents, teachers and managers have to be adept at, if at all they are to play a facilitative role in the development of others, it will be worth our while to briefly dwell on this skill at this stage. Let me elaborate on "counselling" through a real-life example:

An eleven-year-old boy was playing a cricket match in school. It was an important match for his House, and all his House mates were watching the match. At a crucial stage in the match, the boy dropped an easy catch close to the boundary line. He heard boos and jeers from the very friends who had fawned on him earlier when he had been selected to play for the House. He felt like digging a hole in the ground and disappearing. His team mates looked aghast at him, their faces registering a whole range of emotions, from disgust and anger to contempt. Soon after, almost entirely due to his dropped catch, his House lost the match.

138

That evening, and the few days before the term ended, were agonizing for the boy as he was treated like an outcast. While his friends avoided him, others passed derogatory remarks about him well within his hearing. At every meal, youngsters would throw apples at him, shouting "catch". On one occasion, he had to rush out to be sick.

When the boy returned home at the end of the term, he told his parents that he did not want to go back to school. He never mentioned his dropped catch, but talked of various other incidents that he either concocted or exaggerated. This surprised the parents for the boy had seemed so full of cheer in a letter he had written just a week before, and some of the incidents he was now quoting appeared to have taken place much earlier. Nevertheless, the parents merely showed extreme sympathy and understanding, in a genuine attempt to reach out to the boy and share his deep, negative feelings. The mother encouraged the boy to speak more about what had happened in the last fortnight, as to how the exams had gone, and so on. The boy was not very forthcoming. When the father started talking about sports events, he noticed that the boy recoiled almost as if he had been slapped. With some sensitive probing, the boy's real cause for unhappiness began to emerge.

Initially, the boy made out the dropped catch to have been an extremely difficult one. The rest of the school had been mean and unsympathetic, for the sun had been behind the ball, he said. The father agreed how terrible that would have been. The conversation slowly turned to how much fielding practice the boy had had before the match. The boy 's mood began to lift as he started talking about how he would practise catching every day of his life so that he would never again drop a catch. Towards the end of the conversation, the boy even agreed that the catch had been a simple one and that his House mates were justified in castigating him. But he would show them the next term, for he would have practised every day during the holidays. . . Even without consciously realizing it, the boy had made up his mind to return to school next term, and prove to everyone that he was the best fielder in the House.

## INTERPRETING COUNSELLING THROUGH THE "EAST-WEST" MODEL

Let me reinterpret this incident using the terminology of our "East-West" model as also standard terms used by counselling gurus like Rogers and Carkhuff. The boy's threshold springs had been compressed in one massive blow at almost all the need levels. Physically he had been sick, his security needs were denied as he was treated an outcast in his own House, his friends had left him cold, and his erstwhile admirers had begun to boo him, replacing high recognition need satisfaction with denial of even appetite needs. Wishing to withdraw completely from the scene that had caused it, the boy had expressed the desire to leave the school altogether.

*Understanding* that the boy was deeply hurt, the parents began their interaction by extending *genuine* sympathy. By not arguing with the boy immediately, and *accepting* the boy's statements and feelings, the parents included themselves in the boy's condition. Under such non-threatening conditions, the boy's sense of physical, safety and belongingness needs satisfaction regained its balance. In the revived state, when the father took the *initiative* to probe further, with suggestive leads, including sports, the boy's *body language* indicated to the father that he was getting close to the real cause of the problem. Rather than pounce on the cause as if making a great discovery, the father had shown the patience necessary to allow the boy to find it within him to deal with the problem. From that stage onwards, all that the son required was a sympathetic ear as he planned to practise every day and become the greatest fielder ever. The father had merely been a help in enabling the son to learn how to sublimate his energies when confronted by a "failure".

According to Carl Rogers, the three essential qualities or inter-personal skills required in a counsellor are *genuineness, acceptance* and *understanding*. Like the parents in the example, a counsellor ought to exhibit these qualities so that a counsellee feels safe and accepted by the counsellor. This cloak of comfort is necessary for the counsellee to start an honest probe into the real problem facing him or her. Very often, this is all that is required to make a counsellee respond to a problem through appropriate sublimation. In some situations, however, as suggested by Carkhuff, the counsellor has to lead the counsellee into an action-oriented dimension.

In such situations, the counsellor must take the initiative to be assertive, offer directions if and when necessary, and be frank when needed. The counsellor has to decide whether the time is ripe for a feedback to remove a "blind spot", or further counselling to encourage the counsellee to voluntarily lift his or her "mask". In the case of the schoolboy described earlier, the father had deliber-ately taken his time to move into such an action-oriented dimension, realizing that what was required was for the son to lift his "mask" himself, rather than receive feedback that he was avoiding the real problem. The only assertiveness exhibited by the father was to continue talking about sports without flinching, even when the son had recoiled at the first mention of it.

In those instances when a young person stubbornly refuses to lift the mask, or listen to gentle feedback about his or her "blind spot", the parent should eventually become far more assertive, using "frankness" as a method of forcing all cards on the table. The scope of this book does not allow me to dwell on this and other aspects of counselling at greater length. For those interested in pursuing this further, I recommend Fr Joe Currie's primer on the subject, *The Barefoot Counsellor*. As his work took him to many countries, and to diverse groups of people, there is a universal appeal about this book which is almost impossible to match. In the epilogue to the book, the author has also attempted to relate counselling to the Maslovian hierarchy of needs, albeit in a different manner. For more reasons than one, I strongly recommend this book to the reader.

## Identity v. role confusion

That one is different from others, and has a distinct identity of one's own is the next thing to be learnt. When an adolescent's understanding of his or her identity is strengthened by acceptance from parents, siblings, friends and school authorities, it leads to a sense of self-worth as well as strengthening of one's perception of one's own identity. When such an identity is developed out of a healthy resolution of the previous four crises, the adolescent passes from childhood to young adulthood in an easy manner.

It is usual, however, for this passage to be a traumatic one. If a child had failed to resolve any or all of the previous crises in its growth successfully, and is filled with feelings of mistrust, doubt, guilt and/or inferiority, he or she will have a confused sense of his or her identity. 'What do I really like?' and 'What am I naturally good at?' are questions for which the child has no definite answers, and becomes increasingly dependent on others' perceptions, directions and advice. Infantile imitations of others, false fronts and pretension mark the child's behaviour, leading to immense role confusion.

It is at this difficult age that many children are forced to decide on what options to follow in school and immediate community. Conflicting pulls from different people confuse the child. It is not uncommon for children to develop habits of escapism, mob behaviour and indecisiveness. That they behave differently at different times should not surprise anyone, for they are a prey to extrinsic factors rather than intrinsic ones. From this age onwards, most of them become candidates for study by the behaviourists for their intrinsic motivation is almost completely replaced by extrinsic motivation.

## EXPOSURE TO "SHEN" PRODUCTS IS ESSENTIAL FOR GROWTH

At this age, when children are seeking to find their identity, it would be most advantageous for them if they were exposed to the works of those who were clearly self-actualizers. Visits to museums, seeing the creations of great painters and sculptors, listening to classical compositions of the masters, "experiencing" aesthetically pleasing forms such as the Taj Mahal or the Brihadeeshwara Temple in Tanjavoor, rowing down the Thames or the Ganges and listening to self-actualizers on their fields of interests are experiences that leave a permanent impact on children. At a passive level, and in a holistic way, their beings get exposed to what self actualization is all about. The "divine" nature of what the Chinese classification of paintings terms "shen" communicates itself to children who view them. Like one who has tasted nectar, children will, in later life, revert to such rarefied atmospheres by themselves. Whether they return in the passive capacity of a mute audience, or as active self-actualizers themselves, the early memory would have played its role.

To better understand how this may work, it would be essential to know how our brains work, especially in collating and using knowledge and impressions. It has been fairly well established that our brains consist of four parts, the reptilian, the paleomammalean and the left and right brains. Figure 8.3 describes the different functions of the four parts.

## FORMAL EDUCATION USUALLY IGNORES THE RIGHT BRAIN

From a cursory look at the figure, it should be obvious that much of the education that a child goes through today is directed at using and developing the left brain. Many neurophysicians believe that the left brain represents a minuscule fraction of the total capacity of the brain. The right brain, they claim, is the vast reservoir that a human being should learn to dip into.

# TEACHING AESTHETICS AND VALUES LIKE JUSTICE AND FAIRNESS

Only a child with a deep sense of trust and autonomy, with no trace of guilt or doubt in its mental make up will be able to relax in the right brain mode. Its ability to make holistic impressions, feel aesthetic pleasure and displeasure spontaneously, and respond to the outpourings of self-actualizers cannot be explained in a language that the left brain understands, i.e. one cannot trace a clear causal relationship delineating what specific learning led to what action and vice versa. Values such as justice and fairness are also imbibed and retained by the right brain process of learning. When we say, 'It does not seem right', or 'It is not fair', we are making judgments about what is perceived from our notions of right and wrong. A child finds it extremely difficult to relate one with the other, and eventually gives up on its notions if reality as perceived is consistently different from them. Parental role at this phase of development cannot be overemphasized adequately.

Let me relate a remarkable incident concerning a young student in a Japanese school and his mother. The son was relating to his mother an incident in school. A small made friend had been the object of bullying by bigger boys, with the former being reduced to crying and cringing in front of the latter. The mother asked the son if he had not tried to stop the bullies and the son admitted to have been a mere observer, albeit an unhappy one. The mother said she would give him a treat if he took it upon himself to prevent the bullies from getting at the small friend. The next evening, the son returned with the news that he had indeed stopped the bullies. The happy mother kept her promise by proffering a substantial sum of money for the treat. A little while later, before availing himself of the treat, the conscience-stricken son confessed what had actually transpired:

He had gone to school with the resolve of defending his small friend; however, when the bullies started picking on the small friend, courage failed him and he had once again been a passive, unhappy observer. He had, however, wished to look good in his mother's eyes. He had lied about defending his small friend. When it came to accepting the reward, and enjoying the treat, his young conscience had rebelled. Hence the confession.

PARTS OF THE BRAIN AND THEIR FUNCTIONS

| | LEFT BRAIN | RIGHT BRAIN |
|---|---|---|
| **Cognitive style** | analytic, linear | intuitive, artistic |
| **Communication** | verbal, rich vocabulary, grammatical | non-verbal, body language, metaphoric |
| **Will do well in jobs/work that involve** | reading, writing, arithmetic, motor and sensory skills with atomistic approaches | intuition, inspiration, imagination, music, drama, gestalt and holistic approaches |
| **Time sense** | sequentially ordered and measured | primitive, instinctive and spontaneous |
| **Spatial orientation** | relatively poor | superior, for shapes, interiors, environment |
| **Historical figures who were strong in** | Aristotle, Marx and Freud | Plato, Beethoven and Jung |

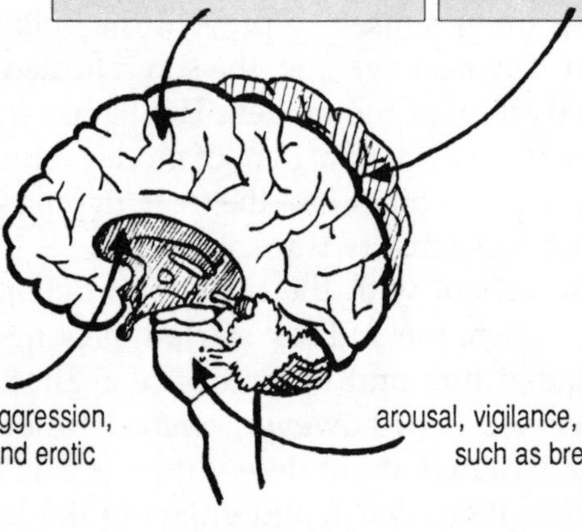

**Paleomammalean**
emotion, appetite, aggression, pleasure functions and erotic desires

**Reptilian**
arousal, vigilance, biological functions such as breathing, feeding and biorhythms

*Figure 8.3*

## TRUST THAT YOUR SON IS A POTENTIAL HERO

The mother's response was perfect. She first communicated to her son that she quite understood him and accepted him for what he had not done first, and for having stated the truth later. She then merely said to him, 'I know you will defend your friend tomorrow, because you dearly want to do it. I also know you will find the courage to do it. So, go ahead and enjoy the treat in anticipation of your doing so'. She kept her promise, in full anticipation and trust that her son was a potential self-actualizer, with the heroic instinct in him to set dangerously low threshold limits at physiological and safety levels (for he would certainly run the risk of being beaten up by the bullies himself) in order to take what his instincts told him was the right action.

The mother did not have to wait too long to learn that her trust was well placed. The son settled the class bullies all right.

There is much to be learnt from this example.

- When a child instinctively reacts to injustice, exhibiting a natural sense of what should be the norms for a world in which trust should exist, and shows signs of taking initiative to follow his instinct, it is a glorious opportunity for a parent to affirm that the child is on the right path.

- Only a rare parent will have the sensitivity to respond to a child in such a manner. One can imagine how many uninitiated parents would have dealt with the situation. 'Keep out of trouble', 'Don't poke your nose into what is not your business', 'Tell the teacher' and 'Tell your little friend to keep away from the bullies' could have been some responses when the son first related the incident. Even if they had encouraged him like the mother quoted in the incident, very few would have restrained themselves from reprimanding the son for lying about having taken on the bullies. Fewer still would have converted it to an affirmation of faith for future action, thus providing the youngster another chance to sublimate his energies through a heroic act.

### Intimacy v. Isolation

A young adult with a pleasant sense of self-worth is an enjoyable person to relate to. Such a youngster is thus in an advantageous position to resolve the next crisis in growth by developing close and meaningful relationships with others. Appetite needs at the belongingness level get satisfied as easily in the outside world as it was within the family when one was a child. When intimacy and love lead to a healthy sexual relationship, the sense of self-worth and wellbeing gets strengthened, and the young adult enters a self supportive, regenerative cycle of positive growth. With the appetite needs at all lower levels adequately satisfied, the young adult is able to unleash his or her intrinsic motivation towards an arena of activity that will allow for self-actualization.

Again, very few find this phase of development an easy stage either. Those who have a confused sense of self identity, or have feelings of mistrust, doubt, guilt or inferiority, find it enormously difficult to develop permanent and meaningful relationships with others. Their masks, or artificial fronts, allow for only temporary relationships—till the mask slips, or the artificial front is pierced—and this leads to isolation. Such people find it difficult to meet their appetite needs for love and belongingness, and are thwarted in their further growth. They begin to level off in the lowest two levels of the hierarchy, expending their energy and time in satisfying high desires at the physiological and safety levels. Their unsuccessful attempts to give and receive love leads to a feeling of resentment against the rest of the world. Recognition by such a world does not matter to them, nor is industrious production for such a world an activity that will have any intrinsic quality to it.

It is about this age that a youngster normally joins a corporation to start a career, bringing with him or her unresolved issues pertaining to all or some of the first six of Erikson's crises. The remaining two of Erikson's eight crises, *generativity v. self-absorption* and *integrity v. despair*, occur when one has passed into middle adulthood and old age respectively. While the corporation can help an individual resolve these last two crises, it can at best try to help the individual recover from and overcome the psychosocial problems his or her early childhood has created.

Most school systems in the world are woefully ill equipped to sensitively deal with children and help them resolve the first six crises properly. The rush to develop the left brain, the race to have students score high marks, the need to conform to archaic forms of conditioning, societal blindness by which teaching is reduced to one of the least attractive professions, and many other factors lead one to believe that schools cannot be trusted to develop psychosocially healthy human beings. With most parents too busy to even attend parent-teacher meetings, let alone develop in themselves the skills of a "barefoot counsellor", parental ability to nurture psychosocially healthy children is also to be doubted. As discussed in Chapter 1, the ability of a formal religion to influence human beings has also been eroded substantially.

## THE ONUS FOR HUMAN DEVELOPMENT IS WITH CORPORATIONS

It appears therefore that it is left to the modern corporation to fill in the void by assuming responsibility for ensuring psychosocially healthy growth of human beings. Without a critical mass of the latter, as we have seen in Chapter 4, no corporation can be sure of producing high-quality products and services. To attract and retain such a critical mass is not possible if the corporation does not have the ability to transform the equivalent of a crooked plant into a full-grown tree. They have to recruit the best of available people from schools and colleges, sensitive to the fact that their recruits are most likely to resemble crooked plants rather than upright ones; for instance, an academically brilliant student of management excited by the extrinsic motivation of fast progress as a marketing executive, claiming to have intrinsic desire to excel in marketing, while the intrinsic motivation could actually be for hard-core Production management.

With high power professionals in the human resources management function acting as the expert horticulturists, corporations will then have to view themselves as *nurseries for human growth*, recruiting young talent like selecting saplings, nurturing their growth carefully almost as if in a greenhouse, and transferring them thereafter to high performance roles rather like transplanting a healthy plant from a nursery to a wide open garden. The garden would have to be weeded regularly, the plant helped to grow to its full form as a tree and transform the garden by its very presence, its fruits and flowers. So also will psychosocially healthy human beings who are trained and developed properly transform the very corporations they had been recruited by. In the next section, we will consider how a corporation could effectively function as a nursery for human growth.

# 9

# THE CORPORATION: THE LAST BASTION FOR HUMAN DEVELOPMENT

For the first time in the history of Man, it is in the selfish interest of those with power and wealth to do their very best for maximizing human development. To remain competitive in today's business world, an organization requires a critical mass of its members to be self-actualizers at their work. As explained in Chapter 2, front-line service employees, knowledge workers and those working in far flung factories and "electronic cottages" will produce quality goods and services only if their lower needs are adequately satisfied (up to their appetite levels) such that they are seeking self-esteem and self-actualization through their work. That this cannot be achieved through fear, authority, manipulation, and so on has been proven over and over again in the earlier chapters. The environmental conditions in corporations must necessarily be made conducive to human development, just as a nursery is designed to protect, nurture and enable the growth of plants.

Ideally, parents should be playing the prime nurturing role for children, supported by a caring education system and enveloped within an enlightened socioreligious environment. When societies were smaller in size, several of them had achieved such a balance successfully. Today, barring a few exceptions, most societies are unable to achieve such an ideal balance. There are several reasons for this failure.

## THE REDUCED ROLE OF PARENTS AND ITS NEGATIVE CONSEQUENCES

With both parents working in an increasingly large proportion of families, parental time available for nurturing of children has been drastically reduced. With the breaking up of joint families and communes, a child is typically brought up in a unitary family today, and he misses the influence of other elders and their care. Rather than hearing of the exploits of Arjuna and Karna from a grand-mother and letting one's right brain conjure up images of days gone by, one switches on a TV to "see Mahabharata", canned and presented in a form that requires no individual imaging. Similar short-cuts in communication, and replacing of direct communication by indirect means have led to alienation of children from their parents and families.

The main influence on children is then peer pressure, and for conformity with peers. Increased use of drugs and alcoholic stimulants, student crime, resistance to parental values (including the Protestant work ethic) and a short-term view of life and its meaning are but signs of the malaise that has set in. That this is primarily due to parents not playing their traditional role of child nurturing is hardly open to argument.

From discussions in the last chapter, it should also be obvious that child psychology is far too complicated for uninitiated parents to bring up children as psychosocially healthy individuals all by themselves. They require help in the form of training and education, time to cope with the problems through flexible working hours, closer association with schools and constant feedback from school teachers to act upon. There are only a few schools that have managed to creatively involve parents in their administration, like the Bombay International School in Chowpatty. From admission to career counselling when students are passing out, parents of children in the school play very active roles. Their sensitivity to the entire process of human development during these crucial years is heightened as a result, and the children consequently feel a sense of security and continuity. But, such schools are a rare exception to the general rule.

## THE FAILURE OF SCHOOLS AND COLLEGES

As the vast majority of schools have become a part of governmental domain all over the world, they are plagued by numerous problems like inconsistent policies, inadequate funds, impersonal administration, a lethargic system that is immune from all attempts to change it, inefficiencies and gross neglect of quality in most aspects. The profession of teaching, once considered and treated as the noblest of all, is uniformly reduced to being one of the poorest paid in almost all countries. Coupled with other problems inherent in the education system, this has led to an exodus of the best teachers from the formal education system.

While teaching at the University of Buckingham, I came across a brilliant student, whose right brain was beautifully developed. In most classes, he would surprise me with his intuitive feel of any case that was being discussed. The sensitivity with which he would state some of the most creative solutions to a case excited me no end. When I talked about him to other faculty, some of them were surprised, for he was a "repeater", i.e. he had failed to clear his papers the previous year and was repeating the year.

Over the next few months, I came to know the student's background. The only son of an extremely successful business tycoon, the boy had been sent to a good, residential school. From a very early age, he had been assessed as requiring "special attention" by the school, a euphemism for what the school considered to be a slow learner. Almost throughout his school days, the boy had been relegated to the company of others who required "special attention" too. It was only when he was about 16 that they found he was suffering from dyslexia, a left brain disease that slows down the speed of communicating through words and symbols. He had managed to pass the school examinations when he had been allowed extra time, to compensate for his problem.

150

When I told the student that Akbar had been a dyslexic, and was actually a functional illiterate in every sense of the term, and that many others had also been afflicted with the problem without affecting their ability to excel in their lives, the student began to unfold himself. After several hours of counselling, the young man began to feel reasonably confident of making a success of his life. 'Is there a possibility that I will be as successful as my father?' was a question that he asked me right at the end, almost rhetorically. I did not have to answer the question, for he was beginning to sound like one who was sublimating his energies.

## ELITE INSTITUTIONS ALSO GET BOGGED DOWN GRADUALLY

Even when elite institutions are built through special funding, and attempts are made to free them of bureaucratic controls, it takes very little time for such institutions to get influenced by the larger environment. An institution like the Indian Institute of Management in Ahmedabad ought to have been a beacon light for quality in education. When it was started in the late '60s, care was taken in the selection of faculty, freedom granted for individual research and experimentation, syllabus was freshly cast with the best of international talent available working on it, and a serious attempt made to guard quality in every aspect associated with the institution. The students who passed out in the 1970s, many of whom are currently in powerful positions across the globe, bear ample testimony to the care taken in those years. Yet, by the late 1980s, the same institution was left without direction for over two years as several conflicting interests delayed the appointment of a director for the institute.

Also, when one views the manner in which the administration of campus interviews is conducted in this and other elite management institutes, one will be appalled at the extent of importance given by students to extrinsic rather than intrinsic factors. Marginal jobs in multinational corporations, with little challenge to either the intellect or for creativity, get top rating almost entirely because of the money and perquisites offered by them. With almost 50% of the students from an engineering background, only an infinitesimal number wish to start careers in production management. The vast majority of students, in all the premier management institutions of India, want to become marketing executives. It is a classic case of the herd mentality. What makes it tragic, however, is the fact that the cream of Indian youth are exhibiting characteristics and behaviour that clearly demonstrate that what motivate them are extrinsic factors rather than intrinsic thrust. Besides, a staggeringly high percentage of them are pure left-brain specialists, with scant regard, and even contempt, for the holistic right brain and its proclivity for the "soft" issues. Anybody trying to talk about the need to balance the left and right brains, the hard with the soft, the yin with the yang, and the masculine with the feminine, will find himself faced with a near empty auditorium.

## UNIVERSAL MALAISE OF THE HIGHER EDUCATION SYSTEM

That the situation is not dissimilar elsewhere in the world is worth emphasizing. In 1980, two Harvard Business School professors, Hayes and Abernathy, wrote an award-winning paper in the *Harvard Business Review*, "Managing Our Way to Economic Decline". Their argument was that overly analytic business schools were partly responsible for a misguided obsession with technique and analysis in practice. In the paper, the authors held that American managerial failure was due to a psychological shift among American managers toward a "super-safe, no risk" mindset. This was characterized by a new Management orthodoxy featured by financial controls, corporate portfolio management (. . . more interested in buying other companies than they are in selling products to customers) and reactive, market-driven behaviour that dampens the general level of innovation in new product decisions.

Commenting on this in a recent book, Henry Mintzberg of the McGill University in Canada said, 'Few disagreed (with Hayes and Abernathy). Well, since then, I have watched business school education become more analytic, not less'. Mintzberg goes so far as to suggest that admission to MBA programmes must be restricted only to those who have working experience. He has himself stopped teaching the MBA class at McGill.

## THE POWERLESSNESS OF OTHER SOCIAL INSTITUTIONS

With schools and colleges also unable to play an important role in the development of psychosocially healthy people, society may have been expected to depend on its religious institutions to assume responsibility. However, as pointed out in Chapter 2, the influence of religion has diminished so woefully that it is more than apparent that this alternative is also not likely to materialize. There are several religious bodies that are gamely trying to do their best, but they are beset with many problems. The main problem is a diminishing work force. Volunteers who join the missionary ranks of religious orders, and stay the full course thereafter, are reducing in number. Another problem is that they are unable to reach the bulk of humanity, for attendance in Church and other similar temples of worship is extremely low.

## THE CORPORATION HAS TO STEP IN TO SOLVE THE PROBLEM

What then is the alternative? If parents, schools and colleges, as well as religious institutions have failed in their roles, can any other institution fill the breach? Social service organizations, help agencies and other voluntary bodies have been trying, but have had only marginal effect so far. The government, as an alternative, should also be discounted on the basis of its inability to deliver through the educational system. It appears as if the only alternative left is the corporation, for it combines several virtues. Corporations have funds at their disposal, are used to taking quick decisions and following them up through implementation, have well defined power structure to support what is considered useful for their profitability and longevity, and are today acutely aware of the fact that their very existence depends on attracting, training and retaining a critical mass of self-actualizing people. As such people are not available in plenty in the employment market, they have no alternative other than to *view* themselves as nurseries for human growth. Further, they have to use their power and wealth to ensure that they *actually become* nurseries for human growth.

Strategically, the most crucial changes that organizations should bring about in order to achieve this are in human resources management and in the attitudes of top and middle management towards both human beings as well as the function of HRM. After having been sidelined as a handmaiden to traditional areas of concentration such as finance, marketing and controls, HRM is poised to move to centre-stage as this revolution in thinking takes place. That the best corporations have already begun to implement this will be quite clear to the reader as this book unfolds.

## STRATEGIC CHANGES REQUIRED IN HUMAN RESOURCES MANAGEMENT

Without trying to write a comprehensive treatise on HRM, as it is beyond the scope of this book, let me just highlight some strategic changes that have to be introduced in the practice of human resources management in four major areas, which can be allegorically separated as

1. *Handpicking the saplings:* Manpower planning, recruitment and selection;

2. *Nurturing the sapling and preparing for transplantation:* Induction, training, career counselling and choice;

3. *Relaying the garden:* The new union-management paradigm; and

4. *Transforming the garden into a new reality:* Creation of a truly evolved corporation.

# 10

# HANDPICKING THE SAPLINGS: MANPOWER PLANNING, RECRUITMENT AND SELECTION

A nursery is only as good as the saplings brought in, and the output only as good as the quality of input will allow it to be. Hence, the crucial first step for a corporation is how it handpicks new recruits, from where and when. I will highlight some essential features that ought to be part of a corporation's approach to this first step, irrespective of which part of which country it is operating in.

## FOCUS ON FRESHMEN RECRUITMENT

From the description in Chapter 8 of what ought to happen, but actually does not happen, to young people even before they complete their teens, it should be obvious that organizations should attempt to recruit as many people as possible at as young an age as society would permit. To use our analogy, the plant or the sapling should be supple enough to respond to the ministrations of a caring gardener. The older the plant, the more difficult it is to straighten it. In selecting young people, two characteristics that should be tested for are:

- A demonstrated ability to trust and follow up on one's intrinsic motivation till the point of achieving easy mastery over their area of interest, whatever be the focus of interest; and
- A demonstrated ability to set even temporarily low threshold limits while following up on one's intrinsic motivational thrusts.

If young people exhibit these two fundamental characteristics, the rest of what is required for success in an organization can be taught through training programmes by the particular organization. What is beyond the scope of most organizations is the revival of these characteristics in young people who appear to show no signs of them at the age of twenty. And, without these two characteristics, human beings cannot grow towards self-actualization. They will grow crooked, and be caught up in "others' domain", played around with like puppets on a string, and produce inferior quality work throughout their lives.

It is not too difficult to spot these characteristics. Those who have a passion for anything at all will instantaneously respond with enthusiasm to questions like, 'What are you passionate about?', 'Is there any activity, author, function, or area that interests you immensely?' and 'Would you like to tell us something about what you spend your spare time on?' They will be able to talk with energy and enthusiasm on their field of interest, with eyes sparkling, body hunched forward and the voice carrying confidence. A student who says he is passionate about Ayn Rand, for example, would be able to reel off almost all the books she had written, talk of Francisco D'Anconia and Howard Roark as if they were long lost friends, and would have actually read all of John Galt's longwinded broadcast. He would also be able to summarize *Objectivist Ethic* and elaborate on the virtues of selfishness. It is not important whether or not the interview panel members are fond of Ayn Rand. What is important is the fact that a student has been able to follow up his interest thoroughly, spend time on it and understood the essence behind it.

Students who do not have this first characteristic in them are also found out easily in an interview process. They are the sort of people who would not have read more than one book of the same author, who would have changed their interests too frequently to allow for any deep knowledge or concern, who would not have done anything beyond what is strictly required by parents, teachers or the system, and who demonstrate no passion at all in whatever they are speaking about. They will also use interviews to find out what they can get out of the organization, rather than discuss what they could contribute. They will not talk of improving their knowledge, expertise and mastery, but rather talk of making available a set of tools for the organization's use as a sort of barter in the extrinsic world they are a part of.

As for the second characteristic, it can be found out through questions like, 'Was there any occasion when you were so absorbed in what you were doing that you were quite lost to the outside world?' and 'Describe to us your daily schedule when you are caught up doing what you enjoy doing most'. Those who have the second characteristic in them will probably close their eyes, smile and start talking about a time that is almost as real to them as if they were doing it then and there. Incidences of skipped meals, shortened sleep timings, personal risks taken, lonely hours spent on unravelling problems and other such experiences will flow out of them, demonstrating their unconscious ability to set low threshold limits when driven by intrinsic motivation.

Those who have lost the ability to set low threshold limits even temporarily will talk of opportunities lost, insurmountable problems, half-done jobs and safe procedures adopted. That they have no sense of autonomy, and are beset with doubts about their own natural abilities will also be evident in interviews. One way of finding out is to ask a student to talk about any assignments undertaken, either in school or college, or while on vacation. There are many who would have left it to their colleagues to do the bulk of the work, positioning themselves as mere passive observers. Or, they will give any number of excuses as to why they could not achieve much owing to the noncooperation of others. 'I was made to wait endless hours without being assigned any project,' or 'The professors (or executives) were too confused to give any specific direction, and I could, therefore, accomplish very little,' they would complain. Unable as they were to risk being taken for a pushy youngster, or be reprimanded for demanding that their time be utilized properly, and prone to taking the easy way out, they would have drifted, where another youngster might have put his all at stake for a piece of action.

To ensure that an organization gets a continuous supply of young, trainable people with the above two characteristics, it is essential for an organization to first cast a proper manpower plan.

## Manpower planning

Far from being a purely quantitative tool devised to excite management theorists, manpower planning is an activity that is of paramount, practical importance. It is the blueprint for human resources management, and its focus, maximizing human development and ensuring organizational effectiveness through adequate and timely manning.

Some essential points to be observed while casting a manpower plan are:

1. First, project manpower needs arising out of expansion and attrition as accurately as possible. If accuracy will mean noncompletion of plans in time, sacrifice accuracy for a rough plan that can be cast in time. Write out the assumptions made for such a rough projection so that it can be refined as assumptions get corrected, or ratified.

2. Project promotability of existing people, backed by necessary education and training; break it down functionwise for each career path.

3. Reduce manpower input points to as few in number as possible, such that each is fed through cadres of freshmen.

4. For each cadre, identify the quality of available raw material, the numbers available/required, the time and extent of pre-employment education and training required, and competition from the market.

5. Plot cadrewise manpower input on a time chart, planning the lead time required for making available each cadre; plan for contingencies of delays as well as advancements.

6. Plan for and enhance training resources to deliver the necessary training; as far as possible, convert slack in line management into additional training resources. Through training activity, create core success teams of mentors and freshmen.

7.  In deciding manpower requirement, productivity norms must be held as tight as possible, but not unreasonably so. While problems arising out of low productivity are well documented, little has been said about the problems arising out of unreasonably high productivity standards. Let me highlight some of them:

    (a) Work will not be done according to quality expectations, or on time.

    (b) The best performers in the team will try to drive everybody else to their limits and beyond, even becoming unreasonable when it comes to granting legitimate leave. Disenchantment and a feeling of having been dealt with unfairly will set in.

    (c) While (b) will not matter if it ends in joint victory and celebration, we are discussing the case of unreasonable productivity standards that will result in failure. The effect of failure on a team that has been subjected to what has been described in (b) is disastrous. The best performers develop what psychologists term "learned helplessness", which is the exact opposite of sublimation. Rather than reacting to failure through sublimation upwards, such people react by desolately accepting the fact that they are incapable of winning.

    (d) New recruits will be denied proper induction, or training, for they will be canibalised into regular work teams. Without adequate preparation, the probability of their making mistakes increases, and they will get reprimanded by superiors who are pressed for time. Negative relationships, antagonism and withdrawal syndromes may result.

I have discussed at reasonable length the problems arising out of unreasonable expectations because this is a crucial reason for human beings starting off on the wrong foot in organizations. Quite often, line managers who wish to show high financial performance try to save expenses by delaying recruitment till the last moment. When work peaks, staff will be pressed beyond their limits, and new recruits canibalised ruthlessly. In a matter of months, the organization will have a sizeable number of inadequately trained, unhappy new recruits, demotivated supervisors and unhappy customers. A classic case of this nature is described here, to add further emphasis to this problem.

A multi-unit Indian organization was going through a business downturn. In November of a year, recruitment was frozen nationally. When the time came for campus recruitment, the freeze was not lifted. The HR manager, using past attrition data, predicted that this would lead to serious manpower shortfall in critical technical areas, amounting to as many as 59 in a particular category by June of the following year.

The management decided not to lift the recruitment freeze but to take actions to minimize attrition, by counselling and other means. By July 1, what had actually happened was this:

1. 58 had left in the particular category of technical specialists, as against the prediction of 59.
2. Several unit managers had directly recruited from campus, outside the normal cadres. In one region alone, three units had recruited 14 classmates from the same technical institute, at salaries ranging from 60 % of previous year's offer at the campus to about 110 %.
3. Several more had been recruited as casuals, contract labour and under various other guises, in a desperate attempt to cope with the spurt in load.
4. Organized training of freshmen had been given up, for the new recruits were required to put their shoulder to the wheel immediately.
5. Of course, the organization's reputation in the campuses had been tarnished almost beyond repair.
6. There were ominous signs that the attrition rate was actually going to increase substantially, for the mood of failure, and unfair treatment of new recruits was having its effect on the general morale of staff.

By September, the organization had advertised through newspapers for the same people they could have recruited from campus in an organized manner, and nurtured them for careers.

To sum up on manpower planning, it is the accurate, quantitative framework that allows for qualitative human development in a planned manner within an organization, achieving organizational excellence through individual fulfilment. It is a dynamic model that has, in its framework, specific design elements that will creatively respond to changes and opportunities that may come up during the plan period.

## SOURCING, RECRUITMENT AND SELECTION

*Sourcing:* Two years before we opened the grand Taj Samudra Hotel in Colombo, Sri Lanka, a Taj management team traversed a wide cross-section of the south-western parts of the island within an arc of about 100 miles from Colombo. The team was visiting schools, colleges, technical institutions and other pockets from where young people could be recruited for careers in the Taj Group of Hotels. Presentations were made appropriately to final and pre-final year students, as also the faculty, elaborating upon the prospective career paths, starting in Colombo and possibly leading elsewhere in Sri Lanka and the world. Thousands of people were thus informed what opportunities for growth existed in the Taj Group of Hotels in particular, and the tourism industry in general. Details of what training recruits would go through, how and where were also explained.

In 1982, a batch of 26 young people, some with experience but many totally raw, were selected to undergo an 18-month familiarization and training programme in India. These 26 were to become the core of highly motivated role models around whom the rest of the hotel manpower was to be built. By exposing them to the best practices in the most sophisticated of Taj Hotels, augmented by special training inputs (including in the Culinary Institute of America in New York State), as well as participation in the opening of another hotel in Goa in India, this group was prepared technically to be at the cutting edge of their profession. They were also exposed to supervisory and management training, besides being taught how to train and supervise others.

By late 1983, they were in a position to return to Colombo and play a major role in recruitment, induction and training of over 500 freshmen. The hotel became a Coaching camp for a few months, as these new recruits were put through their paces and prepared for the hotel opening in the summer of 1984. From the parent hotel in Bombay, less than 30 specialists in various areas were required to be brought in to Colombo for providing the necessary leadership and professional inputs. By 1987, this had been reduced to less than 5. The rest of the hotel was being managed by those who had been locally recruited and trained. A grateful Government even subsided the stipends of freshmen during the training period, for the hotel was solving the unemployment problem through its novel approaches to manpower planning and development.

Even though many of the original 26 had left by the end of the decade, they had played their role as trendsetters, role models and initiators for what was to follow. Despite ethnic strifes in the island, major drop in the tourism flow into Colombo, and political turmoil, the hotel held its own and survived ably. The high morale and motivation of the staff had contributed in no small way to this success.

Similar approaches have been used, with great success in different parts of the globe. A few features of this approach, together with some problems that arise in implementation, are described here.

1. Rather than sticking to traditional sources of recruitment—the employment market for most jobs, and the specialist educational institutions for the professionals—this approach allows for minimizing the numbers to be taken from these sources, and maximizing intake of freshmen from nontraditional sources. As an example, I can point out to the Graduate Training programme of the Taj Group. In 1982, there was resistance from most executives to the starting of this cadre, which was to consist of graduates in any field at all (not catering or hotel management). They were, of course, to be put through a two-year programme to equip them for hotel management careers. The resistance was so much that the cadre was even stopped for a few years. But, by 1989, the graduates of the 1982 batch were among the most successful restaurant managers in the group, with four of them independently managing restaurants in the mother ship of the chain, the Taj Mahal Hotel in Bombay.

2. One should look at the possibility of using lower level cadres to eventually fill much higher positions than conceived before. While recruiting salesmen, if consumer product companies select the kind of young people who have the potential to become sales and marketing managers later, and tell them so at the time of recruitment, they will release tremendous energy in the company. Salesmen who wish to become the best in their profession so that they can eventually become the best sales managers will look at their jobs differently. Also, when they become sales managers, their ability to empathize with newer salesmen will help them in their managerial function. The Taj Group of Hotels has many senior executives who had started out in humbler positions. Their very presence guarantees a sense of security and continuity to the organization and its guests. By projecting them as role models while recruiting apprentice stewards and receptionists, and discussing the

new recruits' possible 20-year careers with the Group on their day of joining itself, their trust is won, security and belongingness guaranteed, and the ground prepared for their concentrating on growing up towards self-esteem and self-actualization.

3. In using highly competitive sources like the entry level MBAs, corporations should take care to ensure that they are selecting intrinsically motivated youngsters, and not mercenaries. The latter will move away at the slightest sign of trouble, either for the company or for themselves. When there is a business downturn, they will be the first to seek jobs elsewhere. When they are faced with a problem at work, either with the boss or with any other factor, rather than trying their best to solve it, they will move out. Such people cause more harm than good to the company.

By restricting the number of such new entrants, and only to intrinsically motivated ones at that, this source can be used advantageously for the organization. They are best suited to early responsibilities that challenge their abilities. They also require experienced bosses who not only complement their inexperience but are also open enough to allow them to give free rein to their initiative and industry. There is a healthy reciprocal brush-off effect when a senior, experienced executive of the old school and a bright young MBA work together as a complementary team. In TELCO, we had attached such MBAs like Executive Assistants to Divisional Managers of Production, Quality Control, Planning, Finance and Accounts and Materials. The experiment succeeded enormously. While resistance vanished almost completely, there was a surfeit of new ideas and approaches. The mutual learning and development was quite visible to everyone.

*Recruitment* Having identified the sources from where freshmen are to be recruited, the next step is the recruitment campaign. The objective of the campaign is, of course, to attract the best quality people from the sources in as many numbers as required. Campaigns that will attract the right kind of people stand apart by their attention to certain important features.

- *Vision:* The corporation's vision for the future will be compelling, and inclusive in the sense that students can identify themselves as being part of the vision. When the Taj Group stepped up its campaign to attract fresh graduates in arts and sciences, the Vision was articulated in a booklet that a student could shove into his Jeans pocket. The message in it was simple:

1. The service industry accounted for over 70% of additional employment in India during the '80s;
2. Hospitality and tourism, the archetypal service industry already accounted for maximum foreign exchange earnings each year, besides having the potential to generate almost 25 % of additional employment in the next decade;
3. The profile for success in the industry was a friendly, extroverted personality who liked people, travel and working hard.

Thousands of young people across the country were invited to attend brief audiovisual presentations followed by question and answer sessions. They came in thousands, and many joined. In Calcutta, the session had to be repeated as the largest banquet hall in Taj Bengal was overfull, and did not even have standing room. During the session, an essential point that was stressed repeatedly was that over 75 % of senior managerial positions in the corporation were filled by those who had joined it at their age. The image projected was one of a happy, dynamic family, with sufficient scope for autonomy, initiative and industry, with the best and the brightest shooting up towards higher and higher job responsibilities and challenge. The money package was not at all stressed. In fact, it was treated as a sort of bonus one received in addition to being given a glorious opportunity to find one's identity and excel.

When Apple aggressively fought IBM in the campuses for the attention of the best and the brightest, Steve Jobs' "vision" captured the imagination of the youngsters. In an article by J P Kahn, "Stephen Jobs of Apple Computer: The Missionary of Micros", the author recounts a speech by Jobs to the Boston Computer Society. Jobs approaches the speaker's podium carrying with him a small beige case. The audience is aware that within the case is the company's new MacIntosh personal computer. Taking an aggressive stance behind the podium, Jobs smiles, his face suddenly illuminated on the giant rear-projector screen mounted behind him. For those in the audience who are familiar with MacIntosh's sci-fi commercial—a take-off on George Orwell's 1984, there is an immediate and delicious irony: instead of Big Brother's (read Big Blue's, or IBM's) intimidating visage staring down from the wall, there is Steve Job's. He begins to speak:

The year is 1958, and a small company has succeeded in perfecting a new technology. It is called xerography. IBM has the opportunity to acquire rights but elects not to. Thus, Xerox is born.

Jobs reads on like a hyped up Edward R. Murrow delivering a condensed history of post-chip technology: 1968—Digital Equipment Corporation introduces the first viable minicomputer, and IBM dismisses the market; 1978—Apple jumps into the home computer field, IBM ignores it; 1981—IBM finally brings out its own personal computer (hisses from the bleachers) and quickly dominates the trade news... Jobs continues to build the tension and finally presents David's answer to Goliath, the MacIntosh personal computer.

Jobs' personal style, almost a natural extension of the American Campus scene, merged with the challenge implicit in a David taking on the might of a Goliath, drew the cream off the American campuses into Apple's fold.

It is not correct to believe that all youngsters in campuses are mercenaries who will go to the highest bidder. A vast majority of them are going to the best bidder for want of sufficiently alluring alternatives that grab their imagination.

- *A career not a job:* Corporations that offer a wide, long-range scope are naturally more inviting. Youngsters who are not too sure of where their interests lie want time at the beginning of their career to feel out various alternatives before finalizing where they wish to concentrate. When recruiters recognize and address this problem candidly by offering a broad-based entry programme, with scope for mutual discussions and finalization of later entry into specific fields, they will find themselves to be far more attractive in the campus.

In TELCO, the graduate training programme at Poona was not attracting sufficient numbers of bright men from the Indian Institutes of Technology in the early '70s. We recast the programme in many ways, one of the essential parts being the manner of decision making as to where exactly an engineer would be placed. We candidly told the engineers in campus that we had been as confused as them at their age, and that we would provide them a broad training programme for 18 months—during which time they will be exposed to different functional areas like production, maintenance, design and development, planning and so on—after which their likes and dislikes would be taken into account while matching organizational needs. Almost 90% of placements could eventually be made with the total acceptance of the young engineers, as well as the divisions they were to be placed in.

Corporations that have had a high success rate of retaining their young recruits, and enabling their growth up the hierarchy, should stress this to support their commitment to human growth. Where it has not been possible in the past, candid admissions of the same together with statements on what changes are being introduced should be made.

One of the key needs for freshmen is to be able to see growth opportunities for themselves. Growth, not in terms of mere hierarchical movement, but in real terms such as responsibilities, challenge and autonomy. That the corporation has clearly laid out human resources management policies that will encourage and enable such growth should be spelt out to freshmen even at this stage.

- *Candid role models as interviewers:* It is not the audiovisuals and printed material that attract and affirm the interests of campus recruits. It is the flesh and blood of their look alikes who have made it good in the corporation they are seeking to join. Their comfort level goes up as soon as they see a few of the successful alumni from their institutions in the interview panel. In selecting for the Tata Administrative Service, care was always taken to ensure that such role models from within the ranks of the TAS were included in the campus interview panels. Informal chats before and after interviews, and over lunch and dinner, increase the comfort level of potential recruits, and an eagerness among them to get selected.

Questions like, "Will we really get an opportunity to influence our final placement, after completing the year's rotation?" could not be answered by anybody other than some of us from the TAS itself. Even if official policy had to be stated as, "The final decision about placement is the prerogative of the management", we senior TAS officers could always wink and say, "Well, most guys manage to wangle what they want . . . we'll tell you how after you join us...but don't quote us to Bombay House".

- *Third party assurances for potential recruits:* When youngsters are unsure about what they should do after passing out, they are dependent on advice from others. At the same time, their trust levels are also low. They are typical cases of children who have failed to successfully resolve Erikson's primary crises of "trust v. mistrust" as well as "autonomy v. shame and doubt", let alone the later crisis of "identity v. role confusion". In their state, they not only depend on others' advice but are also suspicious about it. It is only through careful third party assurance that a corporation can reach out to them and win their trust, thereby reaching first base on helping them resolve the rest of the crises that we discussed in the last chapter.

A corporation should attempt to identify who could ideally influence their career choice and work on it. Teachers and parents could be approached through the candidate in the form of written material that answers anticipated questions. In the selection of Apprentice Stewards (who could become potential manager) from good schools in Delhi, we actually printed out over 1000 letters to parents describing the scope of a career in a hotel, and how we would allow time and facilities for the apprentice to continue his education by correspondence while engaged as an apprentice. The objective was to make conventional middle-class parents open up to the concept of children starting a working career before completing a graduate degree. Also, we wanted the youngsters to have something concrete in hand that they could show and discuss with whomever they trusted. It succeeded very well, with many parents calling on us to discuss the details and thereafter allowing their wards to start on this unconventional route.

Another powerful third party influencer is the candidates' classmate. Corporations that take care of vacation trainees well, and make a good impression on them, will find that when they go to campus for recruitment the next year their stock has gone up. When L & T and TELCO were competing for the best engineers from the IITs in the '70s, TELCO stole a march by introducing a well organized vacation programme for second-year and third-year students, with mentors to ensure that each vacation trainee learnt a great deal and enjoyed himself too. Several of them were tentatively assured of a place in TELCO, and even counselled as to what electives they should take in the following year. They were TELCO's best ambassadors on campus.

At the same time, corporations that try to use this method without getting their act together will face the exact opposite reaction. Word of mouth negative publicity in the campus will effectively counter the jazziest recruitment material they may come up with. "They're not to be trusted," will be the verdict that would have been passed quietly.

## Selection

A common mistake corporations make is to look for perfect specimens of human beings who can be straightaway put on the job. Such people are so rare to come by that it is necessary to be realistic and ensure that all interview panel members share the realism. This is easier said than done. I have drawn the ideal profile that corporations would want to have among their well developed peak performers in Fig. 10.1. Even this figure is not exhaustive, but it is near enough to a godly figure as to allow us to proceed with the description.

The fifteen building blocks on the left of the figure are essential for a corporate citizen to reach his full potential in an executive career. As you move to the right of the figure, you get derived qualities which are essentially built on the foundation provided by one or more of the fifteen building blocks. For example, building blocks numbered 1 to 5 are essential for a candidate to develop a clear "identity and focus". Likewise, blocks 12, 13 and 14 are essential to develop "sensitivity". To develop senior executive skills such as "vision"', "creative insight"', "leadership" and "versatility"', one must not only have all 15 building blocks firmly in place but also have the derived qualities such as "creativity", "sensitivity"', "a global citizen's attitude" and "identity and focus". Another point to be noted is that but for block 3 and parts of block 1, almost all the skills and strengths listed are dependent on a well developed right brain. A comparison of Fig 10.1 with Fig. 8.3 should be interesting.

For a primer on how to develop some of these strengths, there is no better book than Hickman and Silva's *Creating Excellence*. In fact, it is difficult to imagine any in-depth management development programme without compulsory exercises from this marvellous book.

To get back to the selection process, an essential step to be taken before visiting a campus for recruitment, or meeting potential candidates anywhere, is for representatives of organizations to

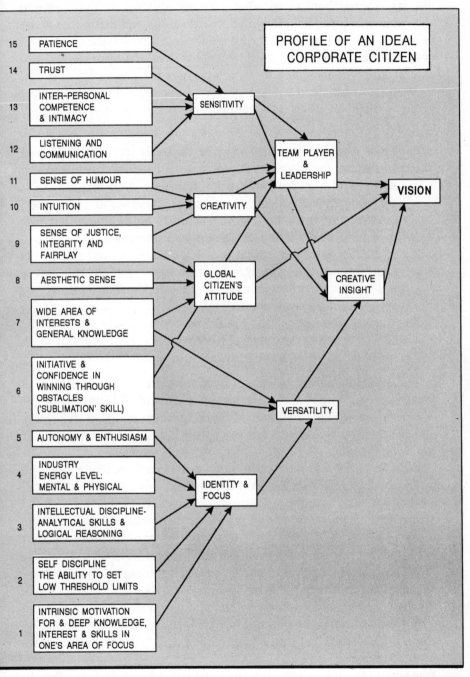

*Figure 10.1*

discuss among themselves what they are looking for and come to a consensus. Of the list of characteristics, skills and attributes given in Fig. 10.1, which go to make an ideal candidate for the CEO of an organization, it will be unfair to expect fresh campus recruits to exhibit all of them in a fully developed form right away, and that too in the one hour of interaction time he gets. Selection panels have to be realistic in their expectations and make three short-lists of characteristics:

1. *Those characteristics that must be evidently well developed* in a freshman: for instance, all entry level recruits would have to demonstrate a clear ability to "focus", which includes in it the two prime characteristics mentioned earlier in the chapter, evidence of intrinsic motivation and the ability to set low threshold limits when driven by such motivation.

2. *Those that he should exhibit potential for, which can be developed later:* for example, management trainees should exhibit potential for versatility, sensitivity and leadership, but not necessarily be fully developed in any of them.

3. *Those that can be developed later, irrespective of whether or not the candidate exhibits any potential, or preference for them at this stage:* for instance, a global citizen's attitude and Vision.

The selection panel members need to participatively arrive at these lists, such that each one accepts them fully. What has to be commonly understood and appreciated by them is that at this stage, one is selecting the equivalent of saplings, and not trees for direct transplantation.

When a corporation prepares such a list participatively, and the interviewers agree to it before the selection process starts, half the job is done. The actual preparation for interviews, conduct of tests, group discussions and other selection processes are beyond the scope of this book. I will merely touch on some major problems that corporations run into as a result of the interviewers themselves.

When interview panel members have high threshold limits, they become a hindrance to the interview process. They try to compensate for their feelings of insecurity by becoming unnecessarily aggressive with candidates. At the slightest hint of disagreement by a candidate, some interviewers get into a rage, thus putting the poor candidate in a state of high stress, an unnatural condition to make a proper assessment in. Sometimes, interviewers try to impress each other in the panel too, complicating the entire process. Unduly high threshold limits for recognition, which demand satiation constantly, lead to such behaviour. It is therefore, crucial for corporations to have ideal corporate citizens (whose personalities resemble the Fig. 10.1 as much as possible) as chairmen of selection panels, and leave it to them to manage the process of selection.

## Concluding the selection process

Mr Dinshaw Malegamwala, for many years the Member Secretary of the Tata Administrative Service, had instituted a sensitive way of completing the selection process. It is worth emulating. At the end of the final interviews, the candidates were asked to wait while the panelists were finalizing their selection. When they had finished, those who were not selected were called in and spoken to with care and concern, the objective being to ensure that they did not feel too despondent. They were helped to sublimate their energies for another try elsewhere. "We have made a selection of people based on our needs, and with a view to matching student profiles with our feel for what kind of person will succeed in Tatas. We are not making any judgement about anyone other than in a purely relative manner. We wish you good luck in your careers," about sums up what Dinshawji used to communicate to them. The selected candidates were called in only after this was done, once again reassured indirectly that they were entering a clean, caring organization. It is very often how those in power deal with those who have none, which shows true humanness. Dinshawji's treatment of those who were rejected was indeed a *genuinely* humane act that never failed to touch others.

# Nurture the Sapling and Prepare for Transplantation: Induction, Training and Career Choice

## PREPARING THE GROUND

Long before the new recruits join, a corporation has to start the preparation for them, laying the ground for the saplings as it were. Let me elaborate what we used to do in the Taj group of Hotels as an example, and thereafter derive some general guidelines from it.

About eight weeks before new recruits were to join, a select number of line supervisors and managers from various departments were released across the country to become auxiliary trainers, to augment the skeletally staffed HR department. These auxiliary trainers were put through a rigorous "train the trainer" programme, some features of which were:

- Theoretical grounding on the psychological state of freshmen, their motivation levels, unresolved crises of earlier years and ways of reaching out and helping them;
- Theoretical and practical sessions on listening, communication and counselling, as the participants were expected to legitimize for themselves the role of a "barefoot counsellor" in the eyes of freshmen trainees;
- Theoretical exposition on "androgogy" as against "pedagogy", sensitizing the participants on how adults learn as against children, for freshmen trainees very clearly fell in the former category rather than the latter;
- Theoretical and practical sessions on persuasive, effective presentations, highlighting use of participative techniques, audiovisual medium, and discussion and workshop methodologies; and
- Development and use of uniform material that combined the virtues of standardization of basics and improvization of 'add-on's.

They were then given practice sessions with peer groups to develop comfortable training styles. They were also made to get familiar with training manuals and material, with permission and encouragement to suggest improvements and changes in them. Thus, a group of line managers, with requisite skills in and enthusiasm for training, were prepared as an essential feature of the new ground readied for the freshmen. One such manager, who liked training very much, and was also extremely good at it, became a full-fledged training manager with a record of significant success. The young lady almost singlehandedly, set up the training function for Taj Bengal Hotel, with many a new innovation. One such was to keep in touch with those selected during the time leading to their joining date. Going through the application forms, she found that two of those selected had birthdays falling during the intervening period. She accordingly organized a simple, but thoughtful cake-cutting ceremony in their honour, with all others selected invited as guests. That the drop-out rate between those selected and those who eventually joined was minimal was not a little due to the personal efforts of the Training manager to keep in touch with the freshmen recruits during this phase.

# THREEFOLD ESSENCE OF THE PRIMARY PHASE

To use Erikson's model and phrases, referred to in Chapter 8, the essence of this phase may be summed up thus:

1.  By involving the line managers in preparing for and actually delivering training, the ground is prepared for developing a "trust" relationship between them and the freshmen, which will stand in good stead later when they have to play a role in helping the youngsters rebuild those of the qualities that their individual childhoods may have failed to help them develop, such as "autonomy", "initiative", "industry", "identity" and "intimacy".

2.  By taking the initiative to build a friendly relationship with the new recruits even before they join, the HR/training executive lays a foundation for legitimizing for herself the role of a friend, philosopher and guide. That this role is crucial will become evident later in the chapter.

3.  With competition being what it is, the closer the rapport between the corporation and the prospective recruit, the greater is the chance that the latter will discuss with the corporation the possibility of alternative job offers if they come up. Many a recruit has joined the Taj Group rather than competition almost entirely due to the intimacy developed during the phase prior to their scheduled joining date. In fact, by using the vacation training period as an advanced sifting mechanism, the Taj Group used to monitor the progress of all potential recruits across the country.

# THE JOINING DAY AND INDUCTION PROGRAMME

In the best of corporations, the joining dates of major cadres are considered to be of great importance. Properly managed, that day could account for the start of several potential senior executives' careers, the start of great friendships and great teams. The objective of the day should be to make the new recruit tell his parent or friend in the evening, "Oh! What a fantastic company I have joined. The people are nice and friendly and I believe I am going to like working with them and growing up rapidly amidst them". Whatever may have been the misfortunes in the individual's childhood, and unresolved crises of youth, the freshman should feel that he is being accorded a glorious second try to correct the course of his own life. Allegorically speaking, the sapling should feel grateful and happy that a straightening stick is going to enable it to redirect itself towards actualizing its full potential.

In the Taj Group of Hotels, we used to typically conduct the events of the day in this manner:

The HR team and the auxiliary trainers would receive and seat the new recruits (sometimes as many as a hundred and fifty at a time) in a large banquet hall, giving each of them a signed welcome letter in the form of a printed brochure but with the new recruit's name written by hand and signed personally by the General Manager. Besides giving the history of the Group, its founding values and beliefs, the letter would make the following personal promise to each new recruit:

> You have been selected because we believe you have the potential and the desire to meet the high standards of excellence that are a hallmark of the Taj Group. We know you have hopes and aspirations of your own., and surely, expectations from us as well. We consider it an obligation on our part to:
>
> —treat you fairly and with respect,
> —ensure that your work opportunities are exciting and interesting,
> —provide open, two-way channels of communication,
> —offer suitable recognition for your dedication and excellence of performance.
>
> Ours is a growing company, continuously improving and expanding. We wish to see you grow along with us.

After they had read the brochure, they would be made to introduce each other, if not in front of the whole group, at least in small clusters so that each would feel recognized. Then the entire senior management team from the Regional Vice-President downwards would join them for an hour. They would individually introduce themselves and extend a personal welcome. As over 70% of them were typically those who had also joined in similar capacities in their youth, they would come through as ideal role models to emulate. This would be followed by an open question and answer session, ending with a tea break when they would have an opportunity to informally mix together. A formal audiovisual programme on the group would follow, and a detailed talk highlighting the future of the corporation as also the place in it for young bright people like the freshmen.

## AN EARLY ASSURANCE ON SATISFACTION OF "APPETITE NEEDS"

By lunchtime on the first day itself, the new recruits would have received verbal assurances as regards the following:

- At the physiological level, they need have no concerns whatsoever, barring insufficient sleep owing to the long working hours;
- At the safety level, assurances of long-term careers, growth prospects and personal concern will have been uttered by senior management directly, supported by the visual, live role models of people like themselves who had made it good in the corporation;
- At the belongingness level, the care and concern, and personal contacts by several Taj staff will have made them feel a part of a large, successful and happy family;
- The very presence of the senior most management, on time and in earnest, making the occasion a special one for the corporation, will have made the new recruits feel they are considered really important;
- Most of the addresses by top management will have centred around the main theme that the only concern any recruit should have is to apply himself or herself diligently and learn to be a master in his or her chosen field; the rest of their needs they need have no concerns about, for the management will make it their personal responsibility to satisfy them on those; however, the fact that life would be one long spell of hard work, of long duration each day and evening, calling for the sacrifice of one's personal and social life will also have been stressed repeatedly; and
- Those of the youngsters with unresolved childhood crises (*à la* Erikson), will have repeatedly heard phrases and words assuring them that they are among people they can *trust*, that they will be encouraged to use their *initiative* and become *autonomous* as early as their own *industriousness* would permit them. They will also have heard assurances that the training programme would allow them the free space to find their true

*identity*—as a chef, a housekeeper, a marketing executive or whatever—as the programme is conducted by those who will make it their work and pleasure to become their *intimate* friends and wellwishers.

## Teaching the wisdom of setting low threshold limits

The afternoon session would be normally used to bring the flying youngsters down to the ground, describing as candidly as possible as to what would happen to them if they did not apply some of the norms voluntarily; for instance, on the question of integrity, it would be made abundantly clear that if an employee was found to be in unauthorized possession of corporate property when leaving the premises, it would mean loss of job even if the said property was a mere pen, or a cookie. The wisdom of setting low threshold limits would be communicated in as practical a manner as possible.

While the rest of the induction programme was not too dissimilar to those conducted in other good corporations, one significant departure in the Taj Group was that I used to conduct the exercise I had described in Chapter 7 for them. They would be made to realize for themselves that the greatest of life's experiences arise from events which seem negative at first. They would then be given a full session on the essential contents of this book's chapters 3, 4, 5, 6 and 7, making them appreciate that

- True motivation is intrinsic to one;
- There is wisdom in developing intrinsic motivation towards self esteem and self-actualization supported by voluntarily set, low threshold limits, and that this is the essence of "producing quality" as well as a meaningful life.
- When they encounter negative experiences, like an uncooperative supervisor, a rude manager, envious colleagues, exhaustion from apparent over work and lack of recognition for work done well, they have a choice of feeling unhappy and sorry for themselves, or experiment with the skill of *sublimation*.

They would then be made to get into a tacit understanding with the HR specialists monitoring their programme that every time they came running with one problem or the other, the latter would have the right to say either, "Goodness gracious" or just, "Good", for the problem could actually be a blessing in disguise . . . to learn all about sublimation.

## THE HR MANAGER AS THE NURSERY GARDENER

Even if the best saplings are procured, and the ground prepared perfectly, the growth and well being of the saplings is crucially dependent on the presence of a well-trained, caring gardener who will provide individual attention to each of the saplings. To play a similar role in an organization is an extremely complex task. As to how complex this task is, and to highlight the variety of skills and knowledge that is required in a human resources executive, I give below a real-life example that occurred in TELCO about fifteen years ago. I have exaggerated a few details to not only enable us to draw a more comprehensive list of qualities required in an HR executive but also to show myself in much better light!

An extremely bright engineer from an IIT had been placed in the Automobile division of TELCO immediately after completing his broadbased introductory training phase. He was working in the propeller shaft line which was just going into stream. One morning, about 8.30, I got a call, 'Mahesh, hi! This is Lalit. I am screwed. Can I see you immediately?' Of course, I could see him immediately, for I could feel the tension in Lalit's voice, which was otherwise extremely calm and assured. I asked him if I could run over to the shop, but he preferred to come over to my office.

He came, looking quite dishevelled and dirty, which was not uncommon for someone from the shopfloor. He said, 'The boss has asked me to leave the Auto division permanently and never again come back. In fact, he insisted that I left immediately.' He was apparently in the shop when the boss had turned up around 7.30. The boss kept screaming at him about the lack of attention to cleanliness, how there was an oil puddle, rags and scrap all over the shop. Lalit had taken it for some time, but as this was going on in front of his workmen and chargemen, he tried to proffer some explanation about the work having been rather rough and time-consuming. This had sent the boss into a wilder outburst of rage. He had begun to insult Lalit and questioned his competence. Then Lalit had lost his cool and said, 'Do you want production, or do you want everyone scrubbing the shop floor?' That had sent the boss round the bend, leading to Lalit's immediate discharge from the division.

I kept listening to Lalit, noticing how tired he looked, and how bloodshot his eyes were. I remarked aloud, "You sound as if you have really been through a grinder. You also look very tired. When did you come to work this morning?" Lalit grinned weakly, and said, 'I have not been out of the shop floor for over 26 hours. There was a problem with the new machine from the Machine Tool Division, and we were trying to set it right all night.' I asked him why he had to hang around, for the maintenance crew could have attended to it. Lalit then commented on the quality of maintenance staff and how little they knew about the new electronic controls. As a specialist in the field (at least theoretically) and a natural engineer who could not keep his hands off a machine, Lalit must have been tempted to try out his expertise, I suspected.

When I asked him if his boss had been aware of the fact that he had been working the whole night, Lalit's reaction was typical. 'Well, he seems to know everything. So, I guess he ought to know about this too. Anyway, that's not a big deal. I have spent several nights in the shop before,' he said. After letting him cool down, I got back to the hurt feeling he was exhibiting. 'You feel hurt by the incident, don't you?' I asked him. He talked of how humiliating it was to be insulted in front of his men, and of what he would like to do to his boss if it were a free world, or some place like his college had been. I let him pour out his emotions, and said, 'So, you are content not to go back to your job in the Auto division.' He kept quiet, and said slowly, 'I love my work. I am an Auto man, and I would give up anything to be able to get my job back'. 'Even swallowing your pride, and saying sorry to your boss for having challenged his right to pull you up for faltering on the high hygiene standards that the plant had set for itself?' I prompted. After some introspection, and with downcast eyes, Lalit said in a low tone, 'Yes, if my boss would let me do it'. I said I would see if that could be arranged. Then, realizing that he was really at the end of his tether, I told him to go home, sleep it off and return the next day.

A few hours later, I casually dropped in at Lalit's boss' office for a chat. As I expected, not even ten minutes had passed before he raised the subject of Lalit. Whenever any of the young engineers were in the dumps, I was normally held responsible, for they were known as my "GTs ( graduate trainees)". When they were doing well, they naturally became, "our boys". I did not mind that, for I dearly wished to reduce the dependency relationship that had grown between the GTs and me.

The boss shot at me, 'Do you know that I have thrown one of your GTs out of my shop. The fellow was so insolent and dared to question my pulling him up for shoddy housekeeping that I had to summarily ask him to go.' I replied, 'Oh, is that what Lalit was talking about? He was so incoherent and sounding so tired—I guess he must have been working overnight again—that I told him to go home, sleep and come back the next day'. The boss was taken aback slightly, for he asked me, 'What do you mean, he had worked overnight? He comes in the A shift'. I kept quiet, for I knew that the boss was already wondering if I could be right. We talked of other things for some time, and the boss got back to the topic of Lalit. 'You said you thought Lalit had been working overnight again. What did you mean by it?' he inquired. I said I was aware that Lalit was known to spend more than a day at a stretch, for he liked to try things out with the new machines whenever they arrived and he normally got time for it only in the C shift. I also said that Lalit had confirmed that he had spent the previous night on the shopfloor too when I asked him why he was sounding so tired. The boss thereupon contacted Lalit's immediate superior and checked my information. On getting a confirmation, he felt really sorry that he had not known about it when pulling up Lalit.

I let him stew in his sorrow for some time, and said, 'Isn't it nice to have a young engineer who takes his work so seriously? I agree that he shoots his mouth off occasionally, but he is going to become a great technocrat one day, I am sure. Also, he wants an opportunity to come and apologize to you for speaking out of turn and questioning you. Will you give him a chance to do so?' The boss agreed readily, adding, 'Lalit is one of my favourite boys. I was also like him at that age. I am sorry that I pulled him up so badly in front of his men. I will make up with him tomorrow. Send him back to me'. Soon thereafter, we were working out how to deal with Lalit's reentry the next day. Within a few days later, Lalit and his boss were as thick as thieves once again.

(While the boss is a director on the board of a large Indian engineering company today, Lalit is an extremely successful entrepreneur in a foreign country, overseeing several corporations independently.)

There are several features of this case that get played back again and again in corporations every day. An eager youngster tries to express his *autonomy* and *initiative*, backed by tremendous *industry*, and a line manager comes around shooting him off his feet for some unintended mistake. Quite often, both are well meaning people, but there is a lack of communication arising out of insufficient sharing of background information, or inadequate managerial skills in the true sense of the term on the part of the boss. To ensure that such interactions of people are converted to positive learning situations, corporations require teams of Human Resources professionals who are specially trained and equipped to do this and much more. Let me highlight some of the qualities, skills and strengths required for such success in this difficult job by dwelling on the finer aspects of the example just quoted.

## AN HR EXECUTIVE'S ESSENTIAL QUALITIES, SKILLS AND STRENGTHS

1. When an employee was in trouble, he could immediately get in touch with me, and be sure of getting my attention and time. *The HR executive must be easily approachable, and employees should have close enough a rapport to wish to avail themselves of this approachability whenever the need arises. Employees should also have sufficient faith and trust in the HR executive's concern to hear them out, skills to counsel and help them, and the organizational clout to render them assistance when their problems are genuine.*

2. I had to let Lalit talk through his problem, give vent to his emotions, including abusing his boss some more, and finally, when he had cooled down, suggest the implications of his parting ways from his boss. I had to baldly state the possibility of life out of the Auto Division so that Lalit would assess what was more important for him—his wounded pride (high threshold limits for recognition and respect from others) or a job that challenged his intrinsic motivation, which would allow him to develop healthy self-esteem eventually. Lalit had to weigh the options and decide himself that he would chose the latter, even if it meant swallowing his pride. *An HR executive must have basic counselling skills to enable him to help others. When it is necessary to probe beneath the "mask", or give feedback on an individual's "blind spot", or use other methods suggested by Carkhuff and Rogers, he should be able to dip into his repertoire and come up with a winner.*

3. Besides hearing Lalit's bald account of what had actually happened an hour earlier, I was actively listening to the full communication—verbal, nonverbal and the body language. His nonverbal communication was all about his feeling hurt, misunderstood and anger at the treatment meted out to him. His body language communicated how tired he was. The whole communica-

tion convinced me that he was at the end of his tether, and close to cracking up. Rather than getting into a long conversation and make him relive the agony of the scene again and again in such a state, I had to decide to take responsibility for his problem while he went and rested. *An HR executive must not only be well versed in the art and science of counselling but also have the practical sense when to use it and when not to do so. By being sensitive to the full message of a "communication" from an employee in distress, the HR executive must decide fast what course of action needs to be pursued, and have the guts to take it forthwith.*

4. In the short time I knew I had to elicit relevant information from Lalit, I gathered the information that he had worked overnight on a legitimate engineering problem, and that his boss may not have been aware of it. *An HR executive's knowledge of work practices and habits of people, as also the setting and context of all relationships, is of crucial importance if his diagnosis of a problem is to be accurate. This means that an HR executive's training should include a long spell of familiarization with the nature, content and context of work in his organization. This makes it inadvisable for an HR executive to consider too many job changes like other professionals. His effectiveness is crucially dependent on his knowledge and feel of the corporation he works in, its products and services, its people and their work habits, its problems and priorities.*

5. The incident that triggered the problem had occurred in the freshman's place of work, and not in a training classroom. It was on the shopfloor, where real-life, industrial activity was going on. The point to observe is that true learning normally occurs when one is engaging oneself in action, and not when one is passively sitting in a classroom. *An HR executive must be sensitive to the fact that his real role is out where the action is, and not merely within the confines of a classroom. While he can use a classroom to lay the framework for learning, teach theory and share available knowledge, he should use what is termed, "on the job training" as the real vehicle for learning. As this occurs under the direct supervision of a line manager, it naturally follows that the line manager plays an even more important role as a trainer than the HR executive during this critical phase. But it is a shared responsibility, and both the line manager and the HR executive need to respect this reality.*

6. I had ready access to Lalit's boss, and a relationship that allowed me to informally discuss the incident of the morning

without having to take, or defend, a stance. I could get the boss to take in the information of Lalit having been tired out after a 26-hour spell of working, without feeling awkward about not having known it in the first place. *An HR executive's effectiveness is crucially dependent on the line management accepting his legitimate role, especially when it comes to such interventions concerning the line manager's treatment of an employee. All too often, the "macho" image of line management interferes with this perception, when it becomes extremely difficult for the HR executive to even acknowledge that he has been a confidant of an employee.* There have been countless occasions when unhappy employees caught within the domain of such macho line managers have first obtained my promise that I would never let their managers come to know that our conversation had ever taken place. In such cases, especially when the organizational culture allows such "macho" images to survive and multiply, an HR executive's role becomes very difficult. *About the only option he has then is to counsel an employee to attempt his way out of the problem through sublimation of his energies. But it is not always possible for young people to manage such crises by themselves. They could fail, and develop what we had earlier referred to as "learned helplessness", or even worse psychological disorders.*

7. Almost as quickly as it had started, I could terminate my involvement with the problem, leaving the line manager and his employee to rebuild their relationship of *intimacy* and mutual *trust*. I had no problem at all about terminating my role, and reducing Lalit's dependency on my intervention to solve his problems. *An HR executive must be as sensitive as a psychiatrist in reducing dependency relationships with himself. He should never enter into a conflict over who the employee should feel closer to. It is the legitimate right of a line manager to attempt to foster the closest relationship with his staff, but it is equally the right and obligation of an HR executive to maintain a relationship that will allow it to be used in case of emergencies, and at the employee's option.*

8. Lalit was exhibiting his *industriousness* ( by working overnight, when he need not have done it at all), *autonomy* and *intrinsic motivation* (as it was his genuine interest that had made him put in the extra hours), *initiative* (for he had taken on the responsibility of a maintenance engineer without being asked to do it by anyone), *the ability to set very low threshold limits at the physiological level* (by skipping sleep and comfort) and his true *identity* as a natural shopfloor manager (by rolling up his sleeves and getting down to

the basics). He was showing every sign of being on the right track. If his brusque, albeit uncalled for, reaction to a short-tempered boss had led to his actual removal from his job, he would have found it very difficult to cope with such an extreme punishment. However, it was necessary for him to learn that he should keep his cool and preserve decorum and manners, if he desired to "belong" to the shopfloor community. As long as he was prepared to learn that, he had every right to be helped to get back where he belonged.

Otherwise, like Freud's horse of Schilda, Lalit's "isolation" would have disintegrated him. *An HR executive should ever be on the look out to see which of Erikson's first six crises is likely to be reenacted, and help a freshman in resolving it anew in a successful manner. If, at the end of an HR executive's intervention, a freshman is left operating at the "self-esteem" level, his threshold limits set at acceptably low points close to his "appetite" needs, the intervention can be considered to have been successful.*

## HELPING ANOTHER FIND HIS TRUE "IDENTITY": THE COMPLEX THREE-STEP PROCESS OF CAREER CHOICE

Another important aspect that an HR executive should pay attention to at this stage is to help a freshman develop his true "identity". Most freshmen who join an organization in their late teens and early twenties are still groping their way towards finding out which arena would match their intrinsic motivation. To better understand the dilemma they are in, let me digress a little and describe the normal process through which one moves while trying to figure out what to do with one's life.

> When one is very young, one makes what can be described as a *fantasy choice* about what one wishes to do in later life. Typically, children fantasize about wishing to be engine drivers, cowboys, pilots and so on. While they will sound quite serious about wishing to convert their fantasy into reality, their parents will probably humour them along, for such "fantasy" choices have no potential for inflicting any permanent damage. In one's teens, when one has to make specific choices about what subjects to take in high school or college, it becomes necessary to make at least a 'tentative choice' about one's career direction. Typically, children decide whether to specialize in the "sciences" or the "arts", medicine or engineering, scholastic pursuits or apprenticeship in a skill/profession and so on. They have some data to go by, based on their own performance and interactions as well as others' advise and observations. This is a very

complicated phase for a child who has failed to resolve some of the earlier crises that Erikson talks about. Even for well-adjusted, psychosocially healthy children, this could be a difficult phase especially if they happen to do well in all subjects at school and excel in extracurricular activities too. When a child is good in many spheres of activity, and he or she is forced to make a choice among those spheres, the situation does become complex.

Having made such a choice, which leads one to procure relevant qualifications to pursue one's chosen career path, it may be expected that the child's problems are over. In actual fact, just the converse is true. For example, even though the top 1% of the student population in India (academic qualifications being the criteria for evaluation) compete against each other to enter the portals of the Indian Institutes of Technology, it is a proven fact that a vast majority of them take a clear decision not to pursue Engineering beyond their basic degree. But they are unclear still as to what would be the best alternative. To broaden their options, and increase their own marketability for careers in the corporate sector, they then decide to compete among themselves for entry into the elite Indian Institutes of Management. The choice is still "tentative'", for they are yet unclear as to what exactly they would like to do if and when they graduate from the IIMs.

Even in IIMs, when they have to make choices as regards what electives they should take, lack of adequate data about future trends as well as their own intrinsic interests leads them to take "safe" decisions that will reduce their risk of making a mistake. As their seniors have by and large specialized in marketing, and most of their colleagues are also planning to do so, it seems the safest route to take as many electives as possible in "marketing". The fact of the matter, however, is that they are still not too sure if they are making the right choice. To move to the final phase, of making a *realistic* choice, one requires adequate information of career opportunities, likely trends in corporate prioritization and focus, as well as one's own intrinsic desires and thrusts. Within the confines of an academic institution, it is almost impossible to get this much-needed information. Thus, most students passing out from the IIMs are still far from definite as to what their *realistic* choice for a career ought to be. If that be the case for the elite among the Indian student population, one can very well appreciate the problems the rest of them face.

## THE PROBLEMS IN MAKING A "REALISTIC" CAREER CHOICE

What is therefore required is for corporations to design a broad based training programme that will have, as its focus, the resolution of this problem of "intrinsic motivation" or "identity" in a freshman.

At the beginning of the graduate training programme in TELCO, the freshmen would identify themselves typically like this: 'I am a GT in TELCO'. Within two years, they would be helped to say, 'I am Machine Tool Designer ', 'I am an Auto man', 'I am a Planning Engineer' and so on. While the detailed process by which we achieved this transformation is beyond the scope of this book, let me highlight a few of the problems HR executives face in managing this transformation.

1. As most corporations fail to cast manpower plans in time, their recruitment is normally done at the last minute, against specific vacancies rather than for careers. Therefore, they have no time to allow for the time required by freshmen to make a "realistic" choice. Freshmen are force-fitted against specific jobs based on an inadequate judgment on their aptitude.

2. Macho line managers do not like the idea of allowing youngsters the freedom to choose their career paths. I have often privately coached trainees such that they make the right impression on the macho manager whose area of work they wish to make a career in. This also meant that I had to keep them away from other managers who might insist on their being "allotted" some engineers. The tendency to treat human beings as commodities is so strong in some managers that managing this phase of matching individual interests and organization requirement in a humane manner is a truly complex process.

3. Many corporations may not have the wide range of activities required to plan such a process. The larger and more diverse a Corporation's interests, the more alluring it is for a freshman to join it, for he sees the opportunity to safely move from his "tentative" choice to a "realistic" one.

## THE LINE MANAGER AS MENTOR AND ROLE MODEL

Young people learn best from live role models. In the early stages of their exposure to the industry, they have to be carefully attached to mentors who will undertake the responsibility to facilitate their wards' growth. A mentor whose lower level needs are satisfied reasonably well, and who is concentrating on deriving self-esteem from his work, or is self-actualizing at work, cannot but have a tremendous impact on a ward. Exposure to how a "shen" product or service is created is about the most powerful way to develop a youngster. It becomes even more so when the youngster is allowed to play a part, however small, in the creation of such a product.

That such products are never the creation of those seeking petty recognition for their own efforts, or those who are scared for any reason, is learnt by observation. On the other hand, the profile of a self-actualizer, who sings and laughs childishly while working at full pace, who is candid, who sets low threshold limits for all his lower needs, who exhibits the heroic in Man through his word and deed, and who is unstoppable in his thrust for excellence, also comes alive in a striking manner.

Such line managers are a rare minority in most organizations, HR executives must take care to ensure that as many freshmen as possible get to work closely with these select few. This has to be achieved diplomatically, for other line managers will insist on their being "allotted" a like number.

## TOP MANAGEMENT'S ROLE IS CRUCIAL

In WIPRO Corporation, for many years now, there has been a practice whereby the Chairman, Azim Premji, personally addresses all new recruits before they have completed their first three months, wherever they may be posted. The focus of the address is the Corporation's value system and core beliefs. On the issue of "integrity" for example, Premji reiterates the corporation's stated commitment to *"govern individual and company relationships with the highest standards of conduct and integrity"*. He assures them that the corporation is extremely serious about it. Despite the environmental contamination, whereby corruption and lack of integrity have become the rule rather than the exception, it has been WIPRO's steadfast commitment to "integrity" that has allowed it to gain the reputation as being one of the "cleanest conglomerates" in India. The Chairman goes on to assure the freshmen that he is not being foolish in insisting on 100 % integrity at all times. Rejecting orders worth millions because a bribe had been insisted upon is not a foolhardy, impractical step. The fact that the best of multinational corporations, like GE, Tandem and Sun Microsystems have chosen to tie up with WIPRO in preference to others could be clearly traced back to WIPRO's reputation for "integrity", he stresses. He also advises the freshmen to refuse to obey orders which they consider unethical, even if it temporarily disturbs their relationship with their immediate superiors. The top management would support them to the hilt when such disputes are referred to them, he assures them.

By the time the new recruits have finished listening to Premji, and have their queries answered, they feel truly elated that they are part of a corporation that is clearly going to be known as the "cleanest conglomerate" in India. The later privations and disappointments which they will encounter, when their best efforts appear to be stymied by a corrupt environment, begin to appear as mere hurdles in the way of an Edwin Moses. The assurance that they will win as a team, and that individually they will have important roles to play in the victory, becomes the beacon for their future endeavours.

Before corporations attempt to emulate WIPRO, let me suggest some caution. One can state the WIPRO kind of Vision only if one is absolutely sure of achieving it. It is dangerous for corporations to make empty promises to or raise impractical expectations among freshmen. The headier they feel on listening to the promise and visualizing the Vision, the greater their disillusionment will be, if and when the promises turn out to be false, and the Vision a mere illusion. Therefore, corporations must be careful in what they articulate in front of freshmen, and be brutally candid. If a corporation has a strong Vision that is true, and achievable with difficulty, it will attract potential self-actualizers like iron filings to a magnet. If it does not have it, it will attract only mediocre people who are destined to wallow in "others' domain". If a corporation holds up promises and a Vision that appear strong, but are actually just marketing gimmicks, it may succeed in attracting good people under a false pretext. But it can never retain them. Self-actualizers will never be part of a false Vision. By definition, the two can never be part of the same whole.

## THE FINAL PHASE BEFORE TRANSPLANTATION—FRESHMEN GET READY TO ENTER THE STATE OF "AUPADESHIKA"

To ensure that transplantation is successful, corporations should place freshmen on a tentative basis in the functional areas where they are most likely to flower, powered by true intrinsic motivation. During this tentative phase, both the freshman and the manager of the functional area must figure out if the placement is working out or not. The HR executive's sensitive intervention is crucial at this stage, to iron out minor problems and facilitate the development of a feeling of "intimacy" between the freshman and his new organizational superior cum "guru". The freshman and his new "guru" must mutually accept the former's state of development as corresponding to *aupadeshika*, when he is ready and eager to receive *upadesa*. His only problem in life, by his reckoning, must be to figure out what he needs to do in order to merit genuine recognition by his "guru", whether it takes five years, or maybe, ten. Slowly, the HR executive should withdraw, almost like a parent after leaving a child in nursery school for the first time, so that new and healthy relationships are formed, and the freshman gets ready to stand on his feet as a self-sufficient person. The allegorical stick, having played its role, has to be removed.

There is a difference, however. An HR executive must retain a channel of communication with the freshman as he begins to grow in his new environment. Occasions almost always arise, if not immediately, at least later in his career, when the same employee might like to have someone to talk to. At such times, the existence of an HR executive who had been a positive influence in one's formative years becomes an important factor. This will become apparent as I spell out, in Chapters 12 and 13, what changes have to be brought about in the larger reality of a corporation if such well-adjusted, psychosocially healthy human beings should take root and flower to reach their full potential through achieving mastery over their work.


## MARCHING OUT LIKE SCHILLER'S HERO, ON COURSE TO VICTORY

Thus, we see how a freshman could be sensitively helped to straighten out whatever turns and knots had been part of his earlier development, resolve the Eriksonian crises anew successfully, learn how to set and manage with low threshold limits, find and give free rein to his intrinsic motivation, and be fully ready for marching out to find his niche in the wider environment of the corporation. If one wishes to depict the mood of such a youngster as he gets ready to march out, one would have to play these lines of Schiller's "Ode to Joy", from the fourth movement of Beethoven's Ninth symphony:

*Brothers, run your course*
*Joyful as a hero to victory!*

# 12

# RELAYING THE GARDEN: THE NEW UNION-MANAGEMENT PARADIGM

A student of physics is used to the methodology of solving a problem by which one first resolves the problem under ideal conditions, and thereafter applies corrections to deal with constraints of reality such as the forces of *friction* and *perturbation*. I have used a similar approach in this book. In the earlier chapters, we have seen how freshmen can be

a)  helped in solving the first six crises of psychosocial growth satisfactorily; and
b)  ideally prepared to enter the state of *aupadeshika*, with strong *will* and *low threshold limits*.

That was, however, within the confines of what is similar to a greenhouse in a nursery or under ideal conditions. To examine what will happen to such people when they enter the larger arena of industrial activity, with pulls and pressures from unions, peer groups, authoritarian line managers, organizational subgroups and so on, one needs to first take a candid view of reality. Only then could one suggest what changes need to be brought about for a new reality to emerge. A paradigm shift is required, which ought to become self-evident as this chapter unfolds.

## UNION POWER AND THE NEED FOR A PARADIGM SHIFT

Most management theorists who advocate faith and investment in human development as a panacea for all evil have unfortunately stopped short of explaining how it should be implemented within the complex reality of union-management relationships. Let me therefore address myself to this issue in this chapter.

To understand the rise of unions, and the awesome power they wield in corporations today, one should focus on how power was wielded historically and the manner in which such power has shifted. A good model to help develop such a focus is the one described by John Kenneth Galbraith in his *Anatomy of Power*. Galbraith contends that there are three instruments which are used in the exercise of power, and three sources from where power emerges, as shown in Fig. 12.1.

*Condign* power is the instrument of punishment. Physical assault, denial of legitimate needs, dismissal and demotion are some common examples.

*Compensatory* power is the instrument of reward. Satisfaction of safety, belongingness and recognition needs through actions such as grant of special increments, promotions and awards, as also just a "pat on the back" are typical examples.

*Conditioned* power is different from the earlier two instruments in that it is not an explicit but implicit exercise of power. In Chapter 10 and 11, I had dwelt at length on how an organization can influence the behaviour of freshmen by proper induction and training. That is a typical example of this instrument of power, whereby an individual is "conditioned" to behave in an appropriate manner without any correlation, or causal relationship with any specific input.

As for the *sources of power*, the first represents the charismatic *personality* who appears to emanate power. People like Gandhi, Lincoln and Churchill leap to one's mind as examples. The second source refers to wealth, or resources of any kind that is a prerequisite for exercising the "compensatory" power. The third source represents the network of people who form the *organization* or structure that collectively radiate power. Union organizations, employers' collectives and associations are typical examples.

## THE ZAMINDAR CONTROLLED ALL SOURCES AND INSTRUMENTS

Let me use Galbraith's model to retrace Indian industrial history with "power" as the central focus. A hundred years ago in India, and some time earlier in the West, when most people engaged themselves in agricultural activity, the common farmhand was well aware of the fact that he was under the control of the local *zamindar* or landlord. The latter had the condign power to mete out ruthless punishment—physical assault, denial of food, maiming and even murder—as also the compensatory power to reward lackeys with loans, greater share of the produce, and an occasional nod of recognition even. As for conditioning, most farmhands knew better than to rock the boat. Acceptance of the *zamindar's* absolute power was dinned into them from birth to death. Tales of what harm had befallen those who had dared to resist were repeated often enough to chill the blood of the roughest youth.

The personality of the *zamindar* overshadowed every other being, while his wealth, and hence his compensatory power, more than outweighed that held by the rest of immediate society. The organizational network that the *zamindar* had at his disposal, including the goon squad, hit men, bouncers, barn burners and other kinds of roughnecks, was all too real for the farmhand to have any doubts in his mind about the third source of power also being centred in the *zamindar*.

Thus, the *zamindar* had all three instruments and all three sources of power at his disposal, projecting a truly awesome power in the eyes of the common farmhand. I have figuratively shown this picture in Fig. 12.2. When industrial undertakings came into being, the owner managers tried to duplicate the example of the *zamindar* by refusing to share any of the sources, or instruments, of power with their workmen. As I had explained in Chapter 2, when such exercise of power went to the extent of threatening satisfaction of appetite needs at the physiological and safety levels, the counter reaction emerged in the form of unions.

## GALBRAITH'S MODEL OF POWER

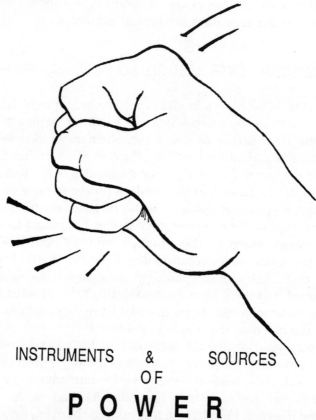

INSTRUMENTS     &     SOURCES

OF

# P O W E R

| | |
|---|---|
| ● CONDIGN | ● PERSONALITY |
| ◆ COMPENSATORY | ◆ PROPERTY |
| ■ CONDITIONED | ■ ORGANIZATION |

*Figure 12.1*

# THE UNION THEN ACQUIRED ALL THREE
# INSTRUMENTS OF POWER

Within the short span of a hundred years, the power scenario has changed drastically, with current reality in over 90 % of corporations in India—public and private sectors included—resembling the picture painted here.

*Condign power*  Most managements have abdicated their right to punish, with unions justifiably taking credit for this successful castration. With help from judges like Krishna Iyer, and enactments such as Sec 11.A of the Industrial Disputes Act 1947, most workmen in India know that the danger of serious kinds of punishment such as dismissal or retrenchment has been almost completely eliminated. In most organizations, unauthorized absenteeism has risen to double figures, with the average in Bihar hovering around 24%. That means, in addition to paid weekly, annual, sick and casual leave averaging 105 days a year, festival holidays of another 7 to 10 days a year, an employee stays away for another 90 days a year without fear of losing his job.

*Compensatory power*  While negotiating a wage settlement, union leaders typically start with demands in the region of a 150 % increase in wages. Managements respond by painting as bleak a picture of economic performance as possible, suggesting a wage freeze, or a paltry increase of say, 1%, as a gesture of goodwill as it were. The union leaders scoff at such a ridiculous response, hold meetings on the "exploitative tendencies of management", shout slogans at the gates such as, 'Management *chor hai'* (Management are thieves), 'Don't deny justice to poor working class' and 'Workers of the industry, unite', burn effigies of senior management, threaten strike action and go-slows and start wearing black armbands. Negotiations continue meanwhile, when management raises its offer to 2 %, while the union condescends to come down to a "reasonable" figure of an even 100 % increase. The drama continues for about six months, during which time, several hundreds of thousands of man hours are lost, and the two parties gradually bridge the gap and come to an agreed raise in wages by about 10%. Union leaders then take out victory processions, exchange garlands, burn incense, throw coloured water around and spread a mood of gaiety. The common worker

ORGANIZATION
A 100 YEARS AGO

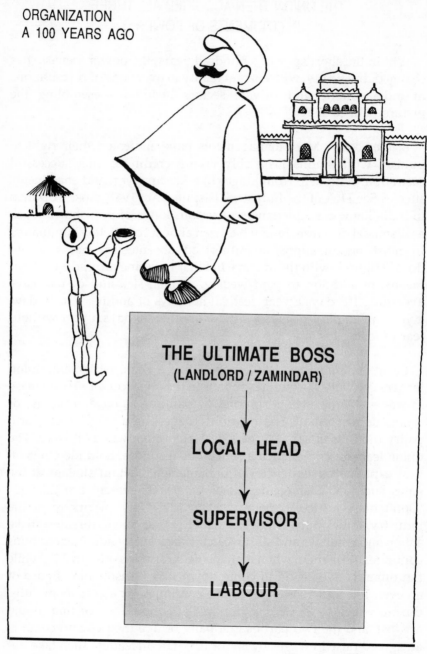

*Figure 12.2*

is left in no doubt at all that he is getting a wage hike of 10% of his salary entirely due to the fight put up by the union against a management that was initially willing to give a mere 1% increase, or even freeze wages.

## WHY UNIONS OBJECT TO REWARD OF INDIVIDUAL PERFORMANCE

In most corporations, performance increments and rewards have also been eliminated at the workmen's level, curiously enough at the instance of unions. The unions have ensured that the management is not allowed to wield any *compensatory* power at all. Even the wage increases are forced sharing of the common wealth generated by the sweat of the brows of workmen, and as such there is no need to feel any gratitude to the management, or so the logic goes. The entrepreneur who risked his name and money to start the enterprise, the managerial input that created the market, designed the product, planned the production, installed systems of control, set up the distribution network and made the whole system work are not to be considered as contributory factors, but as some kind of a birthright for those who are willing to trade their time for money.

*Conditioned power* Most organizations do not have a systematic manner of planning for their manpower followed by the kind of sourcing, recruitment, selection and induction programmes described earlier in the book. Employees are normally engaged against unsanctioned vacancies, as casuals and contract labour, the sole objective being to avoid taking any permanent responsibility for them. From the beginning, employees get to know that their physiological and safety needs will not be satisfied if they are to depend on their employers. When union leaders advise them to keep quiet, let 240 days elapse, and thereafter press for their being made "permanent" employees on the rolls, they naturally understand to whom they should be thankful. By default, most managements have allowed unions to "condition" the employees' minds in favour of unions.

## UNIONS GRADUALLY GRABBED ALL THE SOURCES OF POWER TOO

*Personality* Supervisors of workmen have no visible power at all. They can do nothing to either help, or hurt. Besides, many of them are too visibly scared to stand up to the normally flamboyant personality of an entrenched union leader. In most corporations, the latter hardly comes to work, let alone defile his hands by punching clocks. He comes and goes when he wants, calls for gate meetings whenever he feels like it, abuses the management freely and with no fear at all, and struts around like a peacock wherever he wants to go. Against such a visibly powerful personality, a young supervisor is no match at all. Even senior management appear to be weak compared to the powerful presence of a seasoned union leader.

*Property* As discussed under the instrument, "compensatory power", the common worker is thankful to the union for having fought successfully with the management and wrested an appropriate share from the common wealth. Slogans such as "management *chor hai*" should be understood in this context, for the message is quite literally that. The management are thieves, who attempt to criminally appropriate workmen's share of the common wealth, is the message that is sought to be spread.

*Organization* Managing Directors of public sector Corporations know that their tenure is for very short periods of time, from as little as a few months to a maximum of three years. Expatriate CEOs of multinational corporations also know that their posting is for a limited period of time. Against such transient people are pitted entrenched union leaders whose dearest wish is to never be parted from the power their position affords them. They, with their semipermanent mates, project a sense of continuity and safety. A common workman cannot but be expected to rely on them rather than on a transient management team.

## THE PENDULUM HAS SWUNG AWAY FROM THE *ZAMINDARI* MANAGEMENT

Thus, the pendulum has swung the full arc in less than a hundred years. Now, common workmen in over 90% of Indian organizations perceive that all three instruments of power, as also the three sources of power, are vested with their union leaders. To augment their power, and effectively counter anything and everything that a management attempts to do, unions visibly use external bodies such as the courts, the government, the press, social bodies, communal bodies and almost any busybody at all who has the time and the inclination to fish in troubled waters. While organizations resembled Fig. 12.2 just a hundred years ago, they resemble Fig. 12.3 today. *In such an image of reality, human development cannot take place as envisaged in this book.* It has to be systematically transformed. I will enumerate some essential steps that have to be taken by corporations who wish to transform themselves:

## SHARING THE SOURCES AND INSTRUMENTS OF POWER: REALIGNMENT OF UNION-MANAGEMENT RELATIONSHIP

*Condign power*  In the Taj Group, unauthorized absenteeism was around 8% in 1983, slightly less than industrial average of around 12 %. By 1984, we had brought it down to less than 2.5%. During the years 1984 to 1991, this was brought down to less than 2% per year, while the industrial average in different parts of the country ranged from a low of around 6% in the South to over 24% in the East. The Taj Group had over 40 individual establishments in all regions of India, employees of each establishment being represented by different unions ranging from CITU and HMS to internal unions. These establishments were spread over 10 states and the Union Territory of Delhi, including Kerala and West Bengal. To reduce unauthorized absenteeism to less than 2% and maintain it at that level across the country was not possible without exercising the option of using *condign* power as the last option of an end game. Let me highlight some of the steps we had taken to achieve this result.

Chronic absentees were systematically tracked down and counselled. They were explained what the consequences would be if their record did not improve. For the worst 10% of the absenteeism cases, there was a daily record maintained. If any of them remained absent even for a single day, he was met with immediately on resumption of duty and asked to explain his absence. While his excuse was accepted the first time, from the second time onwards, he was told

## THE PRESENT-DAY ORGANISATION

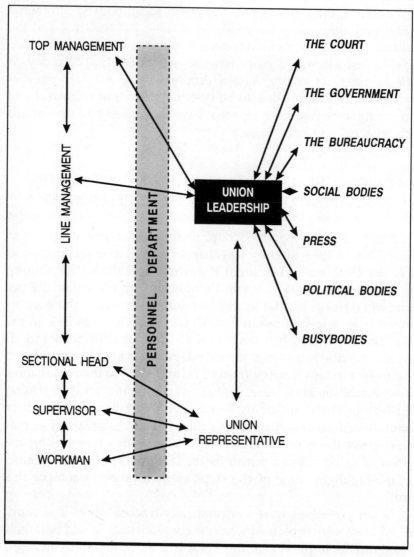

*Figure 12.3*

that he was not permitted henceforth to stay away without prior permission, at least by telephone. Line managers were told that they had the power to refuse requests for leave when asked for without sufficient notice. As the pressure was maintained, the 10 % diminished gradually, till only about 4% could be termed chronic absentees.

## USING "CONDIGN" POWER AS PART OF AN END GAME STRATEGY

These chronic absentees were brought under further pressure. Union leaders and other well wishers who normally turn up pleading the cases of those against whom management was contemplating disciplinary action, were voluntarily sent for by management. They were told that unauthorized absenteeism affected guest service adversely, continuance of which would lead to reduced business and profits, and thereafter, reduced wage increases for employees. They were given lists of chronic absentees and told to counsel them and help them to improve their record. Gradually, records were built, and cases made stronger to warrant disciplinary action. Eventually, as the hard core of unrepentant employees reduced to a very small number, management took disciplinary action following proper enquiry procedures. A few had to be dismissed. Their records were so bad that neither the union nor any other well wisher could step in to stop management action. In fact, the father of an employee actually brought in his son's resignation letter, saying, "You people have been too good for my son. Your personnel officer has spent so many hours and days trying to knock some sense into him. Don't waste time on enquiries. Here is my son's resignation letter".

It took concerted action, sympathetic to start with but gradually stricter and tougher as time went by for each case, to bring unauthorized absenteeism down to negligible figures. That it could be achieved in different parts of the country, in small and large establishments, in new and old establishments, in States like Tamil Nadu which has a reasonably good record of industrial peace as well as states like West Bengal and UP, with internal and external unions, and maintained for over seven years only goes to prove that management can reassert their right to exercise condign power if they go about it the right way . . . using it as the last, necessary resort of a well planned end game.For a more detailed account on "Management of Discipline", I refer the reader to my paper by that title in the July–Sep 1988 issue of *Vikalpa* (vol. 13, No.3), the journal of the Indian Institute of Management, Ahmedabad.

## Management's legitimate use of "compensatory" power

Corporations that have multiple units in different parts of the country must ensure that their employees understand the causal relationship between the economic performance of their respective units and their own wages. In Bombay, when the Taj Group acquired the President Hotel, the employees were represented by a CITU union. They still are. At the time of acquisition, there was a demand that the President Hotel employees should get wages on par with the Taj Mahal Hotel, situated just a couple of kilometres away but older, grander and a better establishment by any yardstick. The management obviously resisted giving in to such a demand, for the rates charged at the President was less than half those charged at the Taj, and the employees were earning even less of a fraction.

Over the years, by patient counselling and sustained resistance, it was gradually brought home to the President Hotel employees and their union that the only way their wages could get close to those at the Taj was by improving the quality of their service as well as productivity. As management matched employee efforts by improving the product substantially, the wages increased and by 1990, the President was on par with, if not better than, the Taj.

Similar cases of success have been recorded elsewhere in the country too, whereby employees were made to realize that while they had a role in influencing the use of compensatory power over them, the management would retain their right in the actual exercise of this instrument of power.

*Using compensatory power to facilitate human development* Another way of exercising compensatory power is through facilitation of employee growth and development such that he is able to assume higher responsibilities and receive legitimate promotions. Corporations that invest substantial energies, time and resources in continuous training and development know that the return on such investment is enormous. As most of available literature in HRD concentrates on this aspect of changing an organizational reality, let me restrict myself to pointing out a few common mistakes committed:

1. Such efforts are normally restricted to non-unionized managerial staff. The focus should be spread to cover all staff. Frontline staff, who are normally unionized, are the very people who should get maximum attention. If and when they develop the feeling that they will one day be the managers/manageresses of their establishment through improved knowledge, skills and competence, their approach to their work, and customers, would undergo a sea change. A professor of management from England who had visited India said, "The Taj Group is the only chain where you can meet a steward or a receptionist who can discuss world economy, ecology and philosophy with you," and asked, "What are such people doing in jobs like that?" My answer was simple: " They are our potential General Managers and they know that. They are learning the frontline jobs as that is where one meets and serves guests".

The last time I had to recruit freshmen for the Taj hotels in Bangalore, in 1990, all I had to do was to pick a few of the 50 odd sectional and departmental heads who had joined as freshmen in 1983 and instruct them to get me their clones! And young people queued up as if the Pied Piper of Hamlyn had begun to play his tune.

2. The rate of change is so fast that obsolescence is a matter of great concern for all corporations. Employees in their mid-40s need to be counselled and encouraged to meet the corporation more than halfway in solving this problem. There is only so much that a corporation can do through formal programmes. The prime focus should shift towards facilitating individual employee initiative to keep himself updated. Special grants should be given for buying professional literature, and for being members of professional bodies. Besides, an atmosphere of learning must be generated such that the entire corporation begins to look upon itself as a learning community. Learning should not be viewed as a peripheral activity which is to be undertaken in one's spare time. It should become, instead, the core activity around which a business community revolves. In short, *Adam Smith's Economic model of Man must be discarded, and the Maslowian model of Self-Actualizing Man must be adopted.*

### Battling unions for reacquisition of conditioned power

I have dealt with the use of this instrument in the earlier chapters in detail. By proper manpower planning, selection of freshmen of the right profile, careful induction and training, a corporation can condition its employees's minds in a positive way. That an employee need not worry about his lower needs at all, and must only concentrate on attaining self esteem level in his chosen area of work is a state of mind that is achieved through careful conditioning by truthful and genuine role models.

Entrenched union leaders quite often object to such attempts at conditioning, for it interferes with their own power base. They will spread misinformation, and their own versions of what reality is all about. New people will be told that they should not produce more than the agreed rates of output, as that is a crucial bargaining point during negotiations. It will also be made quite clear as to what will happen to "rate busters", thus backing conditioned power with explicit threat of condign power being used too. Let me give an example.

*A scene from a "Wild West" film:* We had acquired a running property in an underdeveloped part of Central India, not far from where Rajasekhara had written his *Kavyamimamsa* about a thousand years ago. Sad (as the reader will appreciate later), but true. The local union leader greeted our takeover by visiting the hotel about midnight on the first evening itself, accompanied by four gun-toting youths. He had the bar opened by a barman who was a scared union member, helped himself to several pegs of choice whisky, offered one laughingly to our Security Manager, got up without paying the bill, reached the portico to get into his jeep, and dramatically told his lackeys, 'Announce to the Taj management that I myself have personally visited them.' Immediately, almost as if the whole scene was out of a Wild West film set in Texas in the last century, his men unloaded their ridiculous .202 rifles by shooting into the air, laughed aloud and piled on to the back of the open jeep.

Our security manager politely told the union leader that the next time he came around, he would have to pay the bill. The union leader laughed aloud, appreciating the joke as he believed it was. He then asked the Security Manager to accompany him for a drive, whereupon the latter asked him if four gun carrying lackeys were enough to protect him and if that was so, he would certainly accompany him. The union leader looked hard at the Security Manager and said, 'Oh, you are not the type that wears bangles, I see.' Slightly chastened, in spite of his inebriated condition, he left our premises.

## Career planning for union leaders too

A few days later, I made it a point to visit the hotel and met the union leader and the committee of elected workmen. Having gone through the individual files of each of the workmen, I spent the first hour of the meeting talking of what career each of them could aspire for. 'Ah, your background is exactly similar to the one who is our Front Office Manager in President Hotel. He had also joined as a bell boy . . . And you are an exact replica of our General Manager of this very hotel for he had also joined as a frontline employee in Reception . . . and you remind me of the chap who is our Assistant Restaurant Manager in New York for he was also a waiter and a Union leader just six years ago . . . ', and so on I went. By the time I came around to the imitation gangster cum union leader, I had each member of the union committee imagining himself in better and higher positions within the foreseeable future. I offered a more immediate career change for the union leader who was not an employee. 'With your busy schedule, I am not sure how much time you have to devote to our unit. Even if you can spare about five hours a week, I have a suggestion for you. I would like you to be our public relations and liaison man to spread the message among prospective employees that we are the best employers. Of course, I would like to pay for your time quarterly. . . and in advance of course', I said to him. I gave him a long lecture on what Tatas had done for workmen since the turn of the century, and how we spent much more than the annual sales of that hotel on charitable work, like running hospitals, giving scholarships to students and encouraging cancer research.

## The Union challenge over use of "conditioned" power

The union leader was no fool. He spent the next few days spreading gross misinformation and instigating employees. Finding that some of his closest followers had begun to draw away from their relationship, visioning themselves in positions of organizational responsibility soon, the leader mounted a drastic counter strategy. A departmental head was assaulted by two of his men in the confines of a store room, of course with no witnesses present. They resorted to stout denial when hauled up for it.

We descended on him like a ton of bricks. We announced our intention to chargesheet and suspend the alleged workmen at a meeting with the union committee. We gave them two hours to decide what they wished to do about our decision. They could decide to strike, in which case we would not mind closing the hotel down, for the total sales of the hotel were a mere fraction of what we spent on philanthropic causes each year. Alternatively, they could let the due process of an enquiry run its course. Either alternative was acceptable to us, we said. While they were meeting to discuss their course of action, it so happened that a busload of Taj employees from other hotels arrived, "on a pleasure trip arranged by the company as a sort of reward for good performance". While the union leader may not have believed that statement made by one of the pleasure seekers, the union did agree at the end of two hours that the enquiry could go on with no threat of a strike.

In the next six months, we backed what was essentially a strategic use of *conditioned* power with *condign* and *compensatory* power. While efforts at training for career advancement was the core of our strategy, we had made it quite clear that we would meet gross indiscipline with exercise of "condign" power. We also demonstrated our intention and capability to run the hotel with or without the help of the militant faction in the union. We then chargesheeted and suspended those who had allegedly been responsible for gross misconduct, and showed our commitment to stay and make a fight of it. After the enquiry processes were duly completed, some of the worst offenders were meted out appropriate punishment, which included dismissals. The governmental bodies and law courts supported what was evidently a fair set of actions by the management. At the same time, some of the best performers were sent on training to other and more modern units.

Within a year, the scene had shifted from what had appeared to be a throwback to the mid-19th century, to the late 20th century, as the workmen voted the erstwhile leader out of power, settled down to a collaborative relationship with management, and peace reigned everywhere, including the bar at night.

## Matching the personality of flamboyant union leaders

Either a senior line manager, or a senior HR executive has to match his personality against the flamboyant union leader, win in an eyeball-to-eyeball contest, refuse to back down, call the latter's bluff in public and visibly show that a transfer of power is taking place. The classic example is that of Russi Mody, the former TISCO Chairman countering a union leader at the gate of TISCO's main plant at Jamshedpur.

There was a well attended gate meeting, with a union leader holding forth on management exploitation, injustice, Tata *zamindari* and so on. Russi Mody sat some distance away, behind the audience and began to listen to the union leader. The audience began to get distracted, as first the employees in the back rows, and later the rest, started turning around to see what the Chairman was up to. Having caught the attention of the audience, Mody began to speak too. After some time, he invited the union leader to come up from behind the new alignment and join him. There are countless other examples of Mody having used similar methods to successfully pitch himself and his personality against antagonistic union leaders. Where CEOs do not wish to come to the front themselves, line managers and HR managers should be encouraged to do so. However, unless there is continuity of the specific individual in that role, this will not work. In union-management relationships, where the Union leader normally scores over management is through his longer innings, which alone guarantees continuity and safety in the eyes of workmen.

Similarly, to counter the personalities of shop stewards, line managers and HR officers should be enabled to come through as power centres themselves. Unless they are seen to be vested with, and actually wielding, power, the common workman will not take him or his legitimate instructions seriously. Again, through proper selection and training of line management, backed by adequate delegation of authority within clear and just systems of working, line management can be sufficiently empowered to play effective roles.

## Changing the perception of employees

The effect on the employee must be positive in that he should feel that

- He is in safe, trustworthy hands;
- He has multiple channels open for grievance redressal, including the one of speaking to the HR executive (without incurring the wrath of his line boss);
- His immediate supervisor has not only the power, but also the skills and inclination to help him grow;
- The shop steward does not wield more power than his immediate boss or the HR executive, to either hurt him or help him; and
- That his boss, the shop steward and the HR executive believe in sharing their responsibilities as well as power with respect to his own well-being and growth.

## Management should respect legitimate union role over "property"

While discussing the exercise of "compensatory" power, we dwelt upon this implied source at reasonable length. There is one more aspect to be considered, namely the method of union negotiations. It is high time management and unions gave up the charade of the year-long negotiation for each of the three-year wage agreements. Where unions are encouraged by management to directly seek information about market practices, industry norms and rising competition, their expectations cannot but reduce to reasonable proportions. Besides, if a corporation openly shares financial information of their own budgets, costs and performance, of their future plans and commitments, and voluntarily discloses how fund allocation and disbursement takes place, it is possible to develop an atmosphere of trust and remove suspicion.

At the Fort Aguada Beach Resort, in Goa, a union committee was subjected to a tirade by their general body when they disclosed the likely sum at which their negotiations with management could conclude. A dissident group challenged the competence of the committee and even alleged that they had been "bribed" by the management. The challengers voiced their opinion that they should be authorized by the general body to continue the negotiations. The incumbent committee members took offence at this challenge of their integrity and competence. Tensions heightened, infighting increased, abuses and threats were exchanged and the General Secretary retired from combat by retreating to his distant village, rather like Achilles retiring to his tent on the battle field of Troy.

Several outside union leaders smelt the possibility of entering the fray and successfully adding to their lists of followers. As practitioners know, industrialized countries are plagued by the existence of several unscrupulous union leaders who are ever in search of followers. Any sign of tension anywhere is like a clarion call for them. So, we had several of this kind prowling around, eager to fish in troubled waters.

### Bringing the balance back: Management support for Unions

A Corporate HR team went to the aid of a beleaguered General Manager, and between us, we solved the problem thus:

- We first sent for Achilles from his tent and persuaded him to the view that discretion is not always the better part of valour, for one has to sometimes exhibit valour by openly removing the velvet glove from one's steel fist, assuming that one did have a steel fist of course;

- We called the union committee for a meeting and asked them if they would allow the management to play a complementary role by jointly addressing the employees on the subject of corporate financial performance, expansion plans and high loan repayment liabilities;

- Having got their consent, we asked them to send for the dissident group and addressed them too, in an attempt to convince them that the management's affordability for a wage settlement was indeed abysmally low. The dissident group did not buy our arguments, and kept insisting that management figures were incorrect;

- We persuaded the union committee as well as the dissident group to be present as we addressed all the employees. Our message was simple: "With 43% of the parent company's equity held by Charitable trusts, over 80% of whose income from dividends received went into running the renowned cancer hospital, the Tata Memorial at Bombay, and other such philanthropic activities of the House of Tatas, the management is not interested in denying legitimate rights of employees. None in the management stood to gain by giving less wage increases than the financial performance allowed. We are already the best paid establishment in Goa in our industry, and shall remain so with the co-operation of the employees, their union and its office bearers. A hotel cannot afford to have unhappy employees, for it is the employees' happy smiles that brought back guests. Can't we resolve our differences amicably, like brothers are expected to in families?"

- Patiently, we answered employees' queries, allowed dissident leaders to voice their suspicion, the incumbent leaders to have their say, and took care to ensure that *trust* was rebuilt in an atmosphere of *intimacy.*

- Three days later, we had a wage settlement signed under Sec 12. iii of the Industrial Dispute Act, 1947, in front of the Government's Conciliation Officer . . . with the dissident group signing as witnesses.

## Learning from the Goa experience

The point of this example is not to demonstrate what a talented lot of HR executives we had in the Taj Group of Hotels, or how well we could function as a support group to a line manager calling for professional support. Rather, it is to emphasize the fact that Management should accept the rights of employees to know if the corporation is "fair" and "just" in the way it distributes the wealth generated by the industrial activity it is engaged in. Employees of the Fort Aguada Beach Resort at Goa are the sort that corporations dream of. They are courteous, committed and fiercely loyal. They have never allowed any guest of the hotel to feel the least amount of tension even when the management and union had their differences. The least that the management could do was to accept that such loyalty and commitment deserved repayment with complete trust and sharing of all information. When the management offered such repayment, and kept away from meddling in union leadership conflict, and in fact helped resolve differences among union factions, *trust* was regained. Employees were satisfied that the wealth that was being generated jointly by the management and staff was being properly utilized, in a fair and equitable manner.

This point can bear with some reemphasis. When union and management are open about where, when and how threshold limits are set, and satisfy themselves that there is a sense of fairness while doing so, all the staff in the corporation will find it easy to fall in line with such norms. Granted, there will be disparities, but these should be a function of performance and market worth of an employee as well as equitable sharing based on effort put in. As I had discussed in Chapter 5, one of the most effective ways of setting low threshold limits is by the generation and articulation of a meaningful Vision. It is only when such a Vision is absent, or is tarnished, that employees, and unions on their behalf, object. When employees realize that a CEO is a puppeteer who is primarily interested in exercising power over others (rather like the *zamindar* of yesteryear), they will naturally refuse to set low threshold limits for themselves. When they see incompetent senior executives wielding power, entirely due to their ability to say "yes" and nod to the CEO, and competent executives driven out due to organizational politics, employees will again resist attempts to reduce their thresholds. Employees need to be convinced that all managerial actions are directed at making the organization win in the market place, rather than perpetuating the power of an individual and his coterie.

*Conflicts arise over setting of threshold limits* HR executives and union leaders have very similar roles to play in that both are interested in employee development. However, conflicts arise primarily in reaching an agreement on what constitutes acceptable appetite needs and what are avoidable "desires". As explained earlier in the case of the President Hotel, when a management keeps its promise of ensuring a fair sharing of profits through higher wages and benefits for employees, such conflicts reduce in number and intensity. Gradually, employees will grow in confidence, learn to trust their management and understand the basic truth that management and employee interests are served best when a collaborative, rather than a confrontative, atmosphere prevails in the corporation.

In the example of the Fort Aguada Beach Resort, by ensuring that even the dissident group within the union was persuaded to play a role, the management had only raised the level of collaboration to great heights. Without trying to push through a settlement with the recognized committee under a bilateral arrangement allowed by Sec. 2 (p), the management was bold enough to go in for a conciliation agreement that would have all parties agreeing to it. At the end of the process, there was not a single employee in the Fort Aguada Beach Resort who had any doubts whatsoever regarding the genuine motives of management.

## The new picture: Multiple channels are the key

*Organization* Earlier, I had discussed how the union organization is far more visibly and effectively organized than that of a transient management. One cannot but have mobility and job rotation in the interests of improved corporate performance. Hence, the only way one can counter the lopsided perception in the eyes of the employee is to present an organizational structure with institutionalized systems that are far more visible in its working than the fact that the individual players within the system happen to change. Like a well-rehearsed theater company on tour, there should be a sufficient number of well prepared understudies who can fill the roles of established actors when the latter are unavailable. However, there are only so many understudies who can be used without adversely affecting quality of performance. Thus, a corporation must take care to ensure that replacement planning is done carefully for such crucial roles. Also, it must be realized that while other positions can be filled by understudies easily, it is extremely difficult to replace an HR executive or a line manager who has won the trust of the employees.

Ideally, a corporation should recruit HR specialists ahead of time, use them at the time of recruitment, induction and training, and enable them to legitimize for themselves the roles of friends, philosophers and guides. Together with line managers who are well trained to acquire similar roles for themselves, they should be able to project a combined picture of stability and strength, with the ability to deliver the promise implied in such a picture. The picture that appears in the eyes of the employee should be as described in Fig. 12.4.

Most human beings are uncomfortable when they are at the sole mercy of another human being. For their full development, they need an environment that appears to guarantee protection from unfair treatment, satisfaction of their appetite needs at all levels in a just manner, opportunity to seek mastery over an area of activity that is of intrinsic interest to them and the potential to eventually self-actualize through their engagement in legitimate activities inside and outside the organization.

When an employee knows that he can go to one of several people to voice his grievance if any of the conditions mentioned in the earlier paragraph are threatened, he feels comfortable. Further, when he learns by experience that such grievances will be heard and acted upon in a fair manner, he gradually stops worrying about everything other than the psychosocially healthy growth of himself, his colleagues and family.

## THE ELI LILLY EXAMPLE IS WORTH EMULATING

There are two outstanding examples of how organizations can institutionalize a system that collectively brings employees to such a state. In Eli Lilly, the pharmaceutical giant in the USA, there has been a tradition of selecting and training HR executives, which is worth emulating. Periodically, the organization identifies for every group of about 500 employees, the individual who appears to be

PICTURE AS IT SHOULD APPEAR TO AN EMPLOYEE

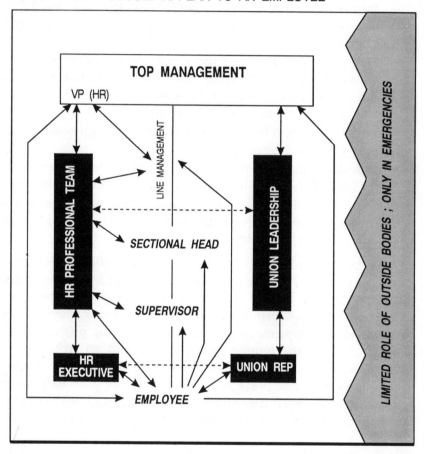

*Figure 12.4*

the most liked. Such an individual is moved to take up the position of a *personnel representative* for the group. He is then equipped with the knowledge, skills and authority required to play the role of a friend, philosopher and guide for the 500 he has been picked from. He is told that his prime objectives will be to

- Build strong and supportive relationships between the 500 and their bosses; act as a safety valve for grievance redressal when line management is unable to deal effectively with employee grievances;
- Play the role of an alternative communication channel, either when employee feelings and views are not transmitted up the line management hierarchy, or when top management views and concerns are not passed down effectively;
- Proactively concern himself with potential grievances and problems and suggest anticipatory steps;
- Provide strong support to the departmental head responsible for his 500, such that he has a happy and effective team; and
- Gradually work himself out of his job when such a team is a self-sustaining entity without the need for a full-time HR man attending to their well being.

It has been a tradition in Eli Lilly to have the HR job viewed as a necessary step for the career growth of line managers. *Macho* line managers do have to play such roles to appreciate that there is a universal "yin–yang" principle that governs all living systems. The hard has to be complemented by the soft, the male principle by a female principle, the hunter by a nurturer and an Arjuna by a Krishna. No amount of lectures will convince macho line managers of this universal principle. Only a two or a three year assignment as a full time HR executive will enable him to appreciate the human dimension and its need for constant and careful nurturing.

## MARRIOTT'S "SPEAK OUT" SHOWS THE WAY

Another good example is the system set up by the Marriott Corporation in the USA. They have an effective method by which employees are made to feel comfortable that they can never be denied justice. Their system is called, *"speak out"*. By this system, which is explained to all employees when they join Marriott, any employee with an unsolved grievance is expected to follow this sequence:

- Seek an appointment with the immediate superior and talk candidly about the problem; if that fails to deliver the goods satisfactorily, then
- Seek out the Personnel Executive he or she feels closest to, and talk about the problem; if this fails too, then
- Seek out the departmental/divisional head and/or the Personnel Manager/Director and voice the problem; if that fails too, then
- Seek out the General Manager of the hotel and have the grievance voiced again; if that too fails, then

*Speak out* by

- Writing or speaking directly to either the Senior Vice President (human resources) or Bill Marriott Jr, the Chairman of Marriott Corporation, at the corporate headquarters in Bethesda, just outside Washington DC; there was no question of this failing as the top management had a 100 % rating on the promptness and fairness of their response.

I met several employees in the Marriott Corporation who confirmed to me that Bill Marriott's responses had always been eminently satisfactory. A barmaid in one of the Marriott hotels in Los Angeles told me that a colleague had written to Mr Marriott about an unsolved problem. Within 48 hours, the problem had been looked into and the general manager of the hotel had called the employee and delivered the solution. When I asked if the GM was not upset that an employee in his hotel had actually gone directly to the Chairman, I got an interesting response: 'Oh, No! Bill Marriott will be very upset if he comes to know that any employee has been discouraged from using the "Speak Out" system . . . and you know, we employees have decided not to have unions because we have enough people to talk to about our problems, including the SrVP (Human Resources) and Bill Marriott himself . . . ', she said. And she had been a Marriott employee for less than two years!

The barmaid actually summed up the essence of the system: When internal channels work well, and no one tries to choke any of the channels—like a line manager getting upset when an employee finds the need to speak to anyone other than himself—employees are *unlikely* to feel the need to speak to someone outside whose normal method of communication is to stand outside the gate, raise banners and slogans and drive away customers.

Combining the learning from the Lilly and Marriott systems, we see that the essence of the new way of organization is

- A supportive line management, who view their own roles as open, developmental and non-authoritarian;
- An effective HR function extending all the way up to a Senior VP or Corporate VP who is visibly part of the top management team of the corporation, and staffed by the kind of people described in Chapter 11 as well as here as the HR man at Eli Lilly;
- A union that plays an effective role to ensure that employees get a fair deal when it comes to setting threshold limits as also when being provided opportunities to grow all the way towards self-actualization at work;
- Freedom for an employee to chose which channel of communication to use, albeit in an acceptable sequence like the Marriott "Speak Out" system; and
- A clearly implied accountability of all those who have power, as to whether it is being used in the interest of individual and organizational development and effectiveness.

## THE CHANGED ROLE OF UNION LEADERS: A NEW PROFILE TO MEET MULTIPLE NEEDS OF EMPLOYEES

We had discussed, in Chapter 2, the genesis of the union movement. It started when employees' appetite needs at the physiological and safety levels were denied by management. Where managements are shortsighted enough to attempt such unjust denials, there is definitely a need for unions to continue to play their traditional role. However, when management consciously change their approach, and genuinely wish to provide a fair deal for their employees, union leaderships should respond by changing their own role too. Unfortunately, that does not happen most of the time. Union leaders have become so used to catering to the lowest two needs of the Maslovian hierarchy that they are unable to cope with the fact that satiation of appetite needs at these levels should be considered as mere stepping stones for further growth of human beings.

A doctor who was a specialist in treating malaria in the 1950s and 1960s should become sensitive to the fact that malaria has been eradicated in most parts of the globe. He should change his focus to acquire new skills and knowledge that would be needed to cope with ailments like stress, cardiac arrests, AIDs and so on. That he would become a sort of museum piece, acting out a forgotten role in an antediluvian play if he continued to specialize in the treatment of malaria alone, is something that his best friends should tell him. Several union leaders, likewise, belong to museums too. Many of them, like their mega counterparts in the erstwhile Eastern Block and Soviet Union, have failed to respond to the change in employee needs.

In the better corporations, which have begun to realize that organizational success is crucially dependent on employee growth up the Maslovian hierarchy towards self-esteem and self-actualization, there is hardly any need for a traditional union leader whose stock-in-trade is limited to making a hue and cry about basic needs being left unsatiated. Without realizing this, such union leaders have resorted to artificial methods of creating crises such that their members are kept continuously threatened at their lower need levels. When union leaders are told that a management will give the maximum allowable limit of 20% bonus, they are quite often disappointed. They request the management to start with a figure of, say 12%, such that employees can be made to feel exploited for a little while till such time as the union leader is able to pick up a row and obtain 20% from management by his efforts. To humour such people, many management representatives continue to play this charade.

### The need for weeding a garden is of paramount importance

The time has come for such union leaders to be ruthlessly removed from corporations the way a gardener would remove weeds. Such union leaders are no different from authoritarian managers who see themselves as puppeteers, rather than as gardeners, for they are also perpetuating their roles by playing with employees' desires. Frightened employees are made to replace their threshold springs with strings which can then be held tight by the puppeteer union leaders. For satisfaction of both appetite and desires, employees are then forced to rely on the union leaders to pull their strings. As we have seen in Chapter 2, unions have traditionally depended on trading employees' output in exchange for compensation in cash. By definition, this exchange takes place in "others' domain", an unsatisfactory arena to produce quality, let alone a means for the true growth of a human being.

What organizations require instead is a different breed of union leaders who will be sensitive to the fact that higher needs have begun to have greater weightage in employee perception. India fortunately has a fair number of such evolved leaders. An outstanding example is the veteran Hind Mazdoor Sabha leader, Anthony Pillai. In the early 1960s, Pillai pioneered the concept of "allocable surplus" for bonus calculation, long before the Payment of Bonus Act, 1965 was enacted. The "set-on", "set-off" formula of that Act is actually derived from Pillai's original contribution while signing a bonus agreement with EID Parry in the early 1960s. During the 1980s, I have negotiated several three-year wage settlements with Pillai, who represented the employees of four of the Taj hotels. Each time, he has suggested innovative ways by which employees could be helped in their growth to full potential. Acceptance of low threshold limits, in the long-term interests of both the establishment and its employees, was understood by him without the management having to do a song and dance about it. In one hotel, he even helped us design a new method of assessing customer satisfaction, and linking it with employee wage and bonus payment.

### Union leaders can teach management organizational priorities

Another example that leaps to my mind was a young union president at the Taj Mahal Hotel, New Delhi. Once, we had been waiting for over 30 minutes to start a union-management meeting because the president of the union had not turned up. Upon checking, I found that while he had come to work, he had apparently been insolent enough not to turn up for the meeting. I angrily asked for him to be brought immediately. Instead, he called for me on the telephone, and this is what he said to me: 'Mr Mahesh, I am unable to leave my post at the coffee shop. There has been high absenteeism in the afternoon shift, and we are only three people manning the place now. There is an unusually large number of guests today, and my leaving the coffee shop will seriously affect service quality. Could we postpone the meeting by an hour please?' My anger evaporated quickly, and we waited for him patiently. We concluded the negotiations rapidly when he did turn up and the employees got a good settlement. That union president went on to greater heights, and is now in a managerial position in a Taj restaurant in New York.

Such union leaders do not happen by accident. Management should take steps to identify potential union leaders among their employees and encourage them to seek and contest Union leadership positions on their own. The ideal profile is one

- Who has a strong "will" and intrinsic motivation to seek mastery in his own sphere of work;
- Who has the potential to come up the organizational hierarchy even while climbing his own Maslowian hierarchy;
- Who has natural leadership qualities;
- Who does not seek favours for himself, but is articulate enough to be able to voice the feelings and expectations of his colleagues;
- Who appears to have low threshold limits, with the heroic streak in him to give up lower needs for higher ones;
- Who appears to have solved the six Eriksonian crises reasonably successfully;
- Who is not only trusted by his colleagues but also he  the requisite skills of listening and counselling; and
- Who has no doubts at all that employee interests and corporate objectives are mutually compatible and supportive.

When such employees seek union leadership positions, and get elected in a free and fair manner, they bring about a sea change in union-management relationships. Whenever I have tried to advise such people to enter the union movement, I have found that they are initially against the idea. The history of union movement is so full of negative doings that a human being of the profile I have just described naturally shies away from it. One has to persuade them and convince them that management genuinely views the position of a Union representative as a good, developmental role for an employee, rather like the personnel representative position in Eli Lilly. Having succeeded in persuading such people to become union leaders, one should desist from attempting to misuse one's organizational clout to thwart their freedom of speech and action as union leaders.

### An HR manager became the Union advisor at their request

If one looks at the profile closely, one will realize that it is not too dissimilar to that of an ideal HR executive trainee. My experience has been that such people make good HR executives in later years. In this connection, let me describe a real-life incident that took place a few years ago in Bombay:

> We were about to start negotiations with a union representing the employees of a unit. The union committee had decided that their earlier advisor was not doing a good job, and were on the lookout for another. The general secretary asked for a postponement of a scheduled meeting because they wanted time to chose a new advisor. During the conversation, he told me that the sort of person they wanted was a personnel executive who had earlier been associated with the unit. The particular executive had since then moved up the hierarchy and was a manager of an HR department in another hotel of the chain in a different part of the country. I jokingly offered to release him for a month if they wanted him. To my great surprise, the union committee promptly took me up on my offer and asked for the executive.
>
> I rang the executive concerned and explained the novel situation. He calmly told me that he would gladly help the union provided I accepted the fact that during the time he was advising the union, he would not be accountable to me. He would act the independent union advisor honestly and negotiate hard with me. I agreed, appreciating and understanding why the Union had so much faith in the particular executive. We began negotiations, my own HR manager sitting across the table from me and speaking on behalf of the union. A good settlement ensued, the union and its members were happy and the management equally so, and the HR manager returned to his position, once again accountable to me!

When a corporation has managed to develop a critical mass of HR executives who can play the role of resident doctors/gardeners, and has the requisite number of the new breed of union leaders, it is in a position to transform the traditional union-management paradigm into a new paradigm, one whose prime focus is human development rather than control.

THE MODIFIED POWER MODEL

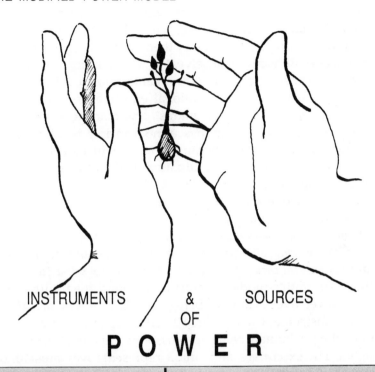

INSTRUMENTS    &    SOURCES

OF

# P O W E R

| ● CONDIGN | ● PERSONALITY |
|---|---|
| ◆ COMPENSATORY | ◆ PROPERTY |
| ■ CONDITIONED | ■ ORGANIZATION |

| ✳ HUMAN *"WILL"* | ✳ THAT WHICH PROGRAMS AND EMPOWERS AN ACORN TO BECOME AN OAK TREE, AND WHICH PROVIDES THE NATURAL THRUST FOR A HUMAN BEING TO SEEK SELF ACTUALIZATION |
|---|---|

*Figure 12.5*

# THE NEW POWER PARADIGM

From the earlier discussions, it should be fairly evident that I am talking of a situation in corporations when all those who have power vested in them—either by virtue of their positions or through their competence—will view themselves as collaborators in an open relationship whose sole focus is to enable human fulfilment in a manner consistent with organizational effectiveness. Management roles will merge with those of unions', line managers will assume staff roles and vice versa, the masculine principle will be balanced by the feminine, and the yin-yang balance will be achieved in a holistic sense. To reach such a situation, Galbraith's power model has to be modified as shown in Fig. 12.5.

I have added one more instrument and one more source. *The fourth instrument is the human will's intrinsic motivation towards self-esteem and self actualization. The fourth source is that which programmes and empowers an acorn to become an oak tree, and which provides the natural thrust for a human being to seek self-actualization.*

While Galbraith's model was primarily concerned with how to exercise power over a human being who is in *others' domain,* the additional instrument and source I have suggested is concerned with enabling a human being to blossom in his *own domain.* Line managers, HR executives and union representatives must understand that their roles are akin to those of specialist gardeners, and not puppeteers. External power has to be used in such a manner that the power intrinsic to a human being propels him or her towards self-actualization. Their role is to erect a wire mesh around a plant to protect it during its infancy, always conscious of the fact that theirs is a facilitative rather than a control function. Like the Lilly HR man working himself out of a job, they too will have to remove the wire mesh when the plant has grown big enough to stand and grow by itself.

In the next chapter, I will discuss a few other crucial areas that have to undergo radical changes in order to convert corporations into true nurseries of Human growth.

# 13

# TRANSFORMING THE GARDEN INTO A NEW REALITY: CREATION OF A TRULY EVOLVED CORPORATION

Having picked the right saplings (Chapter 10), nurtured them (Chapter 11) and also weeded and re-layed the garden to receive the developed plants (Chapter 12), we are now in a position to effect the transplantation and transform the garden into a new reality: *A truly evolved corporation that has a symbiotic relationship with all its stakeholders such as employees, suppliers, customers, shareholders and the neighbourhood, sustaining and encouraging mutual growth in a globally responsible manner.* For a youngster entering the larger arena of a corporation like Schiller's hero marching to victory, the first and most essential requirement is to identify himself with, and truly understand, the Vision that the victory is expected to realize.

## A REVIEW OF THE CONCEPT OF "ALIGNMENT"

In the earlier chapters, I have referred to the important role Vision plays in enabling a human being to voluntarily set low threshold limits and to channel his energy along the natural direction of his "will". That is quite distinctly different from what management theorists refer to as "alignment", whereby members of an organization or team "voluntarily" align their individual efforts along the direction of their organization's goal. One must be cautious while extolling the virtues of alignment of purpose in organizations. Roger Harrison qualified that alignment by itself is dangerous unless it is complemented by attunement, or 'human love expressed as, understanding, caring, nurturance and support'. Besides this correction of Harrison's, I believe there is something far more seriously wrong with the commonly understood version of "alignment". *For a corporation to be successful, its vision must get aligned with the natural direction of the "will" of self-actualizing people, one that is always focussed on universal values such as fairness, justice and integrity.*

## A FAULTY VISION WILL LEAD TO FAILURE:
## THE WRONG "ALIGNMENT"

It is true that all aligned organizations have a powerful impact on their environment as well as on their members, but the net impact will be negative on both counts when the "vision" fails to incorporate, universal values within itself. To better understand this point, let us reflect on what happened to the Nazi party and how their alignment behind Adolf Hitler's distorted "vision" led to disastrous results.

### Yet another analysis of the Nazi failure

As over a million analysts of different persuasions have by now analyzed the Nazi failure, one might wonder why another analysis is required. I am doing so with a view to interpreting undisputed historical data using the East-West motivation model, and to draw some general conclusions on how faulty Visions must inevitably lead to the failure of the very organizations they were meant for. In the early '30s, when the common man in Germany was struggling to find meaning in life, within the constraints of a ravaged economy, many were denied satiation of appetite needs at the lowest of Maslovian levels. An articulate and strong leader who appeared to have a Vision to lead them out of such a morass naturally found audiences to listen to him. In the years that followed, members of the Nazi party found that their needs were met, and desires pandered to:

- At the physiological level, priority was given to having the army well fed and provided for; debauchery at the expense of vanquished countries fed their desires;
- At the safety level, membership in the party accorded them maximum security; they in turn denied the safety of others in a typically criminal fashion: satiation of one's desires at the expense of others' appetite needs;
- At the belongingness level, those who could prove the fact that they had had "appropriate" parentage and genealogy were admitted; even if membership was based on the colour of one's skin, hair and eyes, it was belongingness of a kind. On the other hand, others who did not qualify for membership were again denied basic appetite needs ... for they were denied even the right to live. Again, criminality in the sense of satiating one's desires at the expense of others' legitimate appetite needs was the order of the party;
- At the recognition level, the SS uniform, the marching songs, status symbols in terms of power, cars, property and lackeys fed the party members with a surfeit of quotidian recognition. If one did not belong to the party, one did not qualify for satiation of appetite needs at this level, for others were literally treated as subhuman—*Untermenschen.*

In exchange for all this, all that was expected of party members was to replace their threshold springs with strings and hand them over to the fascist leader so that he could become the greatest puppeteer of them all. The puppeteer, in this case Hitler, then had all his people aligned as he wanted them ... *Along the horizontal, rather than the vertical direction of the East–West model.* In Chapter 6, I discussed what happens to individuals when they transgress reasonable threshold limits. When whole teams of people, an entire organization, or a nation collectively transgress threshold limits in such an aligned manner, disaster has to follow. Just as Adolf Hitler, his Nazi Party members and everybody associated with them, failed in realizing their distorted Vision, so too will any organization that aligns its members behind a wrong Vision fail.

## MAHATMA GANDHI: UNIVERSAL VALUES GAVE POWER TO HIS VISION

On the other hand, a historical figure who was a contemporary of Hitler, but behind whom an entire nation aligned itself offers the ideal example of a Visionary leader. I am of course referring to Mahatma Gandhi. The Mahatma's Vision was one of

- Equality—for harijans and brahmins alike;
- Universal love—including one's enemy;
- Compassion—for one's aggressor;
- A basic belief in the divinity of all beings; and
- *Dharma.*

That millions of people rose to a man to support him and became part of his unarmed band of *satyagrihis* was not surprising at all. Gandhiji's threshold limits were as low as was humanly possible and his "will", unshakeable. Behind such a man, whose Vision combined all the basic, universal values, all human beings who were not permanently twisted in their growth automatically aligned themselves . . . for they could recognize an opportunity for their own redirection—a great learning experience that would reduce their thresholds, realign them along the natural direction of their human "will", achieve psychosocially healthy growth and sublimate their energies towards achieving self-esteem and self-actualization.

## THE COMMON FAILURE OF CEOs: HIGH PERSONAL THRESHOLD LIMITS TARNISH THE IMAGE OF A PROJECTED CORPORATE VISION

While no CEO of an organization has as yet plumbed the depths that Hitler led his Nazi party into, or risen to the heights Gandhiji reached, there are many who do hold up Visions that lack a sound foundation in universal values. When organizational members understand that part of their CEO's Vision is to acquire personal wealth at the expense of the organization, to provide the means for his friends and relatives to live the good life and to derive sadistic pleasure from playing a puppeteer's role, the members are forced into making extremely awkward and difficult choices. A typical case was described by Keitaro Hasegawa in his outstanding book, *Japanese Style Management*. He cites the case of Shingeru Okada, who was the CEO of Mitsukoshi, Japan's oldest—and once most respected—departmental store.

For many years there had been persistent rumours that Okada was far more interested in assuring business profits for a woman with whom he was said to be intimate, than running Mitsukoshi profitably. There were some managers who attempted to play the dangerous role of correcting a CEO, in an attempt to realign the organization's objectives towards universally accepted values such as integrity . . . for Mitsukoshi was not a private company of Okada's but one whose owners were supposed to be shareholders. Okada forced such conscience-stricken managers to leave, one by one.

*Normally, it is not at all difficult to apply pressure on self-actualizing people to leave a corporation. All that is required is for a CEO to become ruthless enough to take away the self-actualizing man's work from him. That is exactly like taking away an oxygen cylinder from a serious heart patient, for it is required as a life supporting device. While anyone who removes an oxygen cylinder from such a patient is likely to be arrested and charged with a deliberate attempt at murder, psychosocial crimes of the nature described are too difficult to prove, or nail down on anyone, especially a powerful CEO.*

All the while that Okada was engaged thus, the major shareholders of Mitsukoshi never even once intervened, or hinted that Okada himself should be removed. A long time lapsed before Okada was eventually dismissed by a unanimous vote of the 16 directors at a board meeting. Okada was then arrested on suspicion of breach of trust and embezzlement. He was charged with having caused losses of about $ 7.8 million to Mitsukoshi.

## SIMILAR CASES OF CEO MISBEHAVIOUR ARE NOT UNCOMMON ELSEWHERE

Barring the final act, when the directors and shareholders bestirred themselves to take corrective action, the rest of this true story must sound familiar to corporate executives across the globe. Let us look into why this happens ever so often in the Corporate world, including in old, established organizations like Mitsukoshi. The fact that an organization has lasted many years is itself normally proof that the entrepreneur who had started the organization must have been one who had a Vision that could inspire and align people along the natural direction of self-actualizers. Normally, with the passing of time, when the founder-entrepreneur either withdraws himself or dies, others who have never had to struggle as much, or lower their threshold limits to the bare minimum appetite levels, move up the organization. The most skilled puppeteer among them, using political and other manoeuvres, acquires power; and to further consolidate his power, eliminates all those who have a strong "will".

## A PUPPETEER USES THE EASTERN CONCEPT OF "HARMONY" TO ELIMINATE CONSCIENTIOUS OBJECTORS: IN INDIA TOO

By definition, a puppeteer cannot coexist with those who are not ready to let him take complete control of their threshold strings. Those who retain threshold springs have to be eliminated from the scene altogether. Gradually, organizations reach a state when no one with a strong "will" remains. This ought to lead to disaster, and it does. How soon such a disaster takes place is a function of several factors, including the culture of the society in which the organization exists. In Japan, and India too, where confrontation is not appreciated, and apparent harmony has to be projected despite real discord among people, those who talk against authority, or "rock the boat" do not receive any support or sympathy. A puppeteer in control is usually acutely aware of this aspect of his culture, and that is very often their life insurance policy. By painting those who oppose him as members of a new generation who have no respect for tradition and harmony, he gains support from the few directors who may be inclined to ask questions. He gains time this way.

Meanwhile, on the strength of the organization's past reputation, and the unfortunate silencing of those who spotted the early warning signals, new recruits join, suppliers continue to supply, and customers continue to buy the organization's products and services. However, as explained in Chapter 4, an organization that has the capacity to retain only those who have no "will" left in them, will find a rapid deterioration in the quality of its products and services. Puppeteers and their puppets cannot survive in a competitive environment for too long as customers will move their clientele to whosoever is able to guarantee a better supply of quality goods and services. Then, the financial performance of the organization will begin to show through, and shareholders will begin to ask questions. Even then, many organizational chieftains will not learn. Okada, for example, is alleged to have used the so-called *sokaiya* (minority shareholders who disrupt meetings for their own ends) to suppress the activity of major shareholders who were opposed to him. Within six months of that attempt, Okada had been ousted from power.

## MONOPOLISTIC CONDITIONS AND PROTECTED MARKETS BREED SUCH CEOs, AND ORGANIZATIONS DECAY AND DIE, LIKE THE OLD, ADYAR BANYAN TREE

In India, where monopolistic conditions and low levels of competition were the order of the day, aided and abetted by earlier governments' protectionist policies that kept international players out of the country, such organizations have continued to survive, and even apparently flourish for many many years. The Okada look-alikes have continued in their positions of unchecked and supreme power for decades. With the introduction of the new policies of the government, and opening of the country to international competition, it is hoped that such chieftains will be eventually found out. But for many organizations, and their people, the rot that has set in is so deep that it may be too late for corrective action. The tree may have grown too crooked and old, and be beyond salvage. A vivid example that comes to one's mind is the grand old Adyar Banyan tree at the Theosophical Society in Madras. The tree was said to be the oldest surviving one of its kind. For centuries, people from all over the world have come to see the grand old tree.

Its root structure extended to an area that was truly staggering. A powerful storm ended the life of the tree eventually, in 1989. For several days, people came to see and mourn over the death of the grand old tree.

As one who had seen it and played under and around it as a child, I too went to see it. The tree was lying on its side, its trunk broken completely. There was nothing inside the trunk. The sap had been eaten out completely. There were only termites inside. All around the dead tree were its offshoots that had independently taken root, and survived.

## CORPORATE VISION MUST ALIGN ITSELF TO THE "WILL" OF SELF-ACTUALIZERS IN THEIR ORGANIZATION: NOT VICE VERSA

*An essential point I am seeking to make is that it is wrong to believe that a corporate management should attempt to "align"its members along the direction of the corporation's Vision. Rather, a corporation should evolve a Vision that is truly of a nature that is aligned to the natural "alignment" of self-actualizing people. When a corporation achieves that, and has the wherewithal to empower human beings to individually and collectively grow up in a psychosocially healthy manner, true "quality" will result from the efforts of that corporation. Conversely, corporations that operate on the basis of a tarnished, false Vision will meet the same fate as Hitler's Nazis, however aligned their puppet force be at the height of their temporary power.*

In all the examples of successful Vision statements, including the several referred to earlier in the book—Mahatma Gandhi, Moolgaokar in TELCO, John Kennedy at the NASA, King Henry in the field of Agincourt and Steve Jobs at Apple—this common feature will be observed. The leader articulated a Vision he was fully convinced about, and which called for a reaffirmation of faith in basic, universal values and beliefs. What such leaders have done is to prove that their Vision drew its energy and power from universal values that the best among them cherished and upheld. Leaders have to get their best people to willingly accept the common goal, and the only way to do so is to convince them that the "alignment" of such a goal is towards universal values. As the "will" of the best among men are naturally aligned towards universal values, they will then accept that working towards achievement of the common goal will be in tune with their personal journeys. Others, the "followers" who constitute the majority of people, will then follow the trend setters and align themselves with them.

## GREAT MIGRATIONS BEGAN WITH A TRAIL BLAZING ENTREPRENEUR, FOLLOWED BY OTHERS WHO ALIGNED THEMSELVES ALONG HIS PATH

We can liken this to the way in which successful migrations have taken place in history. The best among men decide to blaze a new trail, find opportunities for a new way of life, and live it. News of this spreads slowly at first for there are very few "hangers on" in the early stages of such developments. Then, the first lots of followers decide to test out the news. Their confirmation of it starts a wave of followers. People with organizing ability move in, advertise their skills for arranging group movements *in the path of and towards the goal already achieved by the trail blazers,* and the followers sign up. The point to observe in this example is the fact that an organized movement of people succeeds only when the direction of their group's movement is in line with what is acceptable to the self-actualizers in the community.

Let me now extend this to describe how a similar exercise is carried out in organizations that have passed the first phase of the problem in the sense that they have a leader whose Vision is in consonance with basic universal values. In such an organization, those who have reached adulthood with a strong intrinsic motivation for seeking mastery over a specific arena of work will immediately start flowering. They only require the input of knowledge and skills to augment their natural desire for seeking perfection. By placing them under the care of a mentor who will see them through their *aupadeshika* phase, they will be helped to reach the state of *aharya.* Master craftsmen who derive enjoyment from improving machine productivity and longevity, salesmen who are enormously excited when they encounter a difficult customer, secretaries whose self-set standard for information retrieval time is 30 seconds and the Laxmans of the world will abound and thrive everywhere. But such people are those whose earlier years have allowed them to reach adulthood with strong intrinsic motivation.

They constitute a very small percentage of the population in any corporation.

## MANY HUMAN BEINGS REQUIRE HELP FOR REALIGNMENT, LIKE A CROOKED PLANT THAT NEEDS A STRAIGHTENING STICK

The rest of us require the help of an external Vision to tighten our threshold springs, set low threshold limits and let our energies flow up towards seeking self-esteem. In doing so, and provided the Vision is a function of universal values and beliefs, we get suffused with an inner glow rather like the experience of listening to a Beethoven symphony or viewing a Rodin masterpiece. When such experiences are repeated at a fairly frequent rate, there is a good chance that we will develop the ability to sustain inner Visions that will drive us thereafter.

### The case of a young boy in unconscious search of a vision

I remember the case of a young boy who was heavily into drugs, whose father had come to me for help. The boy was the youngest of six children. The other five were well settled, and appeared to be driven by a compelling need for perfection in what they were doing. The father was a highly evolved human being, a mystic, spiritual person. Unfortunately, neither he nor his other children could help the baby of the family find a way out of his state. When the boy came to see me at my office, I had to keep him waiting for a few minutes. When I went out to call for him, I found him fast asleep. It took some time to wake him up. His eyes were bloodshot and out of focus. His emaciated appearance, wild hair, torn jeans and a pronounced hunch merely added to his overall statement on life: 'Nothing seems to make sense. I might as well get enjoyment out of smoking pot'.

Employing a mixture of counselling, insults, browbeating and emotional blackmail, I got him to eventually start talking coherently about his career plans. He had an amazingly creative mind, sharp wit, easy humour and a disarming smile. With all the pampering he had received as the youngest child in a large family, he had never had a problem of satisfying his needs. With resultant high threshold limits, loose threshold springs and a total lack of intrinsic motivation for achieving anything—or so he believed at that time - he was an obvious prey to any influence that could titillate his fancy. Drug peddlers operating near the college gate had got to him and he was almost lost. My diagnosis was that, more than anything else, he required a personal Vision to galvanize his intrinsic motivational energy.

## THE EFFECT OF A VISIONARY BOSS ON THE YOUNG MAN

Through several conversations, and careful orchestration of third party influence by his family, the boy was slowly helped to focus on an area of activity that could challenge his natural strengths. As he grew from boyhood into a young man, he found advertising to be of interest to him. We helped him by getting him to read some of the great pioneers in the field. David Ogilvy and Marshall McCluhan were thrust on him. Gradually he got interested in the emerging field of advertising as a possible arena for starting his career in. But he was far from excited by the field. At this stage, the boy got lucky. He was offered a job by a visionary advertising man who had great ideas about transforming the very focus in Indian Advertising. The agency was also involved in innovative uses of advertising skills for bringing about sociopolitical change, and the young man was sucked into the excitement of it all. Very soon, he was convinced that advertising was indeed the field for him. His energies were focussed on mastering the area, and he began to set high standards of excellence for himself.

In under ten years, the transformation in the young man was complete:

- He had become a voluntary worker against drug abuse;
- He was rated as an outstanding advertising man;
- His natural charm and good humour had made him a much liked and popular person;
- His father had died a contented man  for his favourite young son was well and was on his way to actualizing his amazing potential;
- He was a happily married family man with a perfect sense of balance about his life.

Even such people represent a small minority in that they manage to find a personal Vision quite early in their working career.

## ORGANIZATIONS HAVE TO DESIGN SYSTEMS THAT WILL TAP THE ENERGY RELEASED BY INDIVIDUALS WHEN THEY ARE SUBLIMATING

The third and the largest category of people never really manage to reach a stage when they can be independently on their own. They require constant help and reminders to pull back their threshold limits and strive for mastery of intermittent tasks and smaller goals. Total quality management programmes, quality circles, task forces, monthly targets, cost reduction exercises and various other activities of corporations are *basically geared to providing the means for the vast majority to link in their personal alignment to immediate tasks on hand. Such people require the larger Vision to be reinterpreted in terms of easily understandable short-term goals.* Further, within the limits of such shorter time spans and smaller zones of influence, they need to be given the freedom to express themselves. As they do so, and their interest is held by such specific goals, they achieve a temporary ability to reduce threshold limits and redirect, or sublimate, their energy towards the accomplishment of a task that intrinsically excites them.

*This energy, which gets released when individual human beings are sublimating, is the ever changing, transient energy reservoir that good, participative organizational systems seek to tap. Just as energy is released by electrons when they move from one energy state into another, so also is energy released when a human being pulls back threshold limits at one level and moves up to another need level. In Chapter 5, I referred to this as the "heroic act", a far happier term to use than the prosaic "energy release".*

## ACTIVATING A GOOD VISION: THE JAPANESE CEO LEADS THE WAY

For an organization and its members to release enormous energy through joint acts of heroism its CEO must lead the way. Earlier in the Chapter, I spoke of what ought not to be done, using an example of a Japanese CEO. To make amends, and redress the balance, let me highlight some outstanding features of Japanese CEOs. It is customary for Japanese CEOs to personally guarantee the loans made to their corporations. Among the first duties of a newly appointed president is to affix his seal to such personal *guarantees*. Keitaro Hasegawa, in his *Japanese Style Management*, confirms that while this is not a legal requirement, it is a widely followed common practice. In the event of bankruptcy, the president will forfeit all his private assets to the creditors of the company.

## REDUCING THRESHOLD LIMITS BY CEOs, A NECESSARY FIRST STEP

Hasegawa cites the case of the President of Kojin as an example. When Kojin went bankrupt, the largest company to do so since the war, the personal guarantee system was invoked. The President's palatial residence in Denenchofu, one of the most luxurious residential areas in Tokyo, was seized by the company creditors.

Thus, while the President and the top management admittedly earn more than the common employee, when their corporations face seriously adverse conditions that call for drastic remedial measures, they are expected to first slash their threshold limits. The common employee will be asked to take a pay cut only as a last resort, after the top management and the senior management have first cut their own salaries drastically, followed next by the slashing of dividend payment to shareholders. In short, the leader demonstrates by example that when it comes to cutting down threshold limits, he will lead the way himself.

## CONVERTING ORGANIZATIONAL CRISIS INTO AN OPPORTUNITY FOR GROUP SUBLIMATION

Another closely related feature unique to Japanese top management is the manner in which they attempt to convert adverse circumstances into opportunities for group sublimation. They have shown that it works wonders even when transplanted in a country like the USA, where custom allows top management to keep drawing their million-dollar salaries even while laying off staff, ostensibly with a view to coping with business downturns. A well-documented case talks of how two companies in the beleaguered Steel industry in the USA turned the corner by using typically Japanese practices.

Now, American steel makers have been the butt of corporate jokes for quite some time. A typical anecdote talks of a steel tycoon who was denied entry into Heaven because of the large numbers of people he had laid off. He was therefore sent down to the other place whose entry restrictions were lighter. However, he had to be sent away from there also for, within a very short time, he had begun to shut down furnaces almost by habit. Yet, the *London Economist* (April 2, 1982) cited how two American steel companies had managed to stay solvent, and record profits by adopting Japanese style management practices.

## Japanese style management succeeds in US steel industry

In 1982, when 18 major US steel companies recorded a combined loss of $3.2 billion, the two mini companies, Chaparral Steel and Nucor Corporation recorded profits. Even though Nucor's profits fell from previous year's $34.7 million to $22.2 million while its sales reduced from $545 million to $486 million, the fact is that it stayed profitable. What the Nucor management had done was this:

First, their top management cut down their own salaries by 50%, then the administrative officials responsible for the production division cut their salaries by 35 to 40%, and only then was the income of the hourly staff cut down by 20 to 25%. No one was retrenched, as the entire team converted the adverse situation into a great learning experience for the entire community. That they collectively sublimated their energies towards producing high-quality products at reduced costs, and developed a sense of team worth and intimacy is an obvious conclusion which is reconfirmed by what happened to market shares. In the market for small steel products in California, Japanese used to account for as much as 50% share. That was the case till Chaparral and Nucor decided to eat into the Japanese market share by using their management methods. In 1982, thanks to the success of these two companies, the Japanese share in the market fell to a mere 10 %.

## Harrison Owen's OT thesis supports the group sublimation theory

The American management consultant and author, Harrison Owen has been emphasizing for some years that true organization transformation can take place only when members of an organization go through a joint crisis situation and come out of it. Such organizations take up new structures and forms, with new rites and rituals built around their transformational experience. His classic, *SPIRIT: Transformation and Development in Organizations* is a book that all students and practitioners of management must read. By an odd coincidence, Harrison and I had been invited to address the same audience in Mexico some years ago. I had spoken about the East-West model and how the greatest learning experience almost always arose from traumatic experiences. Immediately after me was Harrison, speaking about how organizational transformation was most effective when organizational members had jointly gone through crises. Naturally, we had the "Ah Ha" experience listening to each other. Comparing notes later, we realized how similar individual and organizational journeys were. It did not surprise us that we had interpreted this passage from Richard Bach's *Illusions* differently, he from an organizational point of view and I, from an individual's:

*What a caterpillar calls the end of the world,*
*The master calls, a butterfly*

## LAYING THE FOUNDATION FOR THE THRUST TOWARDS SELF-ESTEEM

Yet another role that a CEO must play is the way he institutionalizes systems that will encourage and support employee thrusts for achieving self-esteem in their work. In Japan, this is very evident probably because a large number of employees are in a position to seek mastery over their work. Through a combination of life-time employment practices, which guarantee security and belongingness, and providing group and individual recognition carefully, the average Japanese employee is made to feel comfortably satiated at his appetite need levels. Thus many of them are ready and willing to spend their time and energy seeking pride in their work and move beyond "recognition by others" to "self-esteem".

## HOW JAPANESE WORKMEN HAPPILY TRIPLED PRODUCTIVITY

It is customary for a Japanese workman to treat instruction

manuals of new machines as mere starting points, and seek original ways of improving their productivity. Hasegawa cites what happened at the Nagoya Steelworks of Nippon Steel as a typical example. Its hot strip mill commenced operation in 1963, with a life-time expectancy of 20 years during which time it was expected to produce 30 million tonnes of steel. By 1986, it had already produced 50 million tonnes because of innovative improvements, with a further 50 million to come. This threefold increase in the potential capacity of a mill was almost entirely due to innovative risk-taking by workmen assigned to the mill, with active encouragement and support by their plant manager. The latter's role is crucial too, for he has to find ways of not only financing his men's requests for modification but also providing technological support whenever required. His failure to do so will lead to the employees losing trust in his leadership.

## THERE ARE STEPS TO BE TAKEN BEFORE REACHING SUCH A STAGE

Before employees reach such a stage, it is essential that corporations take care to ensure, as in Japan, that the lower needs are adequately satisfied. Properly designed working facilities and humane timings and conditions of work, supported by adequate payment systems will ensure satiation of appetite needs at the physiological level. By guaranteeing continuity of employment and fair treatment, and a system of adequate safeguards against unjust punishment, safety needs can be met. A good manager who understands group behaviour and knows how to develop team spirit will make the employee feel that he "belongs". Empathetic treatment of employees' feelings, genuine concern when he is faced with problems and extending a helping hand when needed will further enhance that feeling of belongingness. Enough and more has been written about these aspects of management, and I do not have to say anything more. Where employers have normally failed is in the manner in which recognition programmes are designed and run. Those who went in for incentive programmes have burnt their fingers, for obvious reasons. Pure extrinsic motivation always has a debilitating effect on intrinsic motivation, and eventually replaces it altogether, with resultant reduction in quality of work. That was proved in Chapter 4.

# RECOGNITION PROGRAMMES MUST CONFORM TO RAJASEKHARA'S *AUPADESHIKA* STATE

The ideal recognition programmes are those that adhere to Rajasekhara's prescription of *aupadeshika*. People who matter must openly recognize merit and perfection when they see it, and encourage the performer to proceed beyond towards self-esteem. The attitude of recognition must be that of a respected teacher to a student who is passing out with First class honours. The latter is aware of his own efforts, is quietly confident of reaching beyond, and is merely seeking the teacher's affectionate blessings and recognition that his self-assessment is correct.

Corporations that have excellent programmes designed along these lines stand out, for they will have a large number of people seeking mastery in their work. An outstanding example is a Far Eastern hotel chain, the Mandarin Oriental. For the past two decades, in almost every listing of the top hotels of the world, the pride of place has been reserved for the Mandarin Hotel in Hong Kong and the Oriental Hotel in Bangkok. Even though the majority of frontline staff in these two hotels are local people who can at best speak halting English, the levels of service they reach are outstanding. Let me cite an example:

# REACHING OUT TOWARDS EXCELLENCE: THE MANDARIN HOTEL EXPERIENCE

After a week's stay at the Mandarin, I had checked out around noon one day. Some hours later, after having attended to unscheduled work elsewhere in Hong Kong, I reached the airport on my own. As I was entering the airport with my luggage trolley, a Mandarin employee suddenly materialized and addressed me: " Excuse me, are you Mr Mahesh, who was our Guest the past week?" I was startled, for I had not expected anyone there, let alone be identified in a crowded place like the Hong Kong airport. He went on, " Soon after you left, a message arrived for you. Could I take you to a telephone and put you in touch with our concierge?" He quietly took hold of the luggage trolley, and led me to a telephone. The concierge was on the line, reading out the fax message to me in no time at all.

I then asked the Mandarin employee how he had known that I

was going to be arriving at the airport at that time, and how he had recognized me. His answer throws a light on what makes Mandarin such a world class hotel:

'While you were checking out, the cashier had been speaking to you. On learning that you were proceeding to Bangkok, he had asked if you would like a room at the Oriental. You had said you were already booked there but would appreciate his confirming your arrival as you were catching a late evening flight. He had asked the concierge to send that message. When the concierge had received another message for you, he remembered that you were on a late flight out of Hong Kong and had called me to locate you . . . and he had described to me how you looked'

In most hotels, messages do not even reach guests who are staying in it. When irate guests scream about having missed important business engagements because some message counter employee had either not taken a message properly, or failed to reach it to him where he had said he would be, all they get normally is a bland,"Sorree . . . but you should have told the message counter that you were expecting an important message". As against that, Mandarin, in their own search for ways to surprise guests with outstanding service, had converted a casual conversation into useful information and delivered a late message in an immaculate fashion.

## A UNIQUE RECOGNITION PROGRAMME THAT WORKS

What supports and encourages such employee thrust for superlative service is the way in which their "Recognition system" works. Every month, each departmental head nominates two employees from his department who are considered to have delivered outstanding service to guests. Such nominations are circulated to all departmental heads, with details of what each of the nominated employees had done. On the first of every month, the General Manager and his departmental heads discuss the merits and demerits of each nomination and reach a consensus on the most outstanding cases, ranging from five to ten a month. A notice is then put up for all to see, proclaiming the "Employees of the month" with their photographs and details of the exact service delivered. The General Manager and the "employees of the month" have a ceremonious lunch in the cafeteria, in front of all the employees. The notice remains for a full month till the next month's list goes up.

## THE MANDARIN DIFFERENCE IS THAT IT ENCOURAGES TRUE UPWARD GROWTH

While most corporations do have recognition programmes, what sets the Mandarin system apart is the way in which they have made the recognition a much sought-after award. Its secret is not the dollars they pay, for that is trivial. It is the manner of public recognition, and the careful selection process that guarantees high value in the perception of all employees. Besides, by disclosing what specific service has been considered to be worthy of such merit, the management communicates in unambiguous terms what it values most. Rather than reducing the recognition programme to a system of extrinsic motivation, Mandarin uses it to highlight how employees seeking perfection in their jobs manage to deliver quality. The rewards are almost as if the management is acknowledging the fact that the chosen ones have already reached their "own domain".

## REMOVING "CROOKED" GROWTH THROUGH ACTIVE PARTICIPATION IN WORK

Let me now turn to some general preconditions for a corporation to be called a true nursery for human growth. What we have discussed so far is primarily directed at helping a nearly fully evolved person to stay in his "own domain", even while engaging himself in an activity that is useful and aligned to the purpose of the organization. As I had stated earlier, such people are a small minority. The rest of us spend our daily lives going up and down the hierarchy of needs, ever so often tempted to add to our desires, unhappy when thwarted in our attempts to satiate expanding desires, and devoid of any excitement in our daily activity. For such of us, the first and most essential ingredient to pull us out of such "crookedness" is active participation in our work, both mental and physical.

## THE SIMPLE SECRET BEHIND SUCCESSFUL QUALITY PROGRAMMES IS THAT EMPLOYEE PARTICIPATION RELEASES "SUBLIMATION" ENERGY

In all corporations that have successful quality assurance practices, whether they term it quality circles, total quality management, small group activity or as Jack Welch of GE terms it, "work out", the underlying principle is to trust that the employee closest to any activity is the best equipped person to suggest ways and means of improving quality and productivity, besides cutting down costs and wasteful actions. When employees who are normally used to receiving instructions suddenly find that their opinion is being sought, they will reorient their energy. Instead of frittering it away on seeking satisfaction of "desires", they will lower threshold limits, and sublimate their energy towards achieving perfection in the arena of work that their superiors have suddenly decided to share responsibility for.

When such employees feel justly treated insofar as satisfaction of their appetite needs is concerned, and are further encouraged to seek perfection in their sphere of activity, there will be hundreds of thousands of innovative ideas that will flow up the hierarchy. The management will then have to merely set up a system to speedily assess the ideas so generated, decide what can be implemented and when, and reply to all, irrespective of their implementation potential.

## "*RINGI*", THE TRADITIONAL BOTTOM-UP COMMUNICATION SYSTEM IN JAPAN PRECEDED THE INDUSTRIAL REVOLUTION

In Japan, there has been a tradition of taking policy decisions from the bottom up rather than top down. It is known as the *ringi* system, the word standing for "requesting a decision". Some claim that this has existed from long before the industrial revolution had touched Japan. Hasegawa believes it existed during the Tokugawa period in the 17th century, when government officials in farflung locations could submit a *ringi* through proper channels on any subject they deemed important. Their ringi would pass through various levels of the hierarchy, each making his comment and applying his seal, before it eventually reached Edo, as Tokyo was then called. Those concerned would study it, and with their comments, read it to the Shogun for his final approval. Then, it would be returned exactly through the same channel it had come up, till it finally reached the official who had originally submitted it.

Despite the then autocratic way of life, the Japanese had even then mastered the art of participation where it really mattered. In modern-day corporations, with advanced telecommunication methods, the speed of reaction to a ringi is naturally that much faster. However, they still practise the age-old method of appropriate routing through proper channels so that everyone gets involved.

As the ringi is taken so seriously, the originator of a ringi takes great care before submitting one. He holds unofficial discussions, known as *nemawashi* (literally, digging around the roots before transplantation) with all concerned people before putting up a ringi. Thus, even before a ringi begins its long journey up the hierarchy, it has received the tacit approval of those who will be affected by it, if and when it is approved for implementation.

## CREATION OF THE FIELD HANDS TO PLAY OUT THE LAST ACT OF THE TRANSFORMATION: THE FLOWERING OF THE GARDEN

A gardener may have a master plan of what his garden should look like eventually (his Vision). He may have taken care to hand-pick the saplings, nurture them, re-lay the garden, and be an ideal role model himself in the manner of his deportment, knowledge, skills, interest and commitment for achieving perfection. Yet, he could be left with a miserable garden at the end of it all, if he fails to equip himself with one vital resource, namely a band of fieldhands who are not only fully in tune with his Vision for the garden but also skilled in ensuring that the plants they are in charge of receive proper care all the time. In the organizational context, that means a cadre of effective line managers in farflung locations who understand the corporate Vision, and are excited by and in tune with it. In the selection, development and empowerment of this crucial cadre of people, there are different approaches and practices. I will describe an effective way we had evolved in the Taj Group of Hotels.

## A SIX-MONTH PROCESS FOR CREATING TRANSFORMATIONAL LEADERS

Every year, the senior management of the group identified about 30 to 35 outstanding young managers in their early thirties who were deemed to have the potential to become senior managers. The top management then went through the list, approved the selection and had them released to go through a six month leadership development workshop. I will describe the workshop in detail, and through it, elaborate on what organizations ought to do so that this final act in the drama is played out successfully.

The workshop was conducted in three separate phases, each consisting of a week of theoretical and experiential inputs followed by about six to seven weeks of practical implementation. While the participants were brought together in one place for the week of inputs, they were sent back to their actual place of work for the duration of the implementation period.

### First, they learnt individual skills and put them into practice

The first phase focussed on the development of individual skills. During the implementation period of the first phase, they were expected to show marked improvement in their ability to

- Effectively listen and respond to, as well as counsel subordinates (for they were taught how to become competent "barefoot counsellors");
- Be more sensitive to other human beings (as part of the implementation phase, they were asked to visit the homes of five of their subordinates, including two who had been identified by them as "difficult");
- Better evaluate subordinates' needs in terms of direction and support and provide the right leadership behaviour and inputs to help them move towards peak performance (thus demonstrating that they had internalized Kenneth Blanchard's superb model of "situational leadership");
- Better organize their time and themselves (following their exposure to time management concepts);
- Ensure discipline in a fair and firm, albeit empathetic manner (for which they were taught the substantive content of this book's Chapter 12); and
- Maintain physical fitness (for the first week, as in the following phases, had a standard component of early morning exercises and yoga).

To enable them to show marked improvement in all these areas without upsetting others through their overenthusiastic behaviour,

244

they had been given a half-day preparation exercise to plan their reentry. Among other things, they were taught not to announce grand plans for the change that they were going to champion. Rather, they were made to realize that the best way to introduce change and gain acceptance for it was to go about the implementation quietly and sensitively, letting their positive actions speak for themselves.

### Then they learnt and practised group facilitation skills

The second phase of the workshop was designed around the need for such potential leaders to develop group skills, an essential ingredient for anyone wishing to transform a collection of individuals at varying stages of development into a high performance team. By the end of the implementation phase of the second phase, they were to demonstrate their new-found strengths to:

- Tap the strengths of each of their subordinates, and get their full contribution at work (for which they had been sensitized through "style flex" and other approaches for identifying different behaviour patterns);
- Conduct participative workshops using techniques such as brainstorming, and to lead focussed discussions, briefings and meetings;
- Work with their teams in identifying priorities for action, and build consensus, harmony and commitment among team members;
- Generate enthusiasm, pride and creativity in work groups;
- Build bridges and healthy interphase relationships between their teams and their internal and external customers; and
- Understand, appreciate, uphold and integrate with the Corporation's culture.

During the implementation period of this phase, an enormous amount of energy was released in various parts of the group. An Executive Chef of a large hotel managed to hold participative brainstorming sessions with all 150 of his staff, section by section. Over a thousand workable ideas "flowed up", were analyzed and a substantial number of them implemented. While food cost crashed, both internal and external customer feedback was extremely enthusiastic and positive on all aspects of product and service quality. Likewise, others began to flex their muscles, and visible effects of a transformation were noticed everywhere.

### The line manager as a "trustee" for human growth: Resolution of Erikson's seventh crisis

An important effect of these two phases of the workshop was on the participants' attitude to their own role vis-a-vis their subordinates. They began to see themselves as *trustees* vested with the responsibility for their subordinates' growth. They had unconsciously resolved the seventh of Erikson's crises, that of *generativity v.self-absorption*. Generativity is the natural impulse of a human being to establish and guide the next generation, an impulse that all species must have in order to transfer the accumulated knowledge and skills of one generation to another. In doing so, one relearns how the Maslovian third level of Belongingness Need actually gets satisfied. It is not met by demanding love from others, but by the giving of oneself to others. As these line managers developed confidence in themselves to stand in front of audiences, present their thoughts cogently, and facilitate others' development, their own sense of self-worth improved. Their popularity ratings improved even as they became more approachable and open in their relationship with others. They gradually became the new locus for change.

### The last phase: Handing over the baton to the youngsters

The third phase of the workshop consisted almost entirely of interaction with the top management. The new change agents were being literally handed over the baton for the next leg of the race. As they listened to corporate plans and were taken into confidence by the top management, there developed in them a sense of responsibility for becoming torch-bearers of the future. At the same time, a sense of "intimacy" developed too, as they felt close to, and part of, the very core of the organization.

This phase ended with a one-day retreat, when they went through an intense life-planning exercise. Each one prepared for himself an agenda for action, one that included all aspects of one's life.

# FIELD GENERALS WITH THE REQUISITE SKILL TO SOLVE THE "ANTINOMY" PROBLEM BETWEEN ORDER AND FREEDOM

By holding such intense workshops each year, for accelerated development of a new generation of leadership, one of our essential objectives was to create field generals who were not only aware of and committed to the overall corporate Vision and strategy but also equipped with the skills to convert them into reality by thinking and acting independently wherever their postings might be. A second objective was to create a cadre of people who could sensitively manage an essential problem of all organizations, that of "antinomy" of order and freedom. There is no better explanation of this problem than that put forward by E F Schumacher, in his *Small is Beautiful*. Towards the end of his book, Schumacher concludes:

All real human problems arise from the antinomy of order and freedom. Antinomy means a contradiction between two laws; a conflict of authority; opposition between laws or principles that appear to be founded equally in reason.

Excellent! This is real life, full of antinomies and bigger than logic. Without order, planning, predictability, central control, accountancy, instructions to the underlings, obedience, discipline—without these, nothing fruitful can happen, because everything disintegrates. And yet—without the magnanimity of disorder, the happy abandon,. the entrepreneurship venturing into the unknown and incalculable, without the risk and the gamble, the creative imagination rushing in where bureaucratic angels fear to tread—without this, life is a mockery and disgrace.

The centre can easily look after order; it is not so easy to look after freedom and creativity. The centre has the power to establish order, but no amount of power evokes the creative contribution. How, then, can top management at the centre work for progress and innovation? Assuming that it knows what ought to be done: how can the management get it done throughout the organization?"

## The Taj answer to E F Schumacher's question on antinomy was the leadership development workshop

Our answer to Schumacher's question was the leadership work-shop. An organization must develop, on a continuing basis, a cadre of young managers who understand and identify themselves with the corporate Vision and strategy, and who are then able to managerially provide the freedom required by the implementors of the Vision to creatively look at the strategy, evolve local plans with happy abandon, and risk their reputation in doing so. In whatever form a corporation does this, such a result must be achieved if it is going to become one of the great corporations of the world. In such a corporation, young entrants who come in like Schiller's heroes will find the right conditions for growing towards actualization of their immense potential.

## THE IDEAL PROFILE OF AN EVOLVED CORPORATION

When a corporation reaches such an evolved state, and sustains itself there for an appreciable length of time, it will begin to seem that the corporation itself has taken a life of its own. Such a corporation will be easily recognized for

- Its collective "will" will be very clearly aligned with basic universal values;
- It will be sensitive in the way it interacts with its physical environment: it will be ecologically sound in its practices, and it would be substantially adding to, rather than taking away from, nature;
- It would protect its societal and physical environment by generating and investing in adequate resources for the same;
- It would be sensitively aware and responsibly conscious of its role as a societal member and take actions that are recognizable as those of an ideal global citizen, with voluntarily set social audit programmes;
- It would offer scope for the development of its employees, suppliers and other stakeholders, recognize the meritorious among them and encourage full human growth among all; to facilitate this, its structure will be flat, and organizational pyramid philosophically inverted (to use Blanchard's phraseology) such that frontline employees feel they are on top, serving and supporting the customers, while the skeletal management are at the bottom, serving their internal customers. . . their people;

- It will have a critical mass of stakeholders whose time and energy is spent on reaching and sustaining mastery over their respective fields of endeavour, which fact will be borne out by the sheer quality of its products and services; and finally,
- Its very existence will significantly add to human, societal and global development with its current and former stakeholders assuming roles as the focus for global transformation.

## THE BASIS FOR OPTIMISM

Throughout this book, I have argued that human beings are intrinsically motivated to reach, or reveal, their inherent nature of Perfection. That it is the powerful new organism of the twentieth century, the Corporation, which is going to invest its power and wealth to enable human beings to actually reach such perfection, is my prediction. While it might sound a wild prediction at first glance, considering the infamy and dishonour that the 20th century corporations have brought upon themselves for over 90 years now, I believe it is not as wild as it may seem at first. To share my optimism with you, I have to talk about the impact and spreading of what Willis Harman has termed, the "second Copernican revolution".

# 14

# CONCLUSION: CORPORATE ROLE IN THE SECOND COPERNICAN REVOLUTION

By the early part of the 16th century, Nicolaus Copernicus had come to the conclusion that the earth was not the centre of the universe. His investigations into the mathematical intricacies of astronomy had led him to believe that the earth went around the sun. This was totally contradictory to the then prevailing Ptolemic theoretical system that held the earth to be the centre of the universe. For fourteen centuries, both religious bodies as well as schools of astronomy had supported each other in perpetuating the belief system which held that the celestial bodies were part of a spherical firmament revolving around the earth, abode of God's chosen creation, Man.

After three decades of thorough investigation, Copernicus published his thesis, On the Revolution of the Celestial Spheres in the year of his death, 1543. A second edition was printed in 1566. By 1600, Copernicus's book was well distributed throughout the

Western world. While a very small number of scientists were convinced that the Copernican explanation was valid, the rest of the world treated it as "scientific heresy".

Those who dared to voice their support for the heresy were hounded, and some were burnt at the stake. Giordano Bruno was the most celebrated of such heretics. Accused of heresy, he had to flee from his Dominican convent at Naples and roam all over Europe. On his return to Italy in 1592, he was arrested by the Inquisition. After seven years in prison, he was burnt at the stake on February 17, 1600 . . . almost symbolizing a century of resistance by the orthodoxy to the spread of the Copernican revolution.

It was to take another century, and the combined genius of Galileo, Kepler and Newton, to convince humanity that, far from being a scientific heresy, the Copernican explanation was indeed the harbinger of a fundamental paradigm shift in the very belief system by which humanity would live and prosper or perish. By 1700, the Copernican revolution had pervaded almost all aspects of human thought. Knowledge was no longer accepted to be the sacrosanct, undisputed privilege of a few. It was to be thrown open to public enquiry, challenged, verified by objective criteria that were to satisfy logical rigour, and validated beyond doubt by scientific analysis and testing before being accepted.

Citing the Copernican revolution in human thought, and the time and agony that accompanied its translation into a common belief system, Willis Harman in 1988 asked, "Suppose a similar transformation were underway today—would we recognize the signs?" He further wondered how we would know whether the transformation was of a minor nature, or of such magnitude as the Copernican revolution. In his study on the subject, *The Transformations of Man*, Lewis Mumford observed that all major transformations of man have "rested on a new metaphysical and ideological base; or rather, upon deeper stirrings and intuitions whose rationalized expression takes the form of a new picture of the cosmos and the nature of man." It is only when people begin to question and change their basic assumptions about "who we are, what kind of universe we are in, and what is ultimately important to us" that we can recognize that a major, new transformation is underway.

## THE "NEW HERESY": CONSCIOUSNESS IS A CAUSAL REALITY

Willis Harman, in his *Global Mind Change*, argues that such a transformation is indeed underway, and that the second Copernican revolution is upon us already. *Central to this "new heresy" is the belief that man's consciousness is a causal reality which not only binds all living organisms but also provides the source of directional energy in them.* It is the energy that provides the intrinsic motivational drive for human will to reach out towards self-actualization, just as it enables an acorn to grow into an oak tree. Harman argues that different branches of knowledge are veering towards this central belief.

Consciousness is a term that defies normal forms of definition. In the Hindu philosophic traditions, most texts and treatises revolve around this central concept. The individual being is viewed as but a sheath of *Brahman* (*"Brahmana Kososi"* is how it is summed up in *Taitreya Upanishad*). The inner self of a being, *Atman*, which is beyond and above body, mind and intellect, is recognized as being immortal and a personification of the great cosmic power, Brahman. *Atman* is *Brahman* and *Brahman* is *Atman*, say the Hindu scriptures. They are but two different manifestations of the Universal Consciousness.

In other systems of thought too, one comes across identical explanations of an all-pervading power that energizes all living beings. Explanations about one's soul, inner reality and tao are but other expressions of Man's search for consciousness. However, as explained in Chapter 2, those who sought truth along these lines were marginalised thanks to the juggernaut set rolling by the combined works of the great classical physicists, Adam Smith, Darwin, the behaviourists and the genetic engineers. Ironically, it is the new developments in the fields of science and medicine that are now heralding the birth of the second Copernican revolution that is placing Consciousness back where it belongs—at the heart of Man's search for the meaning of his very existence.

## NEUROSCIENTIST SPERRY RECOGNIZES THE PRIMACY OF CONSCIOUSNESS

When Roger Sperry of the California Institute of Technology won the Nobel Prize in medicine for his work on the human brain, he was invited to write the lead article for the 1981 *Annual Review of*

*Neuroscience.* In the paper entitled "Changing priorities", Sperry wrote of the importance of the previously neglected area of subjective experience:

> Current concepts of the mind-brain relation involve a direct break with the long-established materialist and behaviourist doctrine that has dominated neuroscience for many decades. Instead of renouncing or ignoring consciousness, the new interpretation gives full recognition to the primacy of inner conscious awareness as a causal reality.

Elaborating upon this theme in a later publication, *Science and Moral Priority* (1983), Sperry wrote:

> ... it becomes increasingly impossible, among other things, to accept the idea of two separate realms of knowledge, existence, or truth: one for objective science and another for subjective experience and values. Did metaphysical dualisms and the seemingly irreconcilable paradoxes that have prevailed in psychology between realities of inner experience on the one hand and those of experimental brain research on the other disappear into a single, continuous hierarchy. Within the brain, we pass conceptually in a hierarchical continuum from the brain's subnuclear particles, on up through the atoms, molecules, and brain cells to the level of nerve-circuit systems without consciousness, and finally to cerebral processes with consciousness. Objective facts and subjective values become part of the same universe of discourse. The hiatus between science and values is erased in part by expanding the scope of science to encompass inner experience and by altering the status of subjective values so that they are no longer set off in an epiphenomenal or other parallelistic domain outside the reach of science.

Towards the end of this fascinating book, Sperry concludes,

> The swing in psychology and neuroscience away from materialism, reductionism and mechanistic determinism toward a new, monist, mentalist paradigm restores to the scientific image of human nature the dignity, freedom, responsibility, and other humanistic attributes of which it has long been deprived in the materialist-behaviourist approach.

In the world of physics, meanwhile, the Newtonian conception of a definite, three-dimensional universe gave way to the quantum theory. The world view of the latter is, among other things, built upon the concept of duality of matter and energy and Heisenberg's *uncertainty principle*. Subatomic matter, according to the quantum theory, sometimes behaves like particles, and at some other times like a wave function. Besides, the more certain an observer is about the location of matter, the less certain the observer can be about the velocity of its movement. Thus, what was an essential pillar of the first Copernican revolution began to be viewed as a gross rather than a subtle view of the world around us, and within us. Fritjof Capra, David Bohm, Dana Zohar and many others extrapolated the new developments in Physics into a larger context which was very clearly philosophical. Dr Deepak Chopra, in his epochal treatise, *Quantum Healing*, has brought the field of Ayurveda and psychopathological cure of terminal diseases into an identical context—a context that derives energy from a well spring within human beings and focusses on achieving a mind-body, yin-yang balance.

Among the world's leading musicians, sportsmen and corporate CEOs, there were many who began to look beyond the objective skills of their walk in life and claimed to have touched a well spring of energy within. Corporate management development programmes elevated the "softer" area of self-development to occupy centre stage.

## THE "PRIMARY PRINCIPLE" OF JC PENNEY'S FORMER CEO

Donald V Seibert, the former CEO and Chairman of the Board of JC Penney Company, Inc. has embodied this paradigm shift in his *Ethical Executive* (1984). In a preamble that sounds disturbingly similar to the trepidations that must have been experienced by the likes of Bruno when voicing the scientific heresy in the sixteenth century, Siebert writes:

> As we move into this discussion of spiritual and moral
> commitments, I feel in a way as though I'm walking on eggshells,
> because it's so easy to be misunderstood. But I consider the ideals
> involved here to be so important that I'm willing to take a few risks
> to get the point across.

As the "primary principle" for success in the corporate world, Seibert states, 'If you want to succeed, it is extremely important to settle as soon as possible on some coherent, comprehensive set of personal values'. He concludes this remarkable book, not surprisingly, with this quotation from Luke (6:38, RSV): ' . . . give and it will be given to you; good measure, pressed down, shaken together, running over, will be put into your lap. For the measure you give will be the measure you get back'.

# LESSEM'S INSIGHTFUL ANALYSIS WITH HIS FOUR DOMAINS OF MANAGEMENT

In his *Global Management Principles,* Ronnie Lessem provides an insightful analysis of what is transpiring in the corporate world. He talks of four domains of management, the primal, rational, developmental and metaphysical, each with its characteristic focus as also global concentration:

- In the West (primarily the USA of the '80s and '90s), the domain of *primal management* is featured by Tom Peters *leadership by wandering around,* a return to basics, to tangible, uncomplicated people and things. Entrepreneurship is the prime force, and everything else is subservient to it. The entrepreneur must have the overriding right to hire and fire people in keeping with the rise and fall of business cycle. The human cost is a necessary part of the system. Steve Jobs, the erstwhile supremo of *Apple* typifies such a primal manager who sets his own rules, is driven by a passion to achieve and quite often suffers by not designing the humanistic counterweights required to balance the system.

- In the North (Western Europe), the domain of *rational management* is featured by a different tone and orientation. Peter Drucker's archetype of the *Effective Executive* thinks, plans and executes the conversion of resources and capabilities into desired results in a methodical, unemotional manner. It is this orientation, articulated further by Humble and Reddin and their system of management by objectives, that has held sway over the traditional management institutes the world over, as it appeals to the young adult who aspires to become a part of a world predominated by Financiers, Marketers and Industrial Engineers.

- In the *East* (typically Japan), the domain of *developmental management,* the focus of the corporate leaders is different. More contemplative and long-term in focus, the developmental manager supplements primal and rational management principles with the view that corporate success is dependent on facilitating human and social development, albeit in a structured manner. The fact that western and northern competitors object to Japanese practices that appear to be those of *Japan Inc.* is proof of this very different focus.

- In the *South* (the developing countries), the domain of *metaphysical management* appears to be on the verge of taking root. For those managers who lead organizations through their Vision and imagination and are transforming the lives of thousands of people who are members of their organizations, something more than primal, rational and developmental managerial principles are required. 'Real' management of this kind, says Lessem, 'draws on natural laws, governing the functioning of all physical and human phenomena, and applies them to the conduct of business enterprise. Placing particular emphasis on energy—that is its flow, velocity, quality and quantity—it draws from a philosophical and experimental base that is now common to both ancient wisdom and modern physics.' Lessem also suspects that 'those of you operating in the South and East may be more receptive to the kind of spirit and energy involved than those of us based, primarily, in the North and West.'

## The hard/soft, yin-yang qualities of the four domains

Lessem has been careful to avoid taking the concept of domains into rigid geographic boundaries. He has been sensitive enough to appreciate and emphasize the subtilities that feature these overlapping domains. He says, 'Each stage of development, and each quarter of the globe, brings both hard and soft qualities into business. The hard ones are enterprise, order, adaptability and vision; the soft ones are community, freedom, harmony, and energy:

Soft and Hard Edges of Management

| State of development | Quarter of the globe | Soft attributes | Hard attributes |
|---|---|---|---|
| 1. | West | Community | Enterprise |
| 2. | North | Freedom | Order |
| 3. | East | Harmony | Adaptability |
| 4. | South | Energy | Vision |

'From ancient times this division between "soft" and "hard" has been considered fundamental to development in life, if not in business. The ancient Chinese introduced the terms "yin" and "yang" to represent these complementary attributes. For some, the division between "feminine" and "masculine" parallels "yin"and "yang", but this association often causes controversy . . . Recent research into the two sides of the brain has revealed some striking similarities between the left brain and right brain, and so-called masculine and feminine traits. Whereas the left brain controls our more analytical and focussed consciousness, the right brain controls our more intuitive and diffuse awareness. At each of the developmental stages, and for such management domain, we require a combination of soft and hard qualities, of a continuously changing nature.'

Throughout history, wherever stability existed, there was sure to be a balance between the hard and soft aspects of organization of life. In primitive societies, while the hunters provided the entrepreneurship and the cutting edge of the harder aspects of life, their womenfolk complemented them with their softer role as gatherers and nurturers of the family and clan. In the cold months of winter, the clan survived only if the womenfolk had played their role adequately, by storing and carefully preserving food and warm clothes. Besides, education, child upbringing, health care and many other essential functions were hers to master and deliver.

Similarly, in the farming community, as described in Chapter 2, while men played the 'hard' roles of ploughing and tilling, women played the 'soft' roles of sowing, nurturing and harvesting. Agrarian lives provided for and demanded that both the roles be played, and harmony existed in the community.

## CONSCIOUSNESS AND THE YIN-YANG BALANCE IN CORPORATE WORLD

In the corporate world, such a balance is yet to be struck globally. By merging and adapting the best principles of primal, rational and developmental management principles within a metaphysical context that envelops and liberates the synergy produced by such a union of views, one can hope to achieve the yin-yang balance in the corporate world. Only then will the global corporation be able to play its vital role in actualizing the second Copernican revolution—and incidentally achieve bottomline results in a competitive, service-oriented world.

All through the book, I have attempted to present a viable way of achieving such an integration that satisfies the practical needs of a competitive business world as also the multifarious, hierarchical nature of human needs. I have refrained from using the word "consciousness" right through for strategic reasons, as such heretic thinking would have kept away supposedly hard-nosed corporate executives. However, by beginning the book with the question, "Is nobility and perfection a natural quality in man, and cruelty and pettiness an aberration, or vice versa?" I have merely used euphemisms for the word "consciousness".

Let me now go over what has been covered so far in the book from the larger perspective of the second Copernican revolution. In doing so, I will further develop the East-West model of motivation and arrive at its final form, with "consciousness" given its due place, as the source from where we come as well as the goal we seek to reach or merge with, besides being the primal form of ourselves during our life journey as well.

In Chapter 1, I argued that the "victory" of human nature was inevitable in the new corporate context. With customer-sensitive service-orientation of front line staff becoming the cutting edge for success in a competitive world, and the bundling of manufactured products with such service becoming the rule, rather than the exception, management of service people has already become the central focus of the modern corporation. In describing the seven elements of the problem facing the modern corporation, I argued that the solution to this problem lies first of all in developing an abiding faith in the potential and willingness of their knowledge workers and front line staff to reach perfection in their jobs. For the first time in the history of economic organizations, the unfolding of human nature to its full potential of perfection has become an unavoidable, critical factor for success. Adam Smith's *Economic Man*, I argued, has to be replaced by an achievable version of Abraham Maslow's Self-actualizing Man.

In Chapter 2, we reviewed historical developments in the belief system that governed Man's view of himself. The unfortunate timing of various developments, whereby the scientific view came to be coupled to those of Smith and Darwin, and later cemented by the behavioural scientists and genetic engineers, led to an impoverished view of Man. With the rise of Marx and the Union movement, Man's innate desire to do something meaningful in life was converted into a tradable commodity called "labour output". Man began to behave exactly like the pigeons in a behavioural scientist's laboratory. Incentive schemes, industrial engineers, and mercenary management practices matched such a world view. However, a silver lining appeared above the looming, dark clouds in the form of Japanese successes in shopfloor management as this was based on trust in and empowerment of workmen.

The next section, comprising Chapters 3, 4 and 5, developed the first stages of an East-West model of motivation that merged Maslow's humanistic model with Eastern traditions in understanding creative development in Man. An important element in this model was the introduction of the concept of *threshold limits*. A comparison was made between the common understanding of heroism and the ability to sacrifice one's lower needs for reaching up towards a higher goal, or Vision. This model also gave the human equivalent to the natural manner in which an acorn grows to become an oak tree. It was also established that the quality of one's endeavour was dependent on two factors. It was primarily dependent on the state of growth one had achieved in one's ability to set adequately low threshold limits for one's lower needs. Secondly, it was also crucially dependent on one's ability to reach out towards a personal or group vision. Experimental research findings on the debilitating effect that extrinsic motivation has on the quality of work were quoted to further emphasize the role of human "will" in one's motivation and ability to reach or reveal one's nature of perfection. In citing the example of Sumant Moolgaokar's achievement in TELCO (Pune), I merely drew a relationship between this seemingly theoretical conception of Man's potential and practical achievement in Corporate India against severe odds.

To understand better the need for strong threshold springs and adequately low threshold limits, Chapter 6 was devoted to the ill effects of transgression of acceptable threshold limits. That corporate world is full of managers and CEOs who try to manipulate this failing by behaving like puppeteers rather than gardeners was also spelt out. To escape the clutches of such puppeteers and temptations that divert one's growth towards the satiation of increased "desires" in others' domain, I argued that one should learn how to "take fate by its throat", rather like Beethovan. In an attempt to further this argument, an exercise was provided for the reader to try out, in order to convince him that our greatest learning experiences do arise out of apparently traumatic events that have the effect of sudden lowering of threshold limits. The learning is essentially one that makes a human being aware that his natural direction for growth is towards self-esteem and self-actualization needs, rather than towards gratification of "desires" at the lower need levels.

In Chapter 7, Freudian psychology was reinterpreted to demonstrate that the "greatest learning" is actually that by which a human being learns how to sublimate his or her energies towards higher goals when life's arrows result in sudden lowering of threshold limits at lower-order need levels. A brief sketch of Beethoven's life and works was presented to demonstrate the connection between the ability to sublimate and the quality of work that ensues while one is sublimating. We thus arrived at Stage 4 of the East-West model of motivation.

## THE FINAL STAGE OF THE EAST-WEST MODEL: CONSCIOUSNESS AS THE BEGINNING AND THE END

At this stage, a question was deliberately left unaddressed. In stage 4 of the model, as in the earlier stages, an essential principle is that of dynamic evolution. An evolution, by definition, connotes transformation from one form to another. In the case of the acorn, the evolution is from the seed to the tree. In the case of a human being, it is from a child to a self-actualizing man. But surely, there is a stage before the child/acorn and after the self-actualizing man/oak tree. Let us suppose that this stage—before and after—is *"consciousness"* and redraw the final stage of the East-West model as shown in Fig.14.1.

What exactly does Fig 14.1 mean? A spark from consciousness gives life to a human form and gives it the directional energy to live out its form in a manner that will allow the original spark to return to its mega form of consciousness. In the life span of the human being, he will have to contend with needs that are fundamental to his form, in the form of physiological, safety, belongingness and recognition needs. By leading a life that engages him in purposive activity, he can learn to maintain low threshold limits on all needs, and develop strong threshold springs to desist from the lure of unnecessary desires. The purpose of action must be towards achieving self-esteem and self-actualization rather than satiating desires at lower-order levels. A man must ideally wish to reach a

## THE FINAL FORM OF THE EAST-WEST MODEL

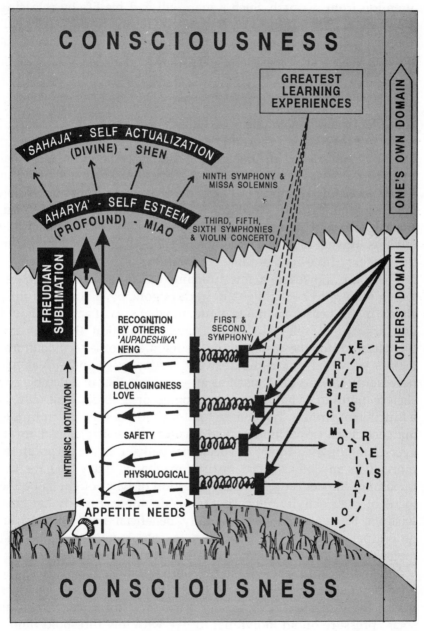

*Figure 14.1*

stage where his energy is almost completely directed towards self-actualization, with no unquenched desires that divert his attention from his path. Such a man will end his life by releasing the spark of consciousness back to where it came from. Others will find the need to return, as unquenched desires (*vasana*) are tantamount to being unfinished business that has still to be attended to.

## Similarity with the scriptures is striking

Students and practitioners of *Advaita Vedanta*, and even casual readers of the *Bhagwad Gita* and the more popular *Upanishads* would have by now picked up the glaring similarity between this final stage of the East-West model and the essential Truth contained in the ancient Hindu scriptures. Nor is it too different from the Sermon on the Mount in its essence. Likewise, students of Spinoza, Kierkegaard and Albert Schweitzer will also spot the remarkable oneness in what has been stated before and what is being stated in the context of the 20th century corporation.

There are, however, a few fundamental contextual differences which require to be highlighted. In days gone by, a child had little choice on his vocational mode of life. In what area of activity should one attempt to self-actualize was not a question that was left unanswered, for the caste, family, religion and other sociocultural factors provided automatic answers. Today, each individual has necessarily to fend for himself as an equal member of a democratic society ought to. What he or she becomes, or is able to do in life, is a function of various dynamic factors. A child's ability and aptitude, matched with opportunities and challenges available lead to an ever-changing assortment of vocational paths. It is the corporation, more than any other social institution, that is likely to have the maximum impact on this crucial question of what ought to be the focus of one's activity. As corporations do not necessarily have the wisdom to appreciate the mutually beneficial need to help an individual find the ideal vocation to self-actualize in, the vast majority of corporate citizens end up as mere puppets on a string.

Yet another difference lies in the manner in which one learns the wisdom of setting low threshold limits. In the olden days, whether it was the Protestant ethic or any other social practice, there was social pressure on an individual to live with low threshold limits. That one should live virtuously was almost axiomatic. That is not the case today. We live in a world that is consumer-driven and market-controlled, and it is legitimately expected that a corporation will create and feed on client desires. It would be natural for a 20th century being to feel the pressure to continuously increase his threshold limits. It is a motorcycle today, an ordinary car tomorrow, an air- conditioned, automated invention later, and a Mercedes Benz after that. That is how desires continuously increase, and no one sees anything wrong with it, especially if you happen to be advertising and selling such products yourself. While corporations are responsible for these increasing desires in people, it is the very same corporation that has to endeavour to create group and team Visions that will galvanize its members to voluntarily lower threshold limits and experience the joy of sublimation. There is an obvious contradiction here, and one that has to be addressed. We will revert to it later in this chapter.

Chapter 8 was devoted to the understanding of child psychology and its reinterpretation using the terminology and content of the East-West model. The first six of Erik Erikson's eight sets of crises that a child faces and attempts to resolve before the age of eighteen were discussed, namely

| Basic Trust | v. | Mistrust |
|---|---|---|
| Autonomy | v. | Shame and Doubt |
| Initiative | v. | Guilt |
| Industry | v. | Inferiority |
| Identity | v. | Role confusion |
| Intimacy | v. | Isolation |

A fundamental premise of this model is that human society should play a role in nurturing a child's intrinsic *will* to reach out towards, or reveal, its intrinsic nature of perfection. In the context of the second Copernican revolution, this merely means that the spark of consciousness in a child should be enabled to lay a basis for its human life so that it can eventually move towards revealing, and merging with, its nature of perfection. Short of such a belief, how can one legitimately expect a child to resolve the crises of *autonomy* and *initiative* before the age of three? In the absence of such a belief, how can a parent trust that his or her child will be able to resolve these crises adequately?

In discussing the crises of *industry v. inferiority*, an attempt was made to introduce the essential skill of counselling and reinterpret it in terms of the East-West model. While discussing the next crises of *identity v. role confusion,* care was taken to stress the point that this crisis is not one of resolving one's vocational walk in life but one of subjectively feeling confident of one's nature of perfection. Ideals such as justice and fair play and aesthetic influences of self-actualizing people's life and works were emphasized. The fact that the right hemisphere of the brain is capable of dealing with this crisis holistically was also stressed.

The last of the six crises of youth, *intimacy v. isolation,* is surely a stage when a youngster learns to not only set threshold limits at the belongingness level but also find the joy in reaching out towards satiating other people's need to belong and be loved.

In Chapter 9, it was pointed out that modern societal institutions, such as the nuclear family, mass educational systems and religious bodies, have failed in their role in enabling a proper resolution of the first six of the Eriksonian crises. Thus, a youngster who joins a corporation for a career is most likely to be one who has struggled and failed to adequately resolve the crises. This imposes a great responsibility upon the corporation to first correct the damage so caused, and thereafter assist a youngster in re-resolving the same crises at a later stage in life. Thus corporations will have to restate their role in society as *the modern nurseries for human growth,* for they alone can ensure that. Concentration of wealth in their hands, and their business need to help in the empowerment of their people, have brought about this fundamental change in their very role in human development.

## HRM and the yin-yang balance in corporations

As a result of these developments, the role of Human Resources Management has suddenly been moved centre stage in the drama of corporate battles for customer satisfaction and retention. It is the responsibility of CEOs and their HRM professionals to ensure that human development takes place while tasks are being accomplished, and to synergistically achieve human self-actualization through organized production of quality products and services. Thus, the harder aspects of management symbolized by marketing, production technology and finance are at last likely to be balanced by the softer thrusts implied in enlightened human resources management and quality assurance through empowerment of front-line and bottom rung employees. The yin-yang balance is likely to be achieved.

As a first step in HRM, Chapter 10 was devoted to manpower Planning, recruitment and selection. Unless a thorough quantitative analysis is made, projecting manpower requirement to meet expansion, attrition and promotional needs, it is not possible to ensure timely recruitment of people in either the required numbers or of a desirable quality. In all aspects of HRM, there is an internal hard-soft balance that has to be struck between the quantitative and qualitative aspect. A model was also presented of the ideal profile of a corporate citizen, one that could be kept as an ultimate target to achieve. As against this, what could be legitimately expected in a freshman from a campus was also highlighted. It was emphasized that one should view such freshmen as saplings being selected for a nursery rather than as full-blown trees for transplantation. Again, a central thrust was the fact that this was a phase in the growth of an individual which required a definite, complementary role to be played by organizations for facilitation of such growth.

Chapter 11 was focussed on a crucial aspect of HRM that is hardly ever dealt with adequately in most organizations—induction, training and career choice. It is in the initial year or two that a freshman is still in a stage when he can be helped to re-resolve Eriksonian crises and also learn how to set low threshold limits with strong threshold springs in place. Again, this is the phase when the all-important problem of identifying the work arena where one can attempt to self-actualize is also solved. The three phases of career choice and the role of an organization in facilitation of the proper, realistic choice being made was also elaborated upon. The multiple skills required of an HR executive, and sensitivity in use of these skills, was also emphasized.

That corporate leaders should articulate and project a "Vision" for freshmen to feel energized and enthusiastic about was also stressed. In fact, this is a primary need in the process of redirecting the equivalent of twisted plants towards proper growth. Youngsters used to high threshold limits, who are thus easy preys for organizational puppeteers, need help in strengthening their threshold springs and setting acceptable threshold limits for their lower needs. Corporate vision has to play a role in facilitating the achievement of this.

## CONSCIOUSNESS AS THE ULTIMATE SOURCE

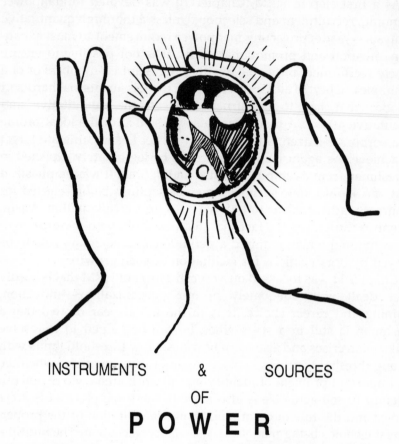

INSTRUMENTS    &    SOURCES

OF

# P O W E R

| | |
|---|---|
| ● CONDIGN<br>◆ COMPENSATORY<br>■ CONDITIONED | ● PERSONALITY<br>◆ PROPERTY<br>■ ORGANIZATION |

| | |
|---|---|
| ✳ HUMAN "*WILL*" | ✳ CONSCIOUSNESS |

*Figure 14.2*

# THE FINAL FORM OF THE POWER MODEL:
# CONSCIOUSNESS AS THE ULTIMATE SOURCE

Chapter 12 addressed itself to the issues governing union-management relationships. Current reality as well as solutions were discussed. John Galbraith's model of power was discussed and a modified power model was suggested. Case histories of successful applications of the revised models were presented, and a general approach towards extricating organizations from the current mess was also suggested. Using the terminology of the second Copernican revolution, one can now redraw Fig. 12.5 by merely giving the right term for the last of the four sources of power, namely *consciousness*, as shown in Fig. 14.2.

In the next chapter, several important issues were addressed. First, the role of the CEO and his articulation of a just Vision by word and deed. No organization can hope to reach and sustain quality for any length of time where the organizational Vision is tarnished by the personal, egocentric needs of CEOs. A classic Japanese case was highlighted to demonstrate this. At the same time, where CEOs rigorously apply far stricter norms upon themselves and lower their personal threshold limits before appealing to others to do so, magic almost always seems to happen. This aspect of CEO behaviour is one that is rarely ever quoted and sought to be emulated when management theorists hold Japan up as an example, possibly because it is the toughest part of what makes Japan so successful.

## The whimsical CEO has to go

Secondly, a brief overview was given on why many Indian CEOs have managed to survive for years on end despite extremely egocentric needs. With the opening up of the economy for competition, the rise of shareholders' role in corporate power balancing and the enhanced importance of customer contact front-line staff, it is unlikely that such CEOs will survive for too long. No longer can CEOs of public corporations brazenly appoint personal favourites as their successors, over the heads of competent alternatives available. No longer can CEOs hope to take whimsical decisions that ignore performance and potential. For, quality has to be produced by empowered, free and liberated corporate citizens who are seeking self-actualization through purposive engagement of their faculties in the creation of quality products and services. If not for any other reason, bottom-line results alone will ensure this.

Thirdly, Schumacher's classic problem of antinomy—between the need for freedom and the need for control—was addressed and a solution suggested for large organizations. The manner in which the Taj Group of Hotels sought to solve the problem through its leadership development workshops was elaborated upon. The core of these workshops was to create a critical mass of line managers who would view their role as trustees for human growth, and equip them with the requisite skills to succeed in such a role. Through this process, a critical mass of potential leaders were helped to resolve the seventh of Erikson's crisis, *generativity v. self-absorbtion*. They were taught how to enjoy giving of themselves and playing substantive roles in the development of people for whom they were responsible.

## Factors that lead to quality

A final piece of the puzzle is yet to be stated, in this complex problem of how to tap into the pure energy latent in people in such a manner that both the corporation and its members benefit. This is best demonstrated through an exercise I conducted recently in a Wipro group company, the Wipro Infotech:

The company, which designs, manufactures and markets computers in India and abroad, was readying itself for a full-fledged launch of a Total Quality Management programme. As part of the startup phase, the entire senior management was put through a two-day workshop. During the workshop, the senior management team was asked this question:

*Look back in time and identify when you were exuding "quality" in the truest sense of the term. Then, describe the circumstances and events that engulfed you at that time.*

They were given about fifteen minutes to write out their answer individually, then discuss amongst themselves in small groups and see if their experiences had anything in common. Sure enough, a strikingly similar pattern emerged, for most of their experiences satisfied the following criteria:

1. A challenge to prove oneself against all odds;

2. A clearly enunciated goal by a team leader (in most cases, the goal was directly related to customer satisfaction);

3. A visibly and totally involved team leader who was leading from the front;

4. The risk of failure was very high;

5. There was an immense sense of personal commitment, driven by a strong intrinsic motivation to succeed, with no thoughts whatsoever for rewards;

6. A small team of close associates with free flow of information, trust and camaraderie;

7. There was very little time to achieve results; and

8. Inherent in the event was tremendous scope for learning.

Using the terminology of this book, the general pattern that emerged could be restated thus:

1. There must be a leader who is capable of articulating and living a challenging Vision;

2. His infectious enthusiasm for winning must reach his team members in no uncertain manner;

3. *Time pressures,* combined with a challenging Vision, must induce his team members to forget about, and sacrifice, lower-order needs in order to indulge in group sublimation of energies;

4. When a group of people reach upwards in such a manner, they will collectively touch a well spring of energy, whose nature is perfection . . . and quality will be the inevitable end result.

Of these four elements, we have discussed all issues pertaining to them in detail through the book barring one factor—*Time pressure.* Let me elaborate on this point and at the same time deal with another problem that must have bothered most readers.

### An exercise for threshold springs

It is a fact that corporate citizens live in reasonable comfort, and are used to much higher threshold limits than others. Most corporations, however, depend on similar people for their clientele as well. If there are not enough people who wish to change cars every three years, automobile corporations will face a problem. If there are not people who like gourmet dinners served in the best possible ambiance, the hotel industry will face a crisis. If clients do not wish for constant improvement of the products and service they receive, the cutting edge for corporate excellence will be blunted. In such an atmosphere, it may appear natural for people to get used to ever-increasing threshold limits.

However, as has been pointed out earlier, the inherent danger in this scenario is that threshold springs will get stretched beyond their elastic limit, and be eventually replaced with *strings* that puppeteers can play and manipulate with. It is essential, therefore, that such people are periodically subjected to short-term bursts of experiences that have the double effect of forcibly reducing their threshold limits, and making them sublimate their energies upwards. That is the only way to exercise their threshold springs and keep them in working condition.

It is just like an athlete who compensates for his overindulgence at the table with a vigorous workout the next day. The chances are, however, that a sensible athlete will resolve at the end of his workout that the next time around, he will indulge less. He alone knows how much effort it takes to sweat out the additional 500 calories imbibed. If he does not have such native sense, he requires a coach and a counsellor to help him. I have suggested nothing different while talking of the roles of the CEO and his HRM advisor.

The reason for time pressure being a crucial factor is two-fold. First, those who have been wallowing in "high" desires are unlikely to respond to any call that demands too much sacrifice. They can take it only in small doses. With every succeeding experience, their ability to sustain themselves for longer periods of denial will improve. Just as an underworked muscle requires warming up exercises and a gradual increase in the strain and stress each day, so also does an unused threshold spring require to be subjected to a series of gradually more strenuous doses of compression and release.

Secondly, there is a much deeper reason why human beings need this kind of time pressure. Most of us are aware of the potential that lies dormant in us, but are somehow afraid to take steps to tap into it. Hermann Hesse describes this phenomenon succinctly in *Steppenwolf*.

The central character of the book, Harry Steppenwolf, is sensitive to the idea that the 'human' is not a finished creation, but a challenge to the spirit, a distant possibility yearned for and feared at the same time. He also appreciates that the way towards such a possibility being actualized can only be trodden in small measure under spells of terrible agony and ecstasy, and by those rare individuals who can face the scaffold today and a monument in their names tomorrow. Harry even walks the path now and then for a little time and for an uncertain distance and pays for it with severe suffering and painful isolation. Yet, he somehow finds himself in dread of the highest challenge, of affirming and aspiring to that ultimate possibility of becoming human.

There is a Steppenwolf in each of us, who knows what needs to be done but recoils from the pain and the effort that accompany all great learning experiences. We can take the pain only in small doses, walk only tentative distances and in limited time frames. And our ability to travel from the sublime to the ridiculous, and back again, allows us the luxury to indulge the whims of the Steppenwolf in us.

Now, there is hardly any corporation that does not already have a marvellous vehicle to piggy-back on, for generating the time pressure. That is the system of monthly, quarterly and annual targeting and evaluation. Unfortunately, however, this system is mostly used for setting production, sales and financial targets, the "hard" area of management. Corporate CEOs can easily complement these hard areas with the softer areas of the process used for setting and achievement of the same targets. Participative management practices need to be used to tap the energies of people such that they voluntarily respond to jointly set targets that are drawn from compelling corporate Vision. Team sublimation of energy will happen, and quality will flow. In fact, the best corporate chiefs are already putting their money on the "process", and TQM programmes that do take off prioritize this in no uncertain manner.

## RESOLVING THE LAST OF ERIKSON'S EIGHT CRISES: INTEGRITY V. DESPAIR

Organizational specialists who market various techniques for Total Quality Management, such as ISO9000, Juran's methodology v. Demming's, quality circles, suggestion schemes and so on, need to delve deeper and discover for themselves that while Ishikawa diagrams, JIT tools and other procedural aspects are certainly important, what is crucial for success is a methodology for tapping into the collective consciousness of groups of people through a series of orchestrated events that will satisfy the criteria for producing quality. There is hardly any doubt that corporate giants like Matsushita, JRD Tata, Alfred P Sloan and Jack Welch have known this secret instinctively and made it the cornerstone of their strategy for achieving and maintaining quality. Such people have spelt out and lived their Vision, challenged their people to join them in the actualization of their Vision, and unleashed the infinite energy within their organizational members.

An outstanding example is Jack Welch, the Chairman of GE, whose senior management spend an enormous amount of time on making his concept of *Workout* a success. 'Workout' is very simply a process by which employees are encouraged to sit together and work out how they are going to substantially improve their performance collectively, be it in the form of productivity improvement, cost reduction, rejection control or customer retention.

When corporate citizens work in such an atmosphere, where they are assisted to repeatedly involve themselves in their own work through sublimation of energy, they are bound to become better people, for they will be enjoying what they are doing, with lower threshold limits and stronger threshold springs. Such people cannot but have an effect on those who they come in contact with outside their organization. Whether it be their suppliers, customers, family, neighbours or their children's school, their infectious enthusiasm and way of doing things will definitely be felt by those they interact with. Such people will be well on their way to solving the last of Erik Erikson's crises, *integrity v. despair*, for their lives will throb with dignity, satisfaction and personal fulfilment. Life will have a meaning and purpose for them and those whom they are able to touch and influence.

## THE JUGGERNAUT OF THE SECOND COPERNICAN REVOLUTION WILL ROLL

As to how their influence will reach beyond their corporation, one can merely speculate. As the model we have been using is one of release of energy, maybe the change that will come about could be along the lines suggested by Ilya Prigogine and Isabelle Stengers in their *Order out of chaos*. Their hypothesis deals with systems that have reached a far from equilibrium stage, which is a good description of most corporations in today's competitive scenario. Prigogine and Stengers say,

> We now know that far from equilibrium, new types of structures may originate spontaneously. In far from equilibrium conditions, we may have transformation from disorder, from thermal chaos, into order. New dynamic states of matter may originate, states that reflect the interaction of a given system with its surroundings.

Corporations that succeed through TQM processes, and apply the principles of 'Just-in-time (JIT)', not only transform the way their suppliers organize themselves but also proactively influence customer behaviour and expectations. When such corporations learn how to tap into the collective consciousness of their constituents—employees, suppliers, customers, immediate neighbourhood and so on—it would not be too wild a thought to imagine that the perturbation caused by them could reach system breaking proportions, thus leading the way to a new, dynamic state of a higher order.

There is hardly any doubt that corporations and their CEOs are today uniquely poised to play the most crucial of roles in the spread of the second Copernican revolution. They have no alternative but to fulfill that role, if only because they have to empower and liberate the energies of their front line staff and bottom rung employees in order to survive and succeed in the market place. When sufficient numbers of giant corporations begin to assume this role, the juggernaut of the second Copernican revolution would have truly begun rolling on its grand journey.

# Bibliographical Notes

To facilitate easy reading, I have deviated from the common practice of marking each reference with a suffix or providing footnotes. Rather, I have chosen to devote this separate section, where I hope to take the more interested, research-oriented reader through the important works I read while working on the book. I have also given a few references of authors whose views differ totally from mine, and of some who have drawn different inferences from almost the same data. Maybe the reader will come up with his own interpretation. The subject matter of the book being what it is, one can be sure that the debate will continue for a long time.

Of the references quoted below, there are many who have specifically given me the necessary copyright permission to quote passages from their publications. These have been marked with an asterisk (*) for which I wish to express my gratefulness. There are others, like Alvin Toffler and Barry Schwartz, from whose written works I have summarized relevant portions to substantiate my thesis. While publishing conventions might not require specific acknowledgements. I believe I owe them a moral debt. I thank these authors but for whose efforts I would have still been floundering.

### Introduction

1. *Keynote* by JRD Tata, ed.; S.A. Sabavala and R.M. Lala, Tata Press Ltd, Bombay, 1986.

## Chapter 1

1. Alvin Toffler's works, *The Third Wave,* William Collins Sons & Co, London, 1980 and *Power Shift* have been extremely useful books that I consulted while writing Chapters 1 and 2. I find AT so readable and definitive that it has been a joy to pore over his works. There has been a mega work from AT for each of the last three decades. In the 70s it was *Future Shock.* The Third Wave came in the 80s, and *Power Shift* in the 90s. I feel it is difficult to either talk of history, or the future without relying upon the research and writing of AT.

2. The data on the service industry in India is drawn from a report I made for the Planning Commission, Government of India, in 1988.

3. Bateson, J.E.G., *Service Marketing,* London Business Managing Services Marketing School, Dryden Press, 1989.

4. John Naisbitt, *Megatrends,* Futura Publications, Macdonald & Co. (Publishers) Ltd, London, 1984.

5. Feargal Quinn, *Crowning the Customer,* The O'Brien Press, Dublin, 1990.

6. Stalk and Hout, *Competing against Time,* The Free Press, Macmillan Inc., New York, 1990.

7. Kenneth Blanchard's remark of inverting the organizational pyramid is taken from an interview by Ron Zemke in *Service Excellence,* an audiovisual production by Nathan and Tailor, Boston, USA.

8. Karl Albrehct and Ron Zemke, *Service America,* Dow Jones-Irwin, Homewood, Illinois, 1985. This is likely to become a classic in the annals of service management.

9. Jan Carlzon, *Moments of Truth,* Ballinger, Cambridge, Mass., 1987. Carlzon is almost a byword in service management already, through his dramatic turnaround of SAS.

## Chapter 2

1. Abinas Chandra Das, *Rig Vedic India,* The Calcutta University Press, Calcutta, 1921. A remarkable work of research on the interpretation of *Rig Veda* suggesting the period when the original civilization of vedic seers existed in India.

2. George Sabine, *A History of Political Theory,* Oxford & IBH Publishing Co., New Delhi, 1973. I recommend this as essential

reading to students of organizational behaviour and change. It gives a marvellous, historical account of Man in society, and how he has tried to control, rule over and use his fellowmen.

3. Adam Smith, *The Wealth of Nations*.
4. Barry Schwartz, *The Battle for Human Nature*, W.W. Norton & Co. Ltd., London, 1986. The title of the chapter is drawn from this book, as also the historical account of developments in Man's understanding of his own nature. A book not to be missed.
5. Charles Darwin, *The Origin of the Species*.
6. Adrian Furnham, *The Protestant Work Ethic*, Routledge, London, 1990.
7. Karl Marx, *Das Capital*, Progress Publishers, Moscow, 1967.
8. Sigmund 'Freud, *Complete Works*, 24 Vols, Hogarth Press, London, 1953-74.
9. B.F. Skinner, *The Behaviour of Organisms*, Appleton-Century, New York, 1938.
10. B.F. Skinner, *Science and Human Behavior*, Macmillan, New York, 1953.
11. K. Matsushita, The secret is shared, *Manufacturing Engineering*, Vol. 100, No. Feb. 2, 1988.
12. R. Pascal and A.G. Athos, *The Art of Japanese Management*, Warner Books, New York, 1981.

Chapter 3

1. The following publications by A.H. Maslow:
   *—Motivation and Personality*, Harper & Row, New York, 1970.
   —Theory of Human Motivation, *Psychology Review*, Vol. 50, pp 370-396, 1943.
   —*Eupsychian Management: A Journal*, Irwin-Dorsey, Home-Wood, Illinois, 1965.
   —*Farther Reaches of Human Nature*, Penguin, 1971.
   —*The Journals of A.H. Maslow*, Vols I and II, Books/cole, California, 1979.

2. Colin Wilson, *New Pathways in Psychology—Maslow and the Post-Freudian Revolution*, Victor Gollancz, London, 1979. The second section of this eminently readable book contains CW's biographical account of Maslow.

3. Henry Ford, *My Life and Work*, Doubleday Page, New York, 1923.
4. Rajasekhara's, *Kavyamimamsa*, edited by C.D. Dalal and Pandit R.A. Sastry, revised and enlarged by K.S. Ramaswami Sastri Siromani and published in 1934 by the Oriental Institute, Baroda. This edition is regarded as one of the more authentic commentaries available. A good interpretation of the relevant portions I have referred to in the book is also available in Ananda Coomaraswamy's, *The Transformation of Nature in Art*, Dover Publications, New York, 1956.
5. Robert Browning, *Andrea del Sarto*. Available in almost any collection of Browning's works, I have taken it from *The poems and Plays of Robert Browning*, The Modern Library, Random House Inc., New York, 1934.

## Chapter 4

*1. Beth A. Hennessey and Teresa M. Amabile, The conditions of creativity, in: *The Nature of Creativity*, edited by R.J. Sternberg, Cambridge University Press, 1988. Tereas Amabile has done considerable work on intrinsic motivation. Readers might be interested to look at her book, *The Social Psychology of Creativity*, Springer Verlag, and her contributions in the *Journal of Personality and Social Psychology*.
2. M. Lepper and D. Greene, Turning play into work: Effects of adult surveillance and extrinsic rewards on children's intrinsic motivation, *Journal of Personality and Social Psychology*, 1975.
3. M. Lepper, D. Greene and R. Nisbett, 'Undermining children's intrinsic interest with extrinsic rewards: A test of the "over justification" hypothesis'. *Journal of Personality and Social Psychology*, 1973.
4. B. Schwartz, *The Psychology of Learning and Behavior*, W.W. Norton, New York.
5. Philip Cushman, 'Why the self is empty,' *American Psychologist*, May 1990. This paper provides almost exactly the opposite view of this book's thesis. Among other things, Cushman says, "There is no universal transhistorical self, only local selves; no universal theory of self, only local theories."
6. B. Schwartz, 'The creation and destruction of values', *American Psychologist*, Jan. 1990. An excellent paper that substantiates and supports the thesis of the chapter, that 'quality'

improves as one progresses up the hierarchy. In this paper the author cites an experiment he conducted with adults where his findings were identical to those of Amabile—that those who are motivated intrinsically outperform those who are motivated extrinsically.

7. Stephen Ray Flora, 'Undermining intrinsic interest from the standpoint of a behaviorist', *The Psychological Record*, Summer 1990. He presents an opposite view, going to the extent of stating that while the practice of imbibing heroin is introduced extrinsically, it is followed through intrinsic motivation. He also suggests that if extrinsic motivation is bad, people who espouse it ought to give up their salary! I wonder what his reaction would be to my distinguishing between appetite needs and desire.

8. Robert W. Goddard, 'The Pygmalion effect', *Personnel Journal*, June 1985.

## Chapter 5

1. Spinoza, *Ethics*. A difficult book to read and digest owing to the author's cryptic style.

*2. P.G. Wodehouse, 'Joy in the morning', from *The Jeeves Omnibus*, Vol. II, Century Hutchinson, London, 1990.

3. Shakespeare, *King Henry V*. The Royal Shakespeare Society has a recording of this with Richard Burton as the king. Whenever line managers have asked for more people, I have been tempted to play this recording. For fear of being lynched, I have actually not tried it.

## Chapter 6

1. Kirk Douglas, *The Ragman's Son*, Simon & Schuster Ltd, London, 1988.

2. Somerset Maugham, *The Razor's Edge*, Penguin, 1963.

## Chapter 7

1. Roy Ochse, *Beyond the Gates of Excellence*, Cambridge University Press, Cambridge, Mass, 1990. Though it contains a wealth of research data, the conclusions and inferences in the book are quite different from mine, from almost the same data. Among other things, he is quite severe on humanists like Maslow.

2. V. Goertzel and M.G. Goertzel, *Cradles of Eminence*, Constable, London, 1962.
3. M.G. Goertzel, V. Goertzel, and T.G. Goertzel, *Three Hundred Eminent Personalities*, Jossey-Bass, San Francisco, 1978.
4. R.S. Albert, Family positions and the attainment of eminence: a study of special family positions and special family experiences', *Gifted Child Quarterly*, 24, 1980, pp 87-95.
5. Romain Roland, *Beethoven the Creator*, Victor Gollacz, London 1929. A remarkably sensitive and readable portrayal of the German composer.
*6. Sigmund Freud, *Two Short Accounts of Psychoanalysis*, James Stratchey, Penguin Books. I have referred to the fifth and final lecture in this book, first delivered by Freud in 1909.
7. Colin Wilson, *A Criminal History of Mankind*, Grafton Books, Collins Publishing Company, London, 1985. A detailed research output from CW, with an interpretation of human behaviour in the author's characteristically candid style.
8. Marc A. Zimmermann,"Towards a theory of learned hopefulness: A structural model analysis of participation and empowerment", *Journal of Research in Personality*, March 1990. Interesting reading, especially when one looks at it as being complementary to the natural skill of sublimation.

## Chapter 8

1. Erik Erikson, *Childhood and Society*, Paladin Grafton Books, London, 1977. This book also gives a complete list of books and papers published by Erikson.
2. Turner and Helms, 'Lifespan development', Holt, Reinhart and Winston, Orlando, Florida. A must for all young and old parents who could dip into it whenever they have a problem with a child.
3. S.J. Joe Currie, *The Barefoot Counsellor*, Asian Trading Corporation, Bangalore, 1981. An outstanding book on counselling for almost anyone who wishes to reach out and help another. The author lived and worked in India for almost two decades as a counsellor.
4. Carl Rogers, 'The necessary and sufficient conditions of therapeutic personality change', *Journal of Consulting Psychology*, 1957.
5. Colin Wilson, *The Bicameral Critic*, Salem House, Salem, New

Hampshire, 1985. A readable book giving an easy-to-understand account of the recent researches into the brain.

*6. Jan Ehrenwald, *Anatomy of a Genius,* Human Science Press, New York. The table given in the chapter is adapted from page 16 of his book. The author has given an interesting analysis of well-known figures from the right/left brain viewpoint. In particular, his interpretations of the characters of Hitler, Stalin and Beethoven are fascinating to read.

## Chapter 9

1. Henry Mintzberg, *Mintzberg on Management,* The Free Press, 1989.
2. Haynes and Abernathy, 'Managing our way to economic decline', *Harvard Business Review* classic that first appeared in the July/Aug. 1980 issue.

## Chapter 10

1. Jay A. Conger, 'Inspiring others: The language of leadership', *Academy of Management Executive,* Vol. 5, No.1, 1991.
2. Craig R. Hickman and Michael A. Silva, *Creating Excellence,* George Allen and Unwin, London, 1985. A book that HR managers and trainers would find eminently suitable in development programs. The authors give almost everything ready made, for use in programs, with exercises and do's and don'ts for each of the six skills they have identified as being the most important for a new-age executive.

## Chapter 11

1. Schiller, Friedrich, *Ode to Joy,* a poem he wrote in the late 18th century which so inspired Beethoven as to give it pride of place in the fourth and final movement of the last symphony he was to compose.

## Chapter 12

1. John K. Galbraith, *The Anatomy of Power,* Houghton Mifflin Co, Boston, 1983.
2. V.S. Mahesh, 'Managing Discipline: A systematic approach', *Vikalpa,* the journal of the Indian Institute of Management, Ahmedabad, Vol. 13, No. 3, 1988. In this paper I have detailed

the methodology we put into practice at the Taj Group of Hotels through which we reduced unauthorized absenteeism from about 9% to 2.5 % and maintained it at that level for over four years.

## Chapter 13

1. Roger Harrison, 'Strategies for a new age', *Human Resources Management*, Fall 1983; In this paper the author talks of alignment and attunement in organizations, which concept I have adapted, with a difference, in this chapter.
2. Keitaro Hasegawa, *Japanese Style Management*, Kodansha International Ltd., Tokyo, 1986. Written by a Japanese professional, this is an insider's view with insights no foreigner can hope to get. I have relied heavily on the author's interpretation of Japanese management practices.
3. Harrison Owen, *Spirit*, Abbot Publishing Co., Potomac, Maryland, 1987. An excellent book with an original insight into human beings and organizations.
4. Richard Bach, *Illusions*, Pan Books, London, 1978.
*5. E.F. Schumacher, *Small is Beautiful*, Harper & Row, New York, 1975.

## Chapter 14

1. Willis Harman, *Global Mind Change*, Knowledge Systems, Indianapolis, 1988. The author and this particular book of his are central to the last chapter. I would consider this book to be essential reading for everyone, irrespective of vocation and interests.
2. Lewis Mumford, *The Transformation of Man*, Harper Bros, New York, 1956.
3. *Taitreya Upanishad*. Among the translations and commentaries available, I referred to Radhakrishnan's and Swami Chinmayananda's.
4. S. Radhakrishnan, *Indian Philosophy*, George Allen and Unwin, London, 1923.
*5. Roger Sperry, *Science and Moral ·Priority*, Basil Blackwell Publications, Oxford, 1983.
6. Danah Zohar, *The Quantum Self*, Bloomsbury, London, 1990.
7. D. Chopra, *Quantum Healing*, Bantam Books, New York, 1989.

8. D.V. Seibert, *The Ethical Executive,* Cornerstone Library, Simon & Schuster, New York, 1984.

*9. R. Lessem, *Global Management Principles,* Prentice-Hall, England, 1989.

10. *Bhagwad Gita.* Among the various translations and commentaries available, I have referred to Swami Chinmayananda's.

11. Soren Kierkegaard, *A Kierkegaard Anthology,* edited by R. Bretall, The Modern Library, New York, 1946.

12. Herman Hesse, *Steppenwolf,* S. Fischer, Germany, 1927.

13. Ilya Prigogine and Isabelle Stengers, *Order Out of Chaos,* Bantam Books, New York, 1984.

# Index